ST. AUGUSTINE

ON NATURE, SEX, AND MARRIAGE

ST. AUGUSTINE
on Nature, Sex, and Marriage

JOHN J. HUGO

SCEPTER PUBLISHERS
Princeton, New Jersey

Nihil Obstat: Rev. Edmund J. Siedlecki, S.T.D.
Censor Librorum
Imprimatur: Rt. Rev. Msgr. Francis W. Byrne, J.C.L.
Vicar General, Archdiocese of Chicago
October 29, 1968

The *Nihil Obstat* and *Imprimatur* are official declarations that a book or pamphlet is free of doctrinal or moral error. No implication is contained therein that those who have granted the *Nihil Obstat* and *Imprimatur* agree with the contents, opinions, or statements expressed.

The acknowledgments and credits on page 237 are an extension of this copyright page.

Composition by Shoreline Graphics, Rockland, Maine
Text composed in ITC Caslon 224 fonts

Copyright © 1969 Scepter Publishers
P.O. Box 1270, Princeton, NJ 08542
Special contents of this edition copyright © 1998 Scepter Publishers
ISBN 1-889334-07-3
Library of Congress catalog number: 70-79795
Manufactured in the United States of America
Second printing, August 1998

Contents

Preface by Ronald Lawler, O.F.M.Cap. 9

Foreword by Bishop John Wright 11

Introduction: Problem or Phantom? 17

Part One: *St. Augustine on Nature and Man*
1. The Marvelous Mating of Soul and Body 31
2. Measure, Form, and Order 44
3. Paradise Lost 53
4. The Force of Disintegration 65

Part Two: *St. Augustine on Sex and Marriage*
5. Marriage and Sexuality 93
6. Marriage Thrice Blessed 118
7. Free and Equal Persons 146
8. To Marry or Not to Marry 167

Notes 189
Appendix—Life and Works of St. Augustine 221
Bibliography 223
Index of Topics 229
Index of Authors 235
Acknowledgments and Credits 237

Quarry the granite rock with razors,
or moor the vessel with a thread of silk;
then may you hope
with such keen and delicate instruments
as human knowledge and human reason
to contend against those giants,
the passion and pride of man.

—J. H. Newman, *The Idea of a University*

Indeed, as a weak and sinful being, [man] often
does what he would not,
and fails to do what he would.
Hence he suffers from internal divisions,
and from these flow so many
and such great discords in society.

—Vatican Council II, *Gaudium et Spes*, no. 10

The joys and the hopes,
the griefs and the anxieties of the men of this age,
especially those who are poor
or in any way afflicted,
these are the joys and hopes,
the griefs and anxieties of the followers of Christ.
Indeed, nothing genuinely human
fails to raise an echo in their hearts.

—Vatican Council II, *Gaudium et Spes*, no. 1

Preface

The year 1968 witnessed the early and most heated battles in many of the culture wars, perhaps most notably in the sexual revolution. And the first casualty reports were devastating for those who fought on the side of the family and divine and natural law. As Pope Paul VI promulgated his encyclical letter *Humanae Vitae* (On Human Life), he faced virulent attack from outside the Church, as well as massive dissent and defections from his own ranks. Hundreds of theologians signed petitions against the encyclical. One American bishop even resigned his office in protest.

All Pope Paul VI had done was to confirm the constant teaching of the Church, from the time of Jesus Christ: that sexual relations were the proper expression only of a lifelong, life-giving monogamous love between a man and a woman. Yet even Christian tradition had come under attack.

Into the fray came a priest from Pittsburgh.

John Jacob Hugo (1911–1985) was a noted scholar, teacher, and spiritual director. Above all, he was a priest—a man who had a generous and even heroic concern for souls. Down through the years, he had gladly taken on unpopular causes. In the 1940s he drew charges of heresy because he preached the universal call to holiness, insisting that the laity were called to the fullness of Christian perfection. In twenty years' time, that notion would become a centerpiece of the Second Vatican Council.

Father Hugo's 1969 book, ST. AUGUSTINE ON NATURE, SEX, AND MARRIAGE, reflects both his pastoral care and his earned reputation as a gadfly. At a time when many prominent Catholics were conceding that chastity and purity were "unrealistic" virtues, and that married love must inevitably be permeated by selfishness, Father Hugo rose up to defend human dignity, the truth of nature, and the power of grace.

His book is not about commandments or prohibitions, but about a certain vision of love and family life. It is a vision full of the promise of profound friendship between spouses, and between spouses and their children, and between men and women and God. Father Hugo recognized that there are actions and motives that are unworthy of such friendship, and he found their antidote in the writings of his beloved St. Augustine, who himself had overcome the ravages of a long-ago sexual revolution.

I am pleased to recommend this book by my friend, John Hugo, and I am grateful to Scepter Publishers for their courage in bringing it again to a public that needs it.

RONALD LAWLER, O.F.M.CAP.
Member, Pontifical Roman Theological Academy

Foreword

One of the welcome results of Pope Paul VI's reaffirmation of the longstanding Christian understanding of marital love may be a re-reading of St. Augustine's teaching concerning sexuality, marriage, and the relations of both to the condition and vocation of humankind. If so, and the thoughtful should fervently hope so, Father Hugo's present book could not be more timely or more helpful.

St. Augustine (like St. Paul and, to risk sounding absurd, Christ Himself) has been perilously close to becoming a casualty of the temper of the times on contraception. Margaret Sanger, angered by Pope Pius XI, dismissed his encyclical on Christian Marriage with quips about the Pope's celibate old age and the influence on him of Augustine, whom she seemed to see as chiefly an anti-feminist Puritan whose philosophical pessimism and personal guilt complex had played havoc with Christian concepts of sexuality.

This undercutting has continued throughout the debate on contraception down to today. It has been given critical apparatus by the footnotes of a few historians not entirely free of their own *parti pris,* a certain passion by writers on theology from the distaff side, and a persuasive air of prestige by the part in the fray of some moralists and lecturers. To put it mildly, St. Augustine has not had a good press this last quarter century: just about every Church teaching distasteful to the contraceptionists has been blamed on the influence of the Bishop of Hippo.

Comes now Father John Hugo, a student of St. Augustine during all the years of his life as a scholar, retreat director, and thoroughly pastoral priest. Father Hugo's mastery of the mind of Augustine is not that of a debater foraging in the pages of the Church Fathers for quotes to support his special pleading; neither is it that of a popular writer publishing under the patronage of routinely granted imprimaturs. Father Hugo has explored every area of the thought of St. Augustine as part of his own effort to arrive at a synthesis of Christian spirituality that would stand up under the test of time and yet meet the contemporary demands of the human condition. In this scholarly work he has successfully (indeed, at times in his life, heroically!) met the trial of contradiction and the testing by that magisterial criticism which forces on the intellectually honest a careful weighing of their conclusions and leads to the kind of solid results reflected in this book.

Father Hugo is, then, the man to interpret persuasively the mind of St. Augustine, even as now is the time for a competent review of the thought of that saintly genius. There is, be it emphasized, no question of "rehabilitating" St. Augustine, despite the discrediting of him attempted in the campaign to establish contraception in the Church. But there is need for renewed appreciation of the contribution of the Fathers generally to the witness of the Church and of the special excellence of the part of St. Augustine in that contribution.

That man always stands in debt to those who before him have wrested some measure of truth from the intellectual chaos around them has been evident to serious scholars at least since Aristotle showed his gratitude to his mentor, Plato. As the early Church, struggling with the Manicheans and Pelagians, had its Augustine, so Augustine had the earlier Fathers; as the Church at the time of the great scholastic synthesis had its Aquinas and Bonaventure, so they had before them the patristic and medieval commentators on the wisdom of the ancients. As the Council of Trent profited from the heritage of a rich age of Catholic theology, so the recent Vatican Council had its vast company of theologians nurtured since the Reformation. Constant development, ever clearer understanding, yet continuity in tradition have characterized the growth of Catholic theology for almost two millennia.

Fully aware that theological development must take place within defined limits if it is to be faithful to the Faith itself, we must study and strive nevertheless to bring to pass ever greater theological understanding of the Faith. Each age finds its own terminology—every era its own emphasis. Problems and questions arise out of the situation in which man is now found, and it is, therefore, in the present that he seeks solutions and answers. To satisfy his eagerness to know, to understand, and, ideally, to live by his knowledge, man is charged to utilize every tool available to him. Yet when dealing with the Faith and our attempts to grasp the intellectual ramifications of its content, man as theologian is necessarily humbled before two realities upon which that Faith intimately depends. The revealed Word of God and the continuous tradition of that Word in the Church remind us that theological commitments, unlike philosophical conclusions, always have a divine "given" upon which investigation must build and against which it must be verified. It is because the teaching accepted as Catholic by the Church has always drawn its sustenance and direction from the revelation given in and through Christ Jesus that the teaching of the Catholic Faith has retained continuity with the first beginnings of the Christian community on the Galilean shore.

Today, in a Church flooded, it sometimes seems, by a paper explosion pouring forth reams and reams of theological material ranging from popularized versions of ecclesiastical gossip to serious compendia of contemporary theology, we are forced to apply with special rigor the criterion of the Faith if we are to identify what is substantial, authentic theology. As in the past, our struggle for renewed theological development will be determined by our fidelity to God's revealed Word and our accurate grasp of the theological expressions of that Word which have won acceptance historically by the Church; then we can safely press on to new theological frontiers, however unknown, however seemingly distant.

Father Hugo's work on Augustine is a reminder of the theological importance of those men whose understanding of the content and meaning of the Word has become so large a part of the mind of the Church. At a moment in the history of Christianity when the great issue is not so much what we mean by God, His life and His love, as it is what we mean by man—and the work of human life and the dignity of human love—it is good that we have easy access to the wisdom of Augustine.

As already noted, his acceptance by the teaching Church has guaranteed his place among those few heralded as the "teachers of the Church." Father Hugo brings special personal experience and expertise to the analysis of the philosophy of

St. Augustine and the explanation of his moral theology. It is always profitable to read sound theological commentary, but when solid reflection on the corollaries and content of the Faith is presented in the direct, readable style of Father Hugo, the profitable experience becomes also pleasurable. ST. AUGUSTINE ON NATURE, SEX, AND MARRIAGE brings to the discussion of the human condition and particularly human sexuality both spiritual sensitivity and unusual common sense. As a result, it makes a notable theological contribution to a discussion not always characterized by awareness of how it is only by the loving use of created goods that men can come to the enjoyment of goods eternal.

JOHN WRIGHT
Bishop of Pittsburgh
Feast of St. Augustine, 1968

St. Augustine
on
Nature, Sex, and Marriage

Introduction: Problem or Phantom?

> So then, every scribe instructed in the kingdom of heaven is like a householder who brings forth from his storeroom things both old and new.
>
> —Matthew 13: 52

> This tradition which comes from the Apostles develops in the Church with the help of the Holy Spirit. For there is a growth in the understanding of the realities and the words which have been handed down.[1]
>
> —Vatican Council II, *Dei Verbum*, no. 8

One would almost think that Augustine is a contemporary. At least his ideas are considered newsworthy by magazines like *Time*, while those of many contemporaries are not. If you go to the public library, as I did in preparing these pages, you find, contrary to expectation, an astonishing amount of material on the saint; and then you are told that your name will be put on a waiting list for some of the books you want; almost as if he were a current bestseller.

To be sure, while Augustine still has his disciples and friends, by no means every mention of him is favorable. Today, in fact, there seems to be a sort of concerted effort to vilify him, or at least to undercut his influence. In one important respect, he offends the modern world or a segment of it: the segment that believes that many of the problems of today can be solved by contraception. Augustine appears to stand in the way of such a solution; his ideas of marriage and sexuality seem outmoded if not false. And these affect his whole view of life, which, we are told, tends to be pessimistic and rigoristic.

Some might ask: Who cares? What difference does it make for us today what Augustine taught in the fifth century? Much water has gone under the bridge since then. The Church itself is now in the throes of an *aggiornamento*. We must solve our problems by our twentieth-century conscience. With all respect and admiration for Pope John XXIII, however, the Church of Christ did not begin with him. One can read contemporary works on moral and theological problems without realizing this: even when carefully footnoted, their earliest reference may be to Karl Rahner or Pierre Teilhard de Chardin. The past can be disregarded by twentieth-century man, arrogant in his possession of vast knowledge; else it can be filled in with a few broad and, as we shall have occasion to illustrate, frequently inaccurate brushstrokes. *Aggiornamento,* for some at least, appears to mean a complete break with the past and a wholly fresh start.

Of course, men today have certain obvious advantages. Rahner and Teilhard and other contemporary thinkers do stand atop a vast accumulation of scientific knowledge. Alongside these stores even men like Augustine and Aquinas in many respects seem primitive. Nevertheless, while our contemporaries may in a sense judge the Doctors of the past, these in turn will join in pronouncing judgment on our contemporaries. Catholic doctrine is a living, evolving truth. It changes, but it also remains the same. Preservation of type, continuity of principles, and power of assimilation are three of the criteria that Newman cites for distinguishing authentic from spurious development.[2]

A child, as he grows up, assimilates many elements into his body; but he rejects others, and he retains his own identity from infancy to maturity. In doctrinal development, the Church assimilates elements from every age, including pagan elements, always retaining its own identity. This assimilation involves a process of catabolism as well as anabolism: some elements are taken into the organism; others are rejected as unassimilable. We make this distinction instinctively every time we eat roast chicken. We must make it also in matters of the mind, especially in the question of a developing theology.

Accordingly, Augustine and Aquinas (not to mention others) will be judges of our contemporaries, despite the advantageous position of the latter. Christians of past ages will be called upon to decide whether material submitted by the moderns is assimilable, whether it is to be retained or rejected, whether it is consistent with the unity and continuing identity of Catholic truth.

To facilitate this living process, we ourselves should try to discriminate between what is digestible and what is not. Our age, despite its pretensions, has also its fashions in thought, although the current fashion may seem, to us, like the final stage of evolutionary progress. Within a short time there will be several other evolutionary "mutations." Consult the books of a few years ago and you will find other "advanced" ideas, now forgotten. A strange thing about most of these ideas is their repetitiousness. As often as not they can be traced to pre-Socratic sages. As the False Gods say of themselves in Edwin Arlington Robinson's poem of that name,

> Howsoever like no other be the mode you may employ,
> There's an order in the ages for the ages to enjoy.

C. S. Lewis, in the dedication of one of his books, thanks a former teacher for telling him that the age in which we live will someday also be considered a period. We would be wise to bear this in mind. It would keep us from running off after every new style in thought. It would caution us that what we now praise as the latest may very soon be dated. Precisely here, knowledge of the past can be of help in discerning what belongs to the inner identity and coherence of Christian truth.

While priding ourselves on the achievements of our age, we might also profitably bear in mind the suggestion of Dom Aelred Graham that "some future Church historian may well record that in the 1960s Catholic theology reached its nadir."[3] To defend this hypothetical historian would no doubt be shadowboxing; although we might at least ask him (hypothetically) why he narrows this judgment to Catholic theologians. Yet the mere possibility of such a historian might well serve to keep us modest, if not humble, as we today make our theological pronunciamentos.

Christian theology is a unified but growing body of truth, the fruit of the Church's endless meditation on Sacred Writ. Augustine made the first really significant contribution to this corpus in the West. In reexamining his work we must determine how far it belongs to his own time, how far he has contributed to enduring truth, how far his teachings are part of our developing knowledge, how far they diverge from it. In doing this, we shall also be helped in assessing the contribution of our day.

Augustine was very much a man of his own age, so different from our own. Manichaeism, Donatism, Pelagianism, and a persisting undercurrent of paganism were his constant preoccupation. In meeting these errors, as he reflected on the Scriptures, and in zealously carrying out his pastoral office of preaching to the people of Hippo, he formulated the principles of what was to be called Augustinian thought. Yet in serving his own age so well he became a man for all ages. His thought transcends the local and temporary because, in the first place, seeking solutions to his contemporary problems, he tried to bring to bear on them the universal light of the Gospel. Moreover, certain heresies and errors, while they have local variations—and we easily become impatient of reading the vagaries of past ages—reveal perennial attitudes of the human mind, persistent tendencies, and recurrent temptations. This is true of the systems combated by Augustine: they are not quite as dead as we would like to think. Consequently, his thought can be of help in meeting these attitudes in other times, including our own, in which some of these wraiths exhibit surprising vitality. There's an order in the ages.

* * *

Were it not for current debates, there would be little excuse for adding more ink to the ocean of Augustinian literature that already exists. But in the vital area to be examined here, little has been written, at least little that is accurate. Catholics particularly have abandoned the field largely to Augustine's caricaturists.

Our inquiry, therefore, will be concerned with one point, or at least it will radiate from one point. Certain contemporary writers, treating especially of marriage, allege that Catholic thinkers have tended to downgrade material nature and, in so doing, have also disdained the sexual component of marriage. These critics hold that in emphasizing the procreative purpose of marriage, there has been a tendency to disparage conjugal love, especially its sexual element, and to equate sexuality exclusively with its biological function, thus producing, in the theology of marriage, a kind of angelism that is unreal and impossible of realization in the human condition. The writers making this allegation claim to trace it to the teachings of St. Augustine, from whom, they say, it derives a spurious authority.

The charge has two parts.

First, St. Augustine introduced Platonism into the exposition of Catholic theology and, in so doing, carried Plato's low esteem for material nature into the stream of Christian thought. As a consequence, it is asserted, he underrated the psychophysical unity of the human person.

Second, Augustine, in his treatment of original sin, is said to have exaggerated its effects, regarding concupiscence as evil. He is, therefore, responsible for the erroneous idea that human nature is intrinsically damaged, especially in its bodily appetites; human sexuality (according to him) would thus be inherently disordered and blameworthy.

As we proceed, we shall cite writers making these charges or criticisms.[4] Some are scholars. Some are journalists who write authoritatively of what they do not know and are unable to verify, thus adding their thin trickle (to borrow a phrase from Bruce Marshall) to the diarrhea of popular theology. We meet here with an anti-Augustinian mood or attitude, of which instances may be found almost daily in the press both secular and religious. Propaganda for contraception, and for a revision of the Church's stand on this question, has tended to reduce Augustine from his position of greatest Doctor of the Church to public villain.

Moreover, attacks on Pope Pius XI's encyclical *Casti Connubii* (On Christian Marriage), made inevitably by those seeking a revision of the Church's teaching on contraception, are also, if not mainly, attacks on St. Augustine, from whom the Pope largely drew in setting forth his doctrine. Margaret Sanger indicated the connection in a remark to which we shall return: "[Pope Pius XI] instructs the faithful how to regulate their conjugal life without the benefit of science and according to theories written by St. Augustine, also a bachelor, who died fifteen centuries ago."[5] Only to the extent that Augustine is discredited can revisionists hope for a change in the Church's teaching.

John T. Noonan, toward the end of his careful survey of the Church's teaching on contraception, speaks confidently of the "rejection" of Augustinian theology.[6] Yet the Fathers of the Second Vatican Council cited Augustine in their sixteen decrees no fewer than fifty-two times, thirty-four of these in the four great Constitutions. Not a slight contribution from the fifth-century Bishop of Hippo to his modern colleagues as they toiled to restate the Gospel message for men of the twentieth century! Moreover, as we shall see more clearly later, the conciliar Fathers explicitly restated the Church's teaching on marriage within the doctrinal framework provided by Augustine. In doing this, they also cited five times the disputed passages in Pius XI's encyclical, which now therefore, rather than being revised or repudiated, has a more precious setting within the decrees of a General Council. Stories of the rejection of Augustine, like Mark Twain's complaint about the rumors of his death, seem to be slightly exaggerated!

In considering criticisms of the saint, Part One of this work, comprising four chapters, will provide necessary background for understanding Augustine's thought. It will meet the first part of the charge mentioned above. Part Two, also divided into four chapters, will, against this background, take up Augustine's teaching on sexuality and marriage.

It should be remembered that Augustine wrote no *Summa theologiae*. His theology grew over a period of some forty years in books, letters, and sermons. Even his books were not systematic treatises but for the most part controversial works (as well as sermons) struck off in moments of the Church's need. His was a developing theology called forth by new needs, and in meeting these, "he had singularly little help from preceding writers."[7] He was still revising and correcting at the end of his life, as shown in the *Retractations*. Nevertheless, his thought, after a short preliminary and formative period following his conversion, quickly reached maturity and developed, not through abruptly different stages, but rather in consistency and refinement. Étienne Gilson, withdrawing a previous criticism, said that even among the many variations in detail in the position of St. Augustine, he has "never discovered the slightest philosophical change in any of his essential theses."⁸ Thus we are dealing with a consistent but not systematic whole. While we will note as far as it serves our purpose the inner growth of Augustine's thought, our chief concern will be with the mature theologian.

Augustine's thought is a synthesis rather than a system—an organic synthesis of principles in vital union rather than a logical and symmetrical system such as the Scholastics were afterward to attempt. Many mistakes made in interpreting Augustine came of ripping elements from his thought and inserting them in later systems, as a builder might pull stones out of one building and place them in another. Augustine does not lend himself to this kind of mechanical transposition: the elements of his thought must be viewed in the living unity in which he sees them. Moreover, in studying Augustine (or any theologian of a former age), it is important not to read history backward. We cannot expect to find in him the developments of later ages. Scholasticism came only later with its refinements. To look for all the modalities and precisions of later thought in Augustine would be absurd. Moreover, his style is not Scholastic but "rather the free flow of later classical eloquence." Above all, his theology is Scriptural; he deals with great Scriptural truths—there is a text ever on his tongue—and, while striving to apply these to concrete problems, he does so only with the still imperfect analytical tools at his disposal, which he greatly improved and extended. Criticism of Augustine must therefore include consideration of his Scriptural sources; he never dreamed of setting up a system of thought independent of the Scriptures, of which his knowledge was phenomenal. No Christian thinker has ever stayed closer to the inspired word than Augustine. Theologians today, seeking to recover a Scriptural theology, can take him as a model. Much twentieth-century theology seems to proceed quite independently of the Scriptures.

The remark of a contemporary scholar is in order: "The influence of St. Augustine on Christianity is sometimes exaggerated. It will be well if we distinguish here his influence on Christianity from the influence of Christianity upon him."⁹

It was Augustine's ambition merely to explain the truths of the Faith that he had accepted. He wrote discursively and often tentatively, at times proposing several solutions to a difficulty. If later followers absolutized some of his tentative opinions, that was scarcely Augustine's fault. He was unyielding only when sure that he was defending the Faith. He closes the first part of his work *On Adulterous Marriages* with this modest remark: "After this rather paltry treatment and discussion of mine, I am not ignorant of the fact that the question of marriage still remains very obscure and involved. Nor I dare say that either in this work or in any other up to the present have I explained all its intricacies, or that I am to explain them now if urged to do so."[10]

Even the greatest theologians cannot escape an admixture of human error. Such errors result not only from the personal and human limitations of the thinkers but also from the restricting limits of knowledge and science of the era in which they live. The social and cultural milieu is the matrix in which theology on its human side is formed and developed. It is the task of reflection and study, separating error, to channel authentic elements into the swelling mainstream of theological truth. Accordingly, the final value of any work is determined by the degree to which it is absorbed into the main tradition. As to Augustine—"while the Church has not adopted all the elements of his doctrine and while it cannot be said without restriction that St. Augustine's theology on the subject of original sin, grace and predestination is the theology of the Church, it is beyond question that all the substance of his theology has passed into her dogmatic definitions, and that he must be looked upon as the founder of supernatural Christian anthropology."[11] The writer is here speaking chiefly of Trent's incorporation of Augustine's teaching into its decrees, and we shall have occasion in Chapter 4 to see his statement verified. Now Vatican II, as noted, has found Augustine's help indispensable even in the twentieth century.

Through Christ we plunge into "the depths of the wisdom and knowledge of God" (Rom 2: 33). No man, whatever his genius, can contain it fully. It is the task of us all, led by those gifted in mind and endowed with spiritual vision purified by holiness, to seek constantly to extend our comprehension of this mystery. Augustine, being a man, made mistakes, and some of his mistakes, because of his authority, had unhappy consequences. He was conscious of his own mistakes; that is why he wrote in his *Retractations,* "Let not those who read these works imitate me in my errors but in the progress they find me making."[12] On this recommendation, therefore, we should not in our pride of more advanced knowledge condemn him but rather try to sift the wheat from the chaff, the assimilable from the unassimilable. We must retain in our growing body of knowledge whatever positive contributions he made. Our eminence today should give us the critical faculty to separate what was mistaken or of merely temporary significance from what is of permanent worth and therefore belongs to the organic growth of the Church's teaching. If our ancestors in the Faith sometimes failed to make this discrimination, we with our better information should not fail to do so now.

St. Thomas will have no difficulty assimilating the positive elements of Augustine's teaching into his own later and more mature synthesis; and the Church will often use his very words in her definitions. It is within this central tradition of the Church's teaching, therefore, that we can find an authentic interpretation of the main elements of Augustine's thought. The value of this thought, conversely, must in the end be judged by his success in setting forth and elucidating Catholic doctrine. By the judgment of the Church in her Councils, including the Second Vatican Council, his score is high.

Finally, it must be emphasized that we cannot interpret Augustine's teaching from the point of view of those who have separated from the main tradition of Catholic theology; of those who have fixed on some particular aspect of his teaching, detached from other principles that act as corrective or counterpoise; who have isolated and absolutized his statements, even his imperfections, as though he were the final and self-sufficient source of theology. Above all, we must avoid the tendency—common in our time, and to be considered in Chapter 3—to interpret Augustine through the eyes of the Reformers and the Jansenists. Those who do so distort Augustine. And because of them, others have tended to regard with suspicion the saintly doctor to whom the distorters attribute such high authority. Although Jansenism was not present for Augustine to refute, we shall see how it falsifies the substance of his teaching. Jansenism—or sub-Jansenism—cannot be accepted as the authentic interpretation of Augustine.

"St Augustine must be numbered among those whose thought is 'open.' Surely many an Augustinian has attempted the task of completion. Almost without exception the effort has only produced a strange variant of the original, and their labors bear the same relation to St. Augustine as those of the NeoPlatonists do to Plato."[13] And Étienne Gilson: "The difficulties which at the present time beset Augustinianism are not an ill for which we need to find remedies, for St. Augustine is not affected by any ill; all that is needed is to return from the Augustinianism of the Augustinians to that of St. Augustine himself."[14] This will be our procedure—a return to the Augustinianism of Augustine—in addressing ourselves to the problem outlined above.

* * *

Readers may wish some information on the works of Augustine. These are quite extensive; what with other things to do, a lifetime would scarcely suffice to read them all. Moreover, the inability to write about anything without writing about everything—which Chesterton confessed as both his weakness and his method—was long anticipated by Augustine: if style, as Newman said, is the thinking out into language, this was the inevitable style of the saint's complex and organic thought. Gilson is not exaggerating when he speaks of Augustine's works as a "labyrinth."

The complete collection of Augustine's works used here for reference is that edited by the Benedictines of St. Maur and published in J. P. Migne's *Patrologia Latina* (vols. 32–47). A great number of these books—but by no means all—are available in English. The Newman Press has currently nine volumes devoted to Augustine in its Ancient Christian Writers series. To date, the Fathers of the Church series contains seventeen volumes of the saint's works. The greatest bulk of his writings in English, however, is still to be found in the eight large volumes devoted to him in *Nicene and Post-Nicene Fathers* (Eerdmans, 1952–56). That this series was published under Protestant auspices is itself enough to make Augustine timely in an age of ecumenical theology; it is a warning against wantonly destroying so valuable a bridge.

Two works, *The Confessions* and the *City of God*, both available in various translations, contain most of the basic and constant ideas of Augustine. The former, which contains the story of his conversion, is also an important source of his teaching. Actually written fifteen years after his conversion and some five or six years after his consecration as bishop, it summarizes his mature reflections and may be considered the matrix of his subsequent works. The *City of God*, in twenty-two books, discursive and even rambling, with the Redemption of mankind unfolding in a vast historical panorama, is the closest thing Augustine has given us to a *Summa*.

Selections from the saint's works, and some complete works, are also available in individual translations.

While usually consulting St. Augustine himself, we shall not neglect capable guides. Chief of these is *The Christian Philosophy of St. Augustine*, by Étienne Gilson, who has accomplished the near-miracle, perhaps for the first time, of reducing the labyrinth to order while preserving the organic character of Augustine's thought. *A Guide to the Thought of St. Augustine*, by Eugène Portalié, S.J., translates a valuable article from the *Dictionnaire de Théologie Catholique;* it is an almost encyclopedic guide to every aspect of the saint's teaching. Dr. Vernon Bourke, the translator of Portalié's work, has also written an analysis of Augustine's more important books within the developing context of his life. Father F. Van der Meer, in *Augustine the Bishop,* takes up the saint's life after his conversion, a part often neglected, and skilfully weaves the story of his life and work as a bishop against the background of the times.

Other works will be cited in context, and a bibliography is provided on pages 223–228.

Part One

St. Augustine on Nature and Man

1. *The Marvelous Mating of Soul and Body*

> For the rest, brethren, whatever things are true, whatever honorable, whatever just, whatever holy, whatever lovable, whatever of good repute, if there be any virtue, if anything worthy of praise, think upon these things.
>
> —Philippians 4: 8

> The Church anchors the dignity of human nature against all tides of opinion, for example, those which undervalue the human body or idolize it.
>
> —Vatican Council II, *Gaudium et Spes*, no. 41

In our time there has arisen a new sense of the psychophysical unity of the human person; this development has brought about a reaction against philosophies that seem to have overemphasized the distinction between matter and spirit in man. In the problem of sexuality the matter is pertinent because sex, it is claimed, has been seen exclusively as a function of the body. Hence there has been overemphasis on the biological function of sex, i.e., procreation, with a corresponding neglect or downgrading of the psychic factor, and therefore of the total love relationship between spouses. (We will not stop here to question the remarkable view that the procreation of a human *person* is merely "biological"; or that the *human* act that determines it could be other than psychophysical.)

Augustine is a natural target of such criticism because he derived his philosophy from Plato by way of the Neoplatonists, who were particularly guilty of exalting spirit and downgrading matter, to the point of regarding the latter as evil. Augustine is thus charged with introducing Platonic, rather than Christian, ideas into his explanation of human nature, and therefore also of marriage.

The question of the influence of Platonism (or Neoplatonism) on St. Augustine has been discussed thoroughly, and the most capable scholars (Portalié, Gilson) have completely disposed of the charge that Augustine's thought was dominated by Platonic rather than Christian principles.[1] St. Thomas had already said, correctly, that "Augustine followed Plato as far as the Christian faith allowed."

There is no denying the Platonic influence on Augustine. As Gilson says, "He did for Plotinus what St. Thomas Aquinas was later to do for Aristotle."[2] But Augustine had a less perfect instrument: "A human instrument, certainly in no way mediocre, but imperfect, blunted and risky, and for its manipulation, a hand, the most perfect, fearful, and pious, intelligent and understanding, strong, prudent, and wise, the irresistible light of the superhuman Spirit—such is the admirable paradox of the wisdom of the Christian Plato."[3]

The Platonist influence is most clearly discernible in his early works, written in the period from his conversion to his ordination (386–391), after the model of the Platonic dialogues. Nevertheless, he had even then established, as Portalié remarks, the fundamental principle of all his subsequent investigation: faith seeking understanding. "I am confident that I will find in the Platonists nothing at variance with our Sacred Literature."[4] In these early years he was perfecting the instrument that he was afterward to use so effectively in the defense and elucidation of revealed truth.

His ordination to the priesthood was an event that precipitated, not indeed a new crisis, but a great religious deepening. He had already written against the Manichees and had completed "that glowing masterpiece, the *True Faith*, perhaps the most beautiful essay of his time on the essence of Christianity," yet he still "looked upon himself as a mere layman" in the service of God's word.[5] This was still true after his ordination, for priests did not then preach; and when Valerius, his bishop, desired him to preach, Augustine asked for and received an opportunity to study. From this time, the mature Augustine emerges, saturated with the Scriptures, his Platonic instruments now fully dominated by his grasp of revealed truth.[6] In his mind the most characteristic doctrine of Plato, that of innate ideas, was completely transformed, and where there was a conflict between Platonic ideas and Christianity, Augustine often apparently did not even notice the difference, for he read with a Christian mind; where Plotinus spoke of "emanation" of creatures from God, Augustine read "creation."[7] Always he assimilated into Christianity whatever of Platonism was useful, rejecting whatever he could not thus assimilate. Despite his admiration for the "Platonists," as he called his mentors, he continually subjects their teaching to sharp appraisal and criticism.[8]

In the matter before us, Augustine was hindered by his Platonism from arriving at the final solution that St. Thomas, with the aid of Aristotle, was to perfect, i.e., the doctrine of the substantial union of body and soul. But Plato had enabled Augustine to conceive the soul as spiritual, and his meditation on Genesis taught him how to demonstrate against the Manichees (and against any excesses of the Neoplatonists in this regard) the goodness of God's material universe.

For Augustine, before he was either a Platonist or a Christian, materialism had been a way of life and a philosophy: he did not need to be convinced of the reality or the attractiveness of the material universe. His conversion involved the realization, first, that all material nature, since it comes from God, is good; and, secondly, that there is an even higher spiritual reality whose presence in the soul endows man with a special likeness to God. He rejected the Platonic notion that the body is a "prison" of the soul—even when he found it in Origen; and he was "inexpressibly astonished that a scholar so versed in ecclesiastical literature" should so contradict "the plain meaning" of Scripture.[9] For his part he believed that God "by a marvelous mating brings a spiritual nature into one that is material and makes the soul and body active and passive principles, respectively, of a single human whole."[10] Man, both body and soul, is destined for God: "For my body lives by my soul and my soul lives by You."[11]

Sin is not to be blamed on the body:

> We ought not, therefore, to blame our sins and defects on the nature of the flesh, for this is to disparage the Creator. The flesh, in its own kind and order, is good. But what is not good is to abandon the goodness of the Creator in pursuit of some created good, whether by living deliberately according to the soul, or according

to the entire man, which is made up of soul and flesh and which is the reason why either "soul" alone or "flesh" alone can mean a man.

Anyone then who extols the nature of the soul as the highest good and condemns the nature of the flesh as evil is as carnal in his love for the soul as he is in his hatred of the flesh, because his thoughts flow from human vanity and not from divine truth.[12]

One wonders whether any modern praise of the body can say more than this, or say it any better. Yet it is not all, for the body (in a passage clean contrary to Plato) will also share the glory of the resurrection: "We do not desire to be divested of the body, but rather to be clothed with its immortality."[13]

Ironically (so far as Augustine's modern critics are concerned), if his Platonism took him a little off-center in the matter of the union of body and soul, it is in a direction opposite that for which he is reproached. He did not believe that the body of itself is capable even of sensation, which he located "entirely in the soul" (i.e., in the soul's attention to impressions on the bodily senses); for him, following Plato, the inferior could not act on the superior. Thus, the soul is deeply, too deeply, involved in all sensation, and this would include that of physical sexuality. There can be in Augustine no question of human bodily activity being divorced from that of the soul.[14]

Nevertheless, if Augustine's explanation of the unity of body and soul is short of the full truth, he never doubted their unity. His knowledge of Scripture prevented error here.

> The better Augustine understood the content of his Christian faith, the better he understood the fact that according to Scriptures, God did not create a soul in creating Adam, but a man: Let us make man (Gen 1: 26); and that the fashioning of Adam's body was actually the fashioning of a man (Gen 2: 7). Merely having to meditate on the dogma was enough to lead Augustine later on to a definition of man quite different from that of Plotinus: man is a rational substance

made up of soul and body . . . Thus Augustine inherited a Platonic definition of man. On the other hand, his Christianity compels him to give staunch support to the unity of the human composite made up of a soul and body.[15]

Augustine's difficulty was that of explaining a Christian truth without adequate philosophical means. The imperfection of his Platonic instrument is here revealed. He is unable to explain the mode of union between body and soul, but he never doubted their unity. "Unfortunately, in Augustine the fullness of Christian truth was always in advance of his philosophy." Gilson, who makes this comment, explains Augustine's technical difficulty and his failure fully to resolve it.[16] Nevertheless, the saint could write, "Only when body and soul are in union can we speak of a man."[17]

What St. Augustine learned from Scriptures concerning the unity of the human person accorded with his own deepest inclinations:

> The *Confessions* is probably the first autobiography in the history of literature. Try to imagine if you can—I myself cannot do so—a St. Thomas writing his memoirs or autobiography. Augustine, interested in man, the self, personality, thereby invented a new literary genre, namely, a detailed account of man's destiny, seen from within, of man's situation in the world, of his reaction to objects and persons and theoretical problems. All this is inextricably linked with a progress which, in the case of Augustine, is a conversation with God.[18]

In the *Confessions,* therefore, we find described, for the first time in the literature of the West, the confrontation of a human person with the Person of God, the first I–Thou dialogue with God, the first existential meeting. It arises from his sense of the uniqueness and unity of the person.

Moreover, this feeling for the person led him to develop the theological doctrine of personality as Catholic theology sees it in the Trinity.

The philosophical discovery of the person was due mainly, if not exclusively, to the pressure and challenge of the Christian revelation of the Godhead. Under this pressure, directed by Augustine's intuition and genius and by the related doctrine of the Incarnation, he was instrumental in substituting man for the world—*Psyche for Kosmos*—as the fundamental analogy whereby to understand and express, so far as possible, the inner life of God.... By this reflective thinking, theological in character, about the Divine Persons, St. Augustine provided Western thought of a later epoch, with the philosophy of the human person.[19]

To the critics accusing St. Augustine of disrupting or neglecting man's psychophysical unity, therefore, the only adequate answer is: "How wrong can you be?"

In the crisis of theological controversy against the Pelagians, Augustine again showed his conviction of man's inner unity. Any fault in his conception of this unity would come to light here; it would lead him astray at this point because, in order to demonstrate the effects of original sin, he is constantly dealing with those texts (Gal 5; Rom 7) which describe the conflict of flesh and spirit. Is this a conflict between body and soul, revealing a split in human nature? Not so, says Augustine; it is a conflict between nature and grace, between the spirit of fallen man and the Spirit of God working in man.

While he recurs to these Pauline texts many times, he provides a full treatment of them in his *Continence*. In chapters four and five he explains the conflict between "flesh" and "spirit" in terms of the Holy Spirit vis-à-vis the whole man, that is, understanding "flesh" as the whole man, body and soul. "How must we understand this 'flesh' if not as 'man'?" Hence, his explanation of "living according to the flesh": "Hear, O man, do not walk according to man, but according to Him who made man."

Consistent with this, the "spirit" whose desires are against the flesh is to be understood, above all, as the Spirit of God in man.

And when we hear, "If by the spirit you put to death the deeds of the flesh, you shall live," let us not attribute this good to our spirit alone, as if through itself it could do these things. . . . So, when by our spirit we put to death the works of the flesh, we are impelled by the Spirit of God.[20]

To be sure, there is in man, by reason of his composite nature, a tension and conflict between his material and spiritual components: and this simply as a matter of fact and observation, not as a postulate of a Platonic dualism. St. Augustine adverts to this inner conflict but declines to discuss it in merely philosophical terms: "This disputation might be of some value," he writes, referring to those who would so consider it in these terms, "in the schools of the philosophers; but we, in order to understand the Apostle of Christ, ought to mark well the way in which Christian writers are accustomed to speak."[21] It is then that he goes on to define "flesh" as the whole man and "spirit" as the Spirit of God working through man's spirit.[22]

Accordingly, when a little later (chapters seven, eight, and nine) he describes the internal conflict within man, it is still in theological terms; that is to say, he is looking at nature, not through an abstract philosophical analysis of its components and their properties, but as fallen from its Paradisal state, with its faculties bearing the punishment of sin:

Indeed in this nature of man, good and well-established and ordered by the Good, there is also war now, because perfect health is not yet. When this feebleness is healed, there is peace. But guilt has incurred that feebleness; nature did not have it. And this guilt the grace of God has already removed from the faithful by the waters of regeneration, but, under the hands of the same Physician, nature is still in conflict with the feebleness.[23]

Augustine, as shall be seen more and more, never varies from this habit of regarding man concretely as he exists, at once bearing the punishment for original sin and the divine restorative of grace. But the point of chief concern here is that he sees the central spiritual conflict between the whole man in his personal unity but fallen, and the Spirit of God. This is of particular interest, since modern authors tend to believe that only they have at length arrived at a correct understanding of these difficult texts (Gal 5; Rom 7) in which the Apostle speaks of the conflict between flesh and spirit. But Augustine anticipates the modern exegesis.[24]

We see here both the originality of Augustine's genius and the perspicacity of his faith. As a student of Plato, he might be expected to conceive nature abstractly in accordance with the divine ideas. Had he failed *per impossibile* to note it in Plato, the notion of a "pure" nature was to be offered to him ready-made (if in an objectionable context) by the Pelagians. He refused it from both sources. As Gilson says, he "never poses the problem of the capabilities of reason or nature in an abstract way."[25] He ever considers man concretely, at first sanctified by God, then fallen, finally restored, but still bearing the wounds of nature, to be healed by grace.

In the following chapter we shall consider the charge of "latent Manichaeism" made against Augustine. For the moment let it be noticed only that such latent Manichaeism, were it to exist, should appear in his explanation of these favorite Pauline texts describing the conflict between flesh and spirit. Here, if anywhere, he would readily succumb to the temptation of seeing evil in bodily nature. Actually, however, he is using these texts against the Manichees. *Continence* was written during the early period of his episcopacy, while he was still fighting Manichaeism. His purpose in it is not only to praise the Christian ideal but also to expose and warn against the Manichaean notion of continence with its rejection of material nature and the body as evil. The Manichees give him precisely the opportunity he needed to affirm the goodness of nature and the unity of flesh and spirit. He made this point with such clarity that afterward, as he tells us himself in the *Retractations*, the Pelagians, who erred in an opposite direction, tried to use some of his anti-Manichaean writings in their own behalf, i.e., to show that man is not afflicted with original sin.[26]

It can be confidently asserted that Augustine, more clearly

than the moderns, describes the actuality of man's moral conflict, seeing as he does the tension between the consequence of sin, concupiscence, and the human spirit under the action of grace. His thought, in dealing with man, is wholly existential. But because of his alleged Neoplatonism he is made the scapegoat for the failure (to be taken up in Chapter 8) of some Catholic thinkers, largely through neglect of Augustine, to stay abreast of progressive knowledge of the dynamic character of human behavior.[27]

The manner in which St. Augustine, despite his Platonism, is saved from any deviations from orthodoxy by his profound meditation on Scripture is well shown in the following passage.

> Who will explain consistently this single statement, that "the Word was made flesh and dwelt among us" so that we may believe in the only Son of God the Father Almighty, born of the Holy Ghost and the Virgin Mary. The meaning of the Word being made flesh, is not that the divine nature is changed into flesh, but that the divine nature assumed our flesh. And by "flesh" we are here to understand "man," the part being put for the whole, as when it is said, "By the deeds of the law that no flesh be justified," that is, no man. For we must believe that no part was wanting in that human nature which He put on, save that it was a nature wholly free from every taint of sin.[28]

Contemporary writers are prone to treat St. Augustine as though he were deficient in faith, orthodoxy, and common sense. On the contrary, our age, despite its accumulation of knowledge, still has much to learn from him. He was not led willy-nilly by pagan sages, but was himself an original and independent thinker. Although he drew on Platonism so far as this was compatible with orthodoxy, which was always paramount in his mind, he nevertheless went to Aristotle, though he considered him inferior to Plato, in developing his teaching on the Trinity, still the peak of his synthesis and indeed of Catholic theology. In formulating his anthropology, however, he laid aside both Plato and Aristotle, setting forth his teaching in historical perspective and in the concrete framework of Scriptural thought and language.

Some go to ridiculous lengths in making St. Augustine responsible for almost every ill in the Church and even in the world. To his alleged Neoplatonism, for example, has been attributed the modern disrepute of manual labor. On the other hand, secular scholars explain our world to their own satisfaction without calling upon Christian thinkers at all. Catholics, for their part, might escape far enough from parochialism to allow that others besides Plato and Augustine have contributed to what Chesterton spoke of as the muddle that is called the modern mind. In any event, Augustine's "view is not identical with psychophysical parallelism or occasionalism, as these are found in the thought of Malebranche or Leibnitz, for instance."[29] Nor is it identical with the dualism of Descartes, whose view of man, as summarized by Jacques Maritain, is that of "an angel driving a machine." The thought of Descartes, if it can in any manner be traced to Augustine, is a deviation;[30] yet it found its way, like that of Malebranche, into Catholic manuals. Neither their theories, nor those of German idealism, which have not been without influence in the modern world, can be blamed on Augustine, or even on Plato.

It thus seems like a vast oversimplification to imagine that theology can be renewed by breaking with "Platonic religion."[31] If for some time Catholic thought has tended to be excessively abstract and static, the fault is not all Plato's. Tendencies arising in later Scholasticism share the responsibility. Plato entered Christian thought through Augustine, and yet the saint, while indebted to Plato for certain metaphysical notions, broke with Plato, as just observed, in his study of man, adopting the concrete, historical, and existential approach that Catholic scholars are now belatedly recovering. Yet this recovery should not mean—must not mean —that under the influence of materialism and pragmatism we abandon the effort to find metaphysical and even mystical meaning in the universe. While our notion of God may be refined in history, God Himself is above history. And while man is subject to history, there is that in him also which reaches out to God, seeking, in Scriptural language, to "see"

Him and even to "share" in His nature (1 Jn 3: 3: 2 Pet 1: 4). Otherwise man, having served history, will merely disappear into the oblivion of history. It was in finding God and then trying to articulate this experience that Augustine learned of the Greek philosopher. Plato, after all, is no villain. His thought was the first great achievement of human wisdom in the West. His vision, for all its limitations and flaws, has become part of our common human heritage. Purified and baptized by Augustine, it has also become part of our Christian heritage. It would be difficult today to imagine Christianity without this contribution, which has given to Christian thinkers tools for exploring the nature of divinity and has stimulated thought, debate, and questioning all these intervening years.

Not all dualism is Platonic or exaggerated. Jesus said, "Do not lay up for yourselves treasures on earth. . . . But lay up for yourselves treasures in heaven" (Mt 6: 19). This is dualism but neither Platonic nor exaggerated. When the Church frequently bids us in her liturgy (which was not written by Augustine) to pray that we may learn to love heavenly things and scorn those earthly *(amare coelestia et despicere terrena)*, this also is dualism, yet neither Platonic nor exaggerated. When St. Paul said (Phil 3: 8) that, losing all things, he counted them but as dung to gain Christ, this also was dualism but was copied neither from Plato nor Plotinus. The Fathers of the Second Vatican Council wrote, "Man judges rightly that by his intellect he surpasses the material universe, for he shares in the light of the divine mind."[32] This is pure Augustinism and dualism, but it is also the Catholic faith. The same Fathers also wrote, "Nevertheless, wounded by sin man experiences rebellious stirrings in his body."[33] This is neither Manichaean nor Platonic contempt of the body, but part of the deposit of faith.

This evangelic dualism, as it may be called, exists in the moral order and is without metaphysical implication other than that there is a hierarchy of being, hence also of goods. It does not imply that any grade of this hierarchy is degraded or evil: what comes from God is inevitably good. But the existence of a hierarchy does offer to men the opportunity for choice and a hierarchical ordering of their own lives. Here indeed is the center and pivot of moral choice and decision: "Mind the things that are above, not the things that are on the earth" (Col 3: 2). The freedom to choose among goods was to be, as shall be seen, the principle guiding St. Augustine in formulating his moral teaching. It is still the guiding principle in Christian morality. Pope John XXIII, in the address opening the Second Vatican Council, stated: "The Church does not offer modern men riches that perish nor promise them merely earthly happiness. Rather, she distributes to them the goodness of divine grace."

If Augustine drew on Plato, as we shall see he did (and St. Thomas followed him) in formulating his doctrine of concupiscence, this was merely to use the tools of reason to explain a doctrine that is Scriptural and Catholic. His procedure was in accord with his conviction, which was to become axiomatic, that theology is faith seeking understanding.

The Scriptures always speak concretely, and indeed Hebrew lacks abstract words. Nevertheless the Greeks, beginning with Plato, have helped us unearth the treasures of Scriptural thought. Modern writers on theology, if they were acquainted with this tradition, might spare us filling the air with dust and pretentiously wasting our time by their learned efforts to "demythologize" anthropomorphic language, which no serious thinker since Plato has understood other than analogically. Nor would they seek to deprive us, by abolishing metaphysics, of the most useful tool we have, short of revelation, which works usefully under revelation, for exploring the unfathomable riches of God.[34]

"The Church also maintains that beneath all changes there are many realities which do not change and which have their ultimate foundation in Christ, Who is the same yesterday and today, yes and forever."[35] That there are eternal values and realities above those of time is of the essence of Christianity, even though Plato has helped us to understand them. It is not Platonic dualism. Many modern thinkers snip away to the breaking point man's anchorage in eternity by an extreme historicism that regards every value as but the development of a mere passing moment in history. This is to jettison, not only what is best and true in Plato, but Christianity itself. "If anyone loves the world, the love of the Father is not in him" (1 Jn

2: 15). Remove such "dualism" from Scripture and there will be, literally, nothing left of its moral teaching and underlying doctrinal truth.

One suspects that some modern thinkers, like certain contemporary artists, have not mastered the tools of their craft and thus airily dismiss the ancient thinkers whom they do not know. This is why, in theology as elsewhere, those who do not know history are condemned to repeat its mistakes. Augustine's thought, with its Platonic ingredient, comes closer to the fullness of Christian truth than the religionless Christianity that, discarding metaphysics and mysticism, gives itself exclusively to the service of the secular city. The ancient saint takes account, at once, of the complexity of the world, the historical process, man's actual state, and his anchorage in eternity. More than fifteen hundred years ago, in the *City of God*—which, beginning with Charlemagne, has so often been misused for political purposes—Augustine set forth his concept of God and His redemption, with some Platonic language indeed, but in the unfolding drama of what in the latest development of theology is called salvation history.

2. Measure, Form, and Order

> God saw that all He had made was very good.
>
> —Genesis 5: 30.

> Though made of body and soul man is one. Through his bodily composition he gathers to himself the elements of the material world; thus they reach their crown through him and raise their voice in free praise of the Creator.
>
> For this reason man is not allowed to despise his bodily life; rather he is obliged to regard his body as good and honorable since God has created it and will raise it up on the last day. Nevertheless, wounded by sin, man experiences rebellious stirrings in his body.
>
> —Vatican Council II, *Gaudium et Spes*, no. 14

Augustine was preoccupied with the problem of evil. Its facile but false solution by the Manichees, who explained it as the result of an evil principle in material nature, held Augustine for a time but did not satisfy him. He broke out of this system through a twofold personal deliverance: first, through the ability, learned of Platonism, to conceive of incorporeal nature; then, as a consequence of this, through the realization that evil is but a limitation, a diminishment; and that moral evil, therefore, is a deflection of the will from the norm of good.

He describes, in his *Confessions*, the anguish of soul in which he made these discoveries, and there, as the term of his probing, gives us a definition of evil, learned from St. Ambrose, which has become classical in Catholic theology: the privation of good, *privatio boni*.[1] He treats the subject fully in a number of works written both before and after the *Confessions*. The solution is always the same: evil is in the will, a defect of the will, a privation of the good. There is no teaching of Augustine clearer or more constant than this.

Metaphysical evil is simply the limitation of good inherent

in creaturehood; and there is no physical evil for him other than that arising from the inevitable limits of every created nature. Corruption can occur in nature, but not to the annihilation of the good; meanwhile, so far as nature remains, it is good.[2] As to moral evil, Augustine never varied from his conception of it as a defect of free will. His discovery that moral evil is simply a lack, a kind of nothingness, takes it completely out of the bodily and material sphere. Whatever he says of sin and concupiscence, therefore, however graphically he describes their force, must be understood against the background of this principle. With endless patience he would repeat to the Pelagians (who already accused him of Manichaeism because of his insistence on original sin and concupiscence) that the difference between man's former state and his present condition is sin: "There would have been none of this shame-producing concupiscence, which is impudently praised by impudent men, if man had not previously sinned."[3] The saint's mere refutation of Manichaeism is his vindication, as good, of the body, sexuality, marriage, and generation: on his principles none of these can contain any substantial taint. By locating moral evil in the will and regarding it as a kind of nothingness, Augustine was prevented from attributing any inherent evil to the body or sexuality.

Conversely, virtue is situated properly also in the will. Continence is not a virtue of the body merely but primarily of the will.[4]

> Virginity is not honored because it is virginity, but because it is consecrated to God; although it is preserved in the flesh, it is nevertheless preserved by religion and devotion of soul. Therefore, even bodily virginity, which a loving chastity vows and preserves, is spiritual. For just as no one uses the body impurely except through wickedness already conceived in the spirit, so no one preserves virginity of body except through chastity already rooted in the spirit.
>
> Moreover, if conjugal chastity, although it be preserved in the flesh, is nevertheless attributed not to the flesh, but to the soul, under whose command and direction the flesh is used in no other except its own

proper union, how much the more, and how much more honorably, is that continence to be numbered among the goods of the soul by which integrity of body is vowed, consecrated, and preserved for the Creator Himself of the soul and of the body.[5]

How can anyone question that for Augustine there could be no inherent impurity or evil in the body?[6]

To suspect Augustine of "latent Manichaeism," as if he continued to believe that there is some intrinsic evil in nature itself, is an outrage. It fails to consider the manner, as well as the completeness, of his conversion; it ignores the thoroughness with which, soon after his conversion, he turned his powerful polemical weapons against the Manichees, continued to attack them tirelessly for some twenty years, and was chiefly responsible for purging their gross errors from the nascent Christian civilization.

This is not to deny that Augustine (and the Church) profited immensely by his Manichaean experience. "He forgets it so little that he makes use of it," says Gilson, showing how he refuted Manichaean materialism from its own principles.[7] The depth of his convictions concerning the excellence of spiritual reality and the havoc of sin, as well as his exaltation of the goodness of creation, also arose from his conversion from Manichaeism. Moreover, the firmness with which he attached procreation to marriage was directly counter to the Manichaean teaching that marriage and generation are evil.[8] The influence of Manichaeism was by way of reaction.

It might be said—in fact this is the point of those who accuse Augustine of latent Manichaeism—that while he was firm enough in refuting the Manichees, he afterward reversed himself in dealing with the Pelagians and asserting against them the destructiveness of original sin.[9] In fact, Augustine achieved the difficult feat of keeping a balance between Manichaean and Pelagian errors, affirming on the one hand the goodness of all created nature and, on the other, the actuality of sin with concupiscence as its cause. That he maintained such a balance is shown by the passage of the *Retractations* in which, when the dust of both controversies was settling, he affirms these two counterbalancing truths, namely, that sin and evil are only in the will, never substantial, and that there is nevertheless in man a concupiscence that causes sin.[10] However, it is not necessary to depend on this or that passage to prove that he maintained this balance. In Chapter 4 we shall show how his whole teaching on concupiscence—which was projected in his early "philosophic" period, developed in his struggle against the Manichees, and matured in the anti-Pelagian controversy—simultaneously and consistently affirms both these truths. In short, the charge of Manichaeism made against Augustine comes from the failure of those who make it to grasp his notion of concupiscence and, in the end, from their failure to keep the balance, which he so carefully preserved, between Manichaeism and Pelagianism.

Both the controversy with the Manichees and that with the Pelagians, if for different reasons, involved marriage and sexuality. The Manichees, regarding matter as evil, also considered marriage and generation evil, since through these the domain of matter is extended. The Pelagians, on the other hand, affirmed the goodness of nature and the body, but in so doing were led to contend that original sin and its effects cannot be transmitted through generation. How Augustine maintained balance between these two extremes may be seen by placing side by side passages in which he refutes both the Manichaean and Pelagian views of the marriage relationship of Old Testament saints. The Manichees claimed to see in the polygamy and concubinage of the patriarchs evidence that marriage is evil. The Pelagians invoked the example of the saintly patriarchs to prove that original sin could not be transmitted through marriage.

Augustine, despite the prejudice that his critics attribute to him against sexuality, eloquently defended the patriarchs against the Manichees. To Faustus he said:

> The origin of sin is in the will; therefore in the will is also the origin of evil, both in the sense of acting against a just precept, and in the sense of suffering under a just sentence. There is no reason why, in your search for the origin of evil, you should fall into

so great an evil as that of calling a nature so rich in good things the nature of evil, and of attributing the terrible evil of necessity to the nature of perfect good, before any commixture with evil.[11]

Against the Pelagians, while not abandoning what he had said to Faustus, he insisted that original sin was transmitted even through the marriages of the Old Testament saints; and as proof of this he cited the fact that their sons had to be circumcised. To Julian he wrote:

> Answer, if you can, why Isaac's soul would have perished from his people if he had not been circumcised on the eighth day by the sign of the baptism of Christ. Explain, if you can, the reason why he would have suffered so great a punishment if not delivered by the sacrament. You cannot deny that God gave life to the dead womb of Sara for the reception of seed, and to the dead body of Abraham for generation in the way in which young men generate, in order that offspring might be born of the old age of the parents. But why did Isaac, born innocent as to personal sins, who would have been born innocent in this respect even if born of adulterers, deserve that his soul should perish from his people if he were not circumcised?[12]

The practice of baptizing infants was of course also the reason why Augustine was so confident that he was defending Catholic teaching in asserting that original sin and its effects are transmitted through generation.

Augustine was really never very deeply committed as a Manichee. His acceptance of that system may have originally stemmed in part from a spirit of rebellion, not uncommon among university students, against "the Establishment"; also against prayerful pursuit by his mother, Monica—from whom he once actually took physical flight.[13] Moreover, Manichaean antinomianism was a convenient cloak for the kind of life that he was then leading—pursuing wisdom on the one hand and, on the other, giving himself over to debauchery. When he really got down to the study of Manichaeism, seeking out Faustus, its chief spokesman, for enlightenment, he was quickly disillusioned and began to detach himself from the sect.[14]

It would be insulting to the memory of this great Doctor to multiply texts "proving" that after his baptism he did not remain a Manichaean. His meditations on Genesis could leave in him no doubt of the goodness of God's creation, and he used the fruit of these meditations almost immediately after his conversion to attack the Manichees mercilessly (against them he wrote two of his three commentaries on Genesis). His insistence on the goodness of nature, including material nature, could be illustrated from every page of his extensive anti-Manichaean writings. What is more important, however, is to understand the principle that governs his thought on this matter throughout his life and was the basis of his refutation of the Manichees:

> For we Catholic Christians worship God, from whom are all good things whether great or small; from whom is all form great or small; from whom is all order great or small. For all things in proportion as they are better measured, formed, and ordered are assuredly good in a higher degree; but in proportion as they are measured, formed, and ordered in an inferior degree, they are less good. These three things, therefore, measure, form, and order, are as it were generic goods in things made by God, whether in spirit or in body.[15]

All things therefore, insofar as they have being—that is, insofar as they are endowed with "measure, form, and order"—are from God and are therefore inescapably good. Evil can corrupt creatures because they are limited in their being, because they are contingent, because they are made from nothingness. Evil is a lapse toward an unattainable nothingness. "The life which wilfully falls away from its Maker, whose being it enjoyed, and desires in a manner contrary to God's law to enjoy the bodily things to which God made it superior, inclines to nonentity."[16]

When therefore it is inquired, whence is evil, it must first be inquired, what is evil, which is nothing else than corruption, either of the measure, or the form, or the order that belongs to nature. . . .

If corruption take away all measure, all form, all order from corruptible things, no nature will remain. . . . But every nature that can be corrupted is some good; for corruption cannot injure it, except by taking away from or diminishing what is good.[17]

As to man:

But to the most excellent creatures, that is, to rational spirits, God has offered this, that if they *will* not they cannot be corrupted; that is, if they should maintain obedience under the Lord their God, so that they adhere to His incorruptible beauty; but if they do not will to maintain obedience, since willingly they are corrupted in sins, unwillingly they shall be corrupted in punishment.[18]

"Against the Manichaeans, who held that a principle of evil in the world limits God's power, Augustine held that God's omnipotence and goodness make impossible the existence of genuine evil."[19] This statement summarizes the saint's teaching admirably: substantial evil, in his thought, is a metaphysical impossibility. In his own words, "Absolutely no natural reality is evil, and the only meaning of the word 'evil' is the privation of good."[20]

How far he was ready to carry his conviction of the goodness of God's creation is shown by a remark that he made (in 421, toward the end of his life) to the Pelagian bishop Julian, who accused him of Manichaeism: "You thought it was necessary to assemble testimonies from Holy Scripture to prove something about which there was no question between us, namely, that man was created by God—which we may not deny about the least of worms."[21] Many years before he had demonstrated to Faustus the Manichee the excellence of his bowels!

Augustine's works are filled with illustrations drawn from nature.[22] To his observations he brought the curiosity and delight of a child combined with the sensitivity of a literary

Measure, Form, and Order 51

artist. (Remember, he had once been a materialist, and the word "rhetorician," used to describe him in his early days, would be better rendered in our language as "literary artist.") He writes (during the period of his later anti-Pelagian works, when he is supposed to have regressed toward Manichaeism):

> What words can describe the myriad beauties of land and sea and sky? Just think of the inimitable abundance and the marvelous loveliness of light, or of the beauty of the sun and moon and stars, of shadowy glades in the woods and of the colors and perfumes of flowers, of the songs and plumage of so many varieties of birds, of the innumerable animals of every species that amaze us most when they are smallest in size. For example, the activities of ants and bees seem more stupendous than the sheer immensity of whales. Or look at the grandiose spectacle of the open sea, clothing and reclothing itself in dresses of changing shades of green and purple and blue. And what a delight when the ocean breaks into storm and can be enjoyed—at least from shore where there is no fear of the fury of the waves.[23]

Of the human *body* he says:

> Nevertheless the human body is a revelation of the goodness of God and the providence of the body's Creator.... There is in a man's body such a rhythm, poise, symmetry and beauty that it is hard to decide whether it was the uses or the beauty of the body that the Creator had most in mind.... I think that in the creation of the human body God put form before function.[24]

His observations on nature were sometimes his own, sometimes drawn from Pliny's *Natural History*—the same source that St. Francis de Sales was to use later. Much more than St. Thomas, whose conviction of nature's goodness is unquestioned but somewhat abstract, Augustine may be considered the harbinger of St. Francis' "devout humanism." His circle of friends was the last humanist group before the barbarian avalanche and until the Renaissance. His was the last of the great Christian-Platonic academies before Pico della Mirandola and Monsilio Ficinio.[25]

Most of the modern objections to St. Augustine seek support from his anti-Pelagian writings where he affirmed and emphasized the consequences of original sin. On the other hand, none of his books is less likely to seem of interest or relevance to a modern reader than that large segment directed against the Manichees. Their fantastic cosmogony and their detailed misinterpretation of the Old Testament, which Augustine followed and refuted in equal detail, seem far remote from our concerns today. Yet it was precisely in these works that he demonstrated the impossibility of evil as a physical or metaphysical reality, a conviction that he held throughout his life, thus establishing the basis of his later strong affirmation against the Pelagians of the reality and destructiveness of sin in *the moral order*. Augustine preserved the difficult and delicate balance between Manichaeism and Pelagianism, as every Catholic must, affirming against the former the goodness of nature, material and spiritual, and against the latter the wounding of nature through original sin. Those who think that at least in his later years he veered toward Manichaeism should watch their own balance and examine whether, under pretext of rejecting Manichaean dualism, they are not themselves drifting toward the Pelagian denial of the effects of original sin. They should reflect that the charge of Manichaeism made against Augustine is not new —it was made against him in his own day, by the Pelagians. Are these critics then really defending nature as if against Augustine—although he defended it more vigorously than they in the Church's actual crisis—or are they, in the naturalistic spirit of the Pelagians, simply refusing to accept the actuality of concupiscence as an effect of original sin? The question will recur. Meanwhile, the next two chapters will be addressed to discovering what is meant in the saint's thought by the "corruption" of nature.

3. Paradise Lost

> If then any man is in Christ, he is a new creature; the former things are passed away; behold they are made new!
> —2 Corinthians 55: 17

> The root reason for human dignity lies in man's call to communion with God. From the very circumstances of his origin man is already invited to converse with God.
> —Vatican Council II, *Gaudium et Spes*, no. 19

> The followers of Christ are justified in the Lord Jesus, because in the baptism of faith they truly become sons of God and sharers in divine nature.
> —Vatican Council II, *Lumen Gentium*, no. 40

1. THE CONSEQUENCES OF THE FALL

We now come to the heart of the problem and the basic reason for the rather thorough modern misinterpretation of St. Augustine.

The starting place for an understanding of original sin and its consequences is the state of man before the Fall. To grasp the nature of the Fall and its effects, we must know what man fell from. In the thought of St. Thomas, which is normative and substantially that of the Church, Adam was originally placed in the order of grace: by grace he was elevated to share in the divine life: for Adam this grace was exclusively elevating grace, *gratia elevans,* raising him to the intimate love of God. His fall, then, since it was from a higher than human state, consisted essentially in the loss of elevating and sanctifying grace. He also lost the preternatural gifts that had been bestowed on him to supplement divine grace. For St. Thomas, neither loss, however disastrous, affected the substance of human nature or its powers.

We are thus left with a relatively optimistic view of nature. However, St. Thomas by no means denies the reality of concupiscence, resulting from original sin. Materially, this comprises all man's desires; it is their exuberant, because vital, tendency to seek each its own good. Before the Fall these appetites caused no trouble: they were kept in harmony and unity by the special gift of integrity under reason and grace. Since the Fall—and here we come to concupiscence in its theological sense—because integrity was not restored with grace, there tends to be anarchy among these desires.[1] As in a family whose members pursue each his own advantage without regard for the good of the whole family, so the desires of fallen man seek each its own satisfaction regardless of the good of the whole man—a wholeness that in the divine order includes his endowments of grace. The desires in man are themselves good, but they are dynamic and no longer respond readily to the control of reason, as reason itself evades the leadings of faith. Hence, as soon as they begin to act, they move into the moral order, where, if indulged, they either divert man more or less from his supernatural end, or, if disciplined and controlled, are drawn into his total effort to obtain that end. Their tendency to disorder, aptly called by the Council of Trent a *"fomes"* (or tinder), remains even in the baptized, "to be wrestled with *ad agonem*," and is therefore ever ready to flame up in disordered and evil actions, although "it cannot harm those who do not consent but manfully resist by the grace of Christ."[2]

In those justified by grace, therefore, concupiscence remains the center and cause of an agonizing struggle for holiness and salvation. All the desires are affected, or wounded, as St. Thomas teaches: the mind by the wound of ignorance; the will, tending toward evil, by the wound of malice *(malitia)*; the irascible appetite by the wound of weakness *(infirmitas)*; and the delectable appetite by sensual concupiscence (concupiscence in a narrow sense).[3] It is because of these wounds that the desires, seeking their own special and connatural goods, tend to do so independently of the good of the whole man, especially as re-created in Christ. The four wounds (together causing concupiscence in the full theological sense) are transmitted with human nature itself because of its loss of the Paradisal gifts; hence, original sin is a sin of nature, as distinct from actual personal sin. The strength of concupiscence is also increased by indulgence leading to sin, and especially by habitual sin. Obviously, too, if the grace of restoration is to be effective, it must have, and does have through the merits of Christ, in addition to its elevating effect, a healing property, remedial grace, *gratia sanans,* by which sin is forgiven and healing aid given to overcome it.

This is the norm, as matured substantially by St. Thomas, and then defined by Trent. In our time both the doctrine and terminology have been corroborated anew by the Fathers of the Second Vatican Council:

> The Council, first of all, wishes to assess in this light [of faith] all those values that are most highly prized today and to relate them to their divine source. Insofar as they stem from endowments conferred by God and man, these values are exceedingly good. Yet they are often wrenched from their rightful function by the taint in man's heart, and hence stand in need of *purification.*[4]

Further on:

> Pursuing the saving purpose which is proper to her, the Church does not only communicate divine life to men but in some way casts the reflected light of that life over the entire earth, most of all by its *healing* and *elevating* impact on the dignity of the person, by the way in which it strengthens the seams of human society and imbues the everyday activity of men with a deeper meaning and importance.[5]

Concerning Augustine, therefore, the question is: How far did he contribute to the doctrine as thus formulated? Did he diverge from it?

First of all, he did not arrive at his position by way of this doctrinal dialectic. He came to it, as described in the *Confessions,* by a long mental and moral struggle, culminating in his conversion through an almost overwhelming experience of grace. This experience of personal weakness and of the power of grace was the matrix of all his further elaborations both of grace and concupiscence. Much of the misunderstanding of Augustine comes from separating his doctrine of grace from his teaching on concupiscence. They must be viewed together, as also in St. Paul, correlative, balancing, and explaining each other. For him, mental darkness and moral weakness—concupiscence—retire only under the action of grace: the desire of the flesh is effectively countered by the desire of the spirit (Gal 5: 17). Concupiscence will always remain to be combated; but it can be dominated and controlled by a will obedient to grace.

It is important to keep in mind this full Augustinian notion of concupiscence. The saint's inclusion of darkness of mind and weakness of will in this concept is sometimes overlooked through preoccupation with his more sensational revelations about himself. Even those who should know better tend to notice only his teaching on sensual concupiscence without reflecting that this stress was forced on him in his polemics against Manichaeans and Pelagians, since in both controversies, if for opposite reasons, sexual concupiscence was a central area of concern. While in the *Confessions* Augustine's account of his struggle with sensuality is candid enough, it is also muted—few details are given to the merely curious. Nevertheless, it is to be feared that it is this part of the narrative that absorbs many readers, who are then inattentive to the real inward process of his conversion. (John Galsworthy once said that it is a mistake for a novelist to stress sex, since this theme, by attracting excessive attention, tends to obscure the artist's overall purpose.) Vernon Bourke in the title of his book well describes the saint's life and conversion as a "quest of wisdom." Augustine was sensitive and complex, as well as passionate, and his conversion was correspondingly complex. For those interested in seeing it whole, its intricate strands are skillfully disentangled by Romano Guardini in his *The Conversion of St. Augustine.*[6]

"The two consequences of original sin which Augustine always associates whenever he mentions them are concupiscence and ignorance."[7] This concupiscence, as Augustine understands it, generally (but not always) results from the wound in the sensible appetites, which St. Thomas also, in a restricted sense, calls concupiscence. But for Augustine, concupiscence (in the larger sense), besides causing ignorance in the mind, affects the will, also a spiritual faculty. It is a key point in his doctrine that man's will is given true liberty, i.e., to attain his end in God, only by divine grace; otherwise it is hopelessly mired down in evil: "Free will is not made void by grace, but is established, since grace cures the will whereby righteousness is freely loved."[8]

The difficulty, as usual, is partly one of semantics. The word *concupiscence,* itself meaning "strong or ardent desire" (Webster), in theology includes all desires, classified by St. Thomas, as just seen, into four basic groups; for all the desires, spiritual as well as sensible, are prone to excess and tend to deflect man from loving God. St. Augustine does not employ the word in this general sense, but rather in the restricted meaning, which we have also seen in St. Thomas, of a disorder in the sense appetites. This restricted use of the word causes Augustine to be misunderstood, as though he acknowledged it only in the sense appetites (and by a further restriction, only in the sexual appetites). Yet the saint, in addition to his stress on the wound of ignorance in the mind,[9] also describes concupiscence in the will. Only through the intervention of the will, indeed, do the desires of the sensible appetites attain moral significance.[10]

Man's will, then, is all-important. If it is rightly directed, the emotions will not be merely blameless but even praiseworthy. The will is in all these affections; indeed, they are nothing else than inclinations of the will. For what are desire and joy but the will in harmony with things we desire? And what are fear and sadness but the will in disagreement with things we abhor?[11]

Hence, although later terminology differs from that of St. Augustine, his notion of concupiscence includes all the desires and is in fact identical with that of St. Thomas. Accordingly, the Angelic Doctor gives short shrift to the objection that Augustine's teaching on the results of original sin differs from his own.[12] We must simply make allowance for Augustine's different terminology—or for lack of a developed terminology in Augustine's time.[13]

2. JANSENISM

In the next chapter we shall complete the Augustinian notion of concupiscence and consider how it affects the desires. It is necessary to state as much as we have now in order to see how for the saint the Fall affected human nature. This is the heart of the problem of Jansenism and of Augustine's relation to this system.

Because of his own experience—and because of his polemics against the Pelagians—there is in St. Augustine great stress on grace as remedial. The important question here is whether he understood that grace also effects an elevation "to share in the divine nature." Did Augustine believe that Adam possessed *gratia elevans*? On the saint's position here depends his whole doctrine of the Fall and its consequences. Accordingly, this point is absolutely decisive for the correct understanding of his anthropology. At this point, precisely, Luther and Jansenius went off the path, claiming Augustine's authority for the erroneous view that original sin has left human nature flawed intrinsically. From this misunderstanding has come also the sub-Jansenistic misinterpretation of Augustine current among many Catholics.

There can be no doubt that St. Augustine was convinced of the supernatural character of grace in man's restored state as in Adam before the Fall. We encounter here, however, a difficulty common in studying Augustine's writings. It comes from his discursive method, his lack of the later more developed terminology, and from his concrete, historical viewpoint, which is not concerned to draw an abstract distinction between nature and grace. Nevertheless, he affirmed that "from the very beginning, Adam, in the state of innocence, possessed these gifts that are called praeternatural and supernatural."[14] Because of Augustine's method, it requires, to establish this point in detail, an extensive foray into his works. But Jacques Maritain provides a useful summary:

> Still it is well to add that the difference [from St. Thomas's view] is purely modal, that St. Augustine taught as clearly as possible, the ontological value of the distinction between nature and grace, that he

clearly affirmed such a distinction, even for the state of innocence; that, for him, grace is the root of Adam's supernatural privileges as of his corporal immortality, hence, it is also supernatural; it is positively and intrinsically ordered to the Beatific Vision, which is not due to any created intelligence, not even to the angelic; it is distinct from nature, even in the case of the angels (*simul condens naturam et largiens gratiam*).[15]

It is worthy of note that St. Thomas thus understood Augustine; his assimilation of Augustine's teaching on the wounds of nature necessarily implied that he regarded Augustine's understanding of grace to be identical with his own (elevating as well as remedial). It was the loss of St. Thomas's thought, superseded as it was by nominalism and deviant forms of Augustinianism, that caused later errors.

Most of the modern misunderstanding about Augustine comes from looking back at him through the eyes of the Jansenists. And yet Jansenius's "fundamental error consists in disregarding the supernatural order: for Jansenius, as for Baius, the vision of God is the necessary end of human nature; hence it follows that all the primal endowments designated in theology as supernatural or praeternatural, including exemption from concupiscence, were simply man's due."[16] In Catholic thought Adam was placed from the beginning in a supernatural state; his fall therefore, a loss of gratuitous endowments, left his nature intact. For Jansenius, on the other hand, Adam was created only in a natural state; his fall therefore affected his nature and its powers, damaging them intrinsically. Quesnel, a follower of Jansenius, drove this principle to its ultimate odious conclusion when he held that even the prayer of a sinner is but another sin.[17]

How could St. Augustine's doctrine be confused with such an utter distortion of it? How could Jansenius claim the great Doctor's authority?

The answer, in Gilson's words, is, in the first place, derived from one of the "essential characteristics" of Augustinianism: "its fundamental condition of incompleteness"; for this reason it is "exposed to all sorts of deviations"; and "Jansenius,

Malebranche, Gerdil, are so many tangents of Augustinism; they are not St. Augustine."[18]

Moreover, St. Augustine did not approach this problem as later Scholastics did; his terms must be transposed into theirs (and ours) with care—a care rarely observed. The Scholastics usually regard abstract nature in its metaphysical essence: what it is or ought to be. But Augustine viewed man concretely—as he actually appears in history. He does not distinguish abstractly a state of pure nature and study its relationship to grace. He does not describe, in purely abstract terms, either man's elevation or his fall. Indeed, for Augustine, man's state before the Fall was his natural state, since it was the state originally given to him by God (another source of semantic difficulty).

The Jansenistic misreading of Augustine has produced a miasma that has spread over the modern Catholic world. Even the scholarly, it is to be feared, tend to look at Augustine through this distorting atmosphere.[19] The Abbé Klein, writing the history of heretical "Americanism," called it a "phantom heresy": a combination of errors found, not in the teachings of the accused, but in the accumulated imputations of the accusers.[20] What is commonly known as Augustinism—a gloomy view of nature, overemphasis on original sin, exaggeration of concupiscence—is likewise a phantom heresy. Moreover, this phantom causes Catholics to neglect and even to deny, at least in practice, what are in fact teachings of St. Thomas and even of the Church.

For example, there is a common misunderstanding about the wounds of nature. The idea of a nature wounded is attributed to St. Augustine, although it comes directly from the *Summa* of St. Thomas, which contains Augustine's teaching *eminenter;* and it is then interpreted according to the Jansenistic mentality. The wounds of nature are thus thought to imply some intrinsic damage to nature: "darkness," "malice," "weakness," can be misleading—especially malice, which St. Thomas describes as an inclination to evil, *pronitas ad malum,* justifying this from Scripture. The use of this phrase in catechisms has undoubtedly contributed to a falsely Augustinian, or more specifically, to a Jansenistic outlook, i.e., a failure to relate these words to man's original elevation through grace. This may be seen especially in older catechisms, where grace and the divine indwelling are considered *after* the account of the Fall: a procedure that allows the Fall to look like a fall from nature, so that grace appears to be, in the Jansenistic manner, only a remedy for sin, with its elevating effect lost sight of.

Thus the misunderstanding of Augustine is a pretext for neglecting the important practical teachings of St. Thomas on the wounds of nature; and this in turn leads to glossing over the Church's doctrine on original sin and its consequences, defined, as we shall see, largely in the very words of Augustine, by the Council of Trent. The modern attack on St. Augustine, therefore, is tantamount to an attack on the Church.

By uncritically identifying Augustinism with its Jansenistic misinterpretations, modern Catholics expose themselves to the errors of Augustine's Pelagian opponents.

Concupiscence is healed by *gratia sanans:* loss of fear for concupiscence means loss of the sense of need for this remedial grace: "The role of grace is only understood," Gilson remarks, "in terms of the evils it is to cure."[21] Accordingly, the doctrine Augustine fought so hard for—and which has also been substantially incorporated into the teachings of the Church—is carelessly thrown away. Father Bernard Häring's one-volume summary of moral theology (*Christian Renewal in a Changing World*) does not mention concupiscence. Catholic moral theology is thus presented without the crucial dynamic principle that governs the whole Christian life in its central struggle. (In his three-volume text Häring devotes only a few pages to this important subject, with another eight pages given to the capital sins.) Of course Father Häring speaks of the effects of original sin, but in a general way, as selfishness, pride, egotism. He insists on the need for mortification, dying with Christ, self-denial, and detachment. He places purification, or purgation, in its normal place (at the beginning) of the Christian ascent to holiness. In view of this it may seem like mere caviling to make a point of his avoidance of the word "concupiscence." But as we shall see, this word—with the idea it contains—focuses attention sharply, as no other yet suggested does, on the dynamic and real cause of sin.

Writers who, in treating of sin, trace its causes to "selfishness" or "egotism," are dealing with the problem superficially, or rather, evading it. "Egotism" and "selfishness" are already moral dispositions, if but incipiently formed. The same is true of the capital sins, which are vices or evil dispositions.[22] This is to say, they already belong to the moral order and, instead of explaining sin, must themselves be explained. The explanation is to be found in concupiscence, the *fomes* of sin, as the Fathers of Trent called it, but of itself not actualized, therefore not yet belonging to the moral order although constantly threatening to enter there. To meet this threat and to contain concupiscence, directing its underlying energies to a life serving man's supernatural end, remedial grace, together with a suitable response to this grace, is required.

Neglect of remedial grace, following disregard for concupiscence, cannot but lead to the neglect of elevating grace. We shall have occasion to speak of this connection later, although meanwhile it should be evident. Both the elevating and the remedial effects come from the one sanctifying grace merited for us by Christ. Nor can we, in our fallen state, enjoy the benefits of elevating grace except to the extent that we are purified by remedial grace. Accordingly, eloquent praise of elevating grace, as found in authors who like to emphasize exclusively the "positive," cannot compensate for the practical harm done by forgetting the need for remedial grace (and the personal response demanded by it) in eliminating the negative effects of sin.

Jansenism has become such a bogey to Catholics that it has driven modern Catholic thought off center. Fear of the oblique Manichaean spirit implicit in Jansenism, which would see nature and its powers intrinsically damaged and evil, has prevented due recognition of the evil that, without implying any inherent evil in nature, results from original sin. Because Augustine insisted on the threat of concupiscence, the Pelagians called him a Manichee. By echoing this cry modern Catholics expose themselves to the danger of Pelagianism and would deprive the Church of Augustine's intuition and of a key contribution he makes to Catholic moral theology.

Jansenism and Pelagianism are opposing forms of naturalism; we gain nothing by allowing ourselves to be pushed from one extreme to the other. Jansenism, holding that man's state is but natural in God's plan of salvation, and admitting that the Fall involves the whole of mankind, inescapably concludes that our common nature is deeply and internally damaged; for the Jansenists, grace is necessary to restore nature —but only to its own natural plane. The Pelagians, likewise asserting that man's state in God's plan is but natural, see in Adam's sin no consequences for mankind except a bad example; they believed, therefore, that, except for those actually sinning, men can be saved without grace. Only those guilty of personal sin, according to the Pelagians, require grace—for forgiveness, and thus to restore them to their natural state. Catholic truth, an eminence between these opposing errors, holds that man's state, as planned and effected by God, is supernatural: Adam's fall, therefore, which does affect mankind, on the one hand leaves nature intact (as the Pelagians—and Augustine—rightly believed); but, on the other, it leaves us in a disordered state—a disorder that the Pelagians denied and the Jansenists exaggerated by making evil substantive, but that in Augustine's (and Catholic) thought becomes actually evil only when it enters the moral order and entices the will away from its true final good in the order of grace. This is why the Pelagians called Augustine a Manichee; on the other hand, the Jansenists, erroneously claiming Augustine, called Catholics Pelagian. It seems time to call a halt.

When the Jansenists claimed that man fell from a state of nature, they could, by citing Augustine's emphasis on remedial grace, make a specious claim to his authority. Nor could they do other than conclude, in placing Adam but in a state of nature, that the Fall had damaged this nature intrinsically. In this case, grace would be necessary to restore man *even to the state of nature;* and they could again appeal plausibly to Augustine's teaching on remedial grace (forgetting its elevating effect) in his polemics against the Pelagians, to prove that it accomplishes only this. Modern Catholics, by talking recklessly of Augustine's "latent Manichaeism" and by allowing the Jansenists exclusive rights to interpret him, deprive the Church of his insight into that weakness, resulting from the Fall, which hinders our enjoyment of those benefits won for us at such cost by the Savior.[23] And they align themselves with the Pelagians both in a denial of the danger of concupiscence, and the consequent practical denial of the need of remedial grace to overcome it in order that we may "in truth" share the divine life.

However, the problem of original sin and its consequences can be fully understood only in the light of St. Augustine's developed doctrine on concupiscence. To its consideration we now turn.

4. The Force of Disintegration

> Put on the Lord Jesus Christ, and as for the flesh, take no thought of its lusts.
> —Romans 3: 4
>
> Therefore, man is split within himself. As a result, all of human life, whether individual or collective, shows itself to be a dramatic struggle, between good and evil, between light and darkness.
> —Vatican Council II, *Gaudium et Spes*, no. 13

I. THE MEANING OF CONCUPISCENCE

In the previous chapter we considered the background of St. Augustine's teaching on concupiscence. It remains to examine the nature of concupiscence, as he saw it, and the manner of its operation.

Viewed in the context of man's original state, where he was raised to share the divine life through grace and destined to find final fulfillment in God, concupiscence in the thought of Augustine is simply the recoil of man's natural appetites upon themselves after the loss of grace and the other supporting gifts of his Paradisal state: It "is the rebellion against our own selves, proceeding from our very selves, which by a most righteous retribution is rendered only by our disobedient members."[1] It comprises all the natural desires that, good in themselves since they come from the Creator, are wounded by sin through the loss of their original elevation and orientation by grace to God; hence these desires are also prone to deviate even from their true natural good as defined by reason and to fall into actual sin. With his elevation lost, his mind deprived of the highest wisdom, his will no longer attuned by grace to his true end, and his lower faculties left to their own dynamisms, man finds that his life on earth becomes a personal anarchy. When grace is restored, but the other gifts withheld, he is enabled once more to live on the divine plane but must engage in endless conflict with his rebellious faculties. Nature itself, however, together with its powers, is left substantially intact.

Thus Augustine's teaching is not "exaggerated"; indeed, via St. Thomas, he has given the Church, as shall be seen, its developed notion of concupiscence. Here again he begins with his own experience: his long struggle against mental blindness and sensuality is never forgotten, nor the deliverance effected in him by God's grace. Later he tirelessly attacks the Pelagians with their proud assertion of nature's capacity to live a sinless life. He asserts against them in a thousand ways nature's inability to obtain salvation without the healing balm of grace. He is guided by the text: "Whatsoever is not from faith is of sin" (Rom 14: 23). He sees the influence of concupiscence pervasive in human actions. Later theologians would teach that nature is capable of some good natural actions but that man cannot observe the natural law in its entirety for any considerable length of time without the aid of grace.[2] The Church condemned the Jansenists for holding that all natural actions are sinful. Does St. Augustine hold this Jansenistic tenet, or does his teaching imply such a view? The Jansenists, indeed, claimed his authority, but their claim was based on their misunderstanding of his teaching.

Misunderstanding arose from shifting the discussion from Augustine's context and point of view to that of later Scholasticism, which starts from an abstract conception of nature. "To the best of our knowledge, at least, a definition of what man's metaphysical essence could have implied as belonging by right to his nature is not to be found in Augustine. The point of view he takes is always, so to speak, historical and purely factual."[3] Since he does not distinguish a state of pure nature, he does not discuss whether man of himself is capable of good moral actions. However, he allows that the pagans had virtues—although spoiled in practice by defects into which man, relying on himself alone, inevitably falls.[4] He sees concupiscence, which resulted from the actual Fall, as pervasive, ever-threatening, constantly infiltrating our actions, and certain, unless restrained by a will responsive to healing grace, to lead into sin. Yet it is not itself actually sinful. He can maintain this position because man, in his thought, fell from the state he enjoyed before the Fall. Our natural powers, although prone to disorder, remain sound. It is a mark of Augustine's genius that even without the metaphysical notion of nature, he avoided the excess into which the Jansenists afterward fell.

Augustine's notion of concupiscence and of how, without being actually sinful, it leads to sin, is manifest from his notion of sin.

The ordinary descriptive definition of sin, taken from St. Augustine, and still used in our catechisms as well as in theology manuals, is "a word, deed, or desire against eternal law." This definition is comprehensive and theological ("against eternal law") rather than merely moral. Yet it gives no insight into the etiology of sin. Another definition, from an early work in which the subject is studied extensively, does provide such an insight. Here it is in St. Thomas's version: "Sin is nothing else than the neglect of eternal things in the pursuit of temporal things."[5] In *The Problem of Free Choice*, from which this definition is taken,[6] St. Augustine describes how man is placed between the goods of this world and those of eternity. Life demands of him a choice: if he chooses the higher over a lower good, he makes an act of preference, the beginning of love, and he acts virtuously, drawing toward God; but if he prefers the lower good over the higher, deflecting from the higher, then he sins. Sin, although evil, comes from embracing a good. No one, including a sinner, acts except from the desire for what he regards here and now as good. This is how concupiscence, although proceeding from a natural appetite that is itself good and seeking that which is good, can, by transgressing the limits set by God for the use of created goods, lead to sin. There is no need to postulate a dark strain, a downward bias, in human nature, or its faculties. The wound of *malitia* in the will, although an inclination to evil, is still a desire for good: a desire that is disordered because it chooses a lower good over the higher.

St. Thomas adopts this conception as his own, denying an alleged conflict with the other descriptive definition of sin (given above), which he had also taken from the one he always regarded as his master.

Concupiscence, therefore, in Augustine's thought, is the disorderly pursuit by the several appetites of their proper natural goods, a pursuit that, since the loss of integrity, is difficult even for the grace-filled will to contain within the prescribed limits. This concupiscence, tending to exuberance and turbulence (one of Augustine's favorite words), leads readily to disorder, diverting the will from God. There are always the two elements: a turning to creatures that causes a turning from God. Concupiscence is not, therefore, as the Pelagians maintained, a merely natural vigor by which the faculties appropriately seek their own goods; it is a powerful vital energy that spontaneously rises to excess, tempting the will from God. The diversion from God constitutes its formal evil.

St. Augustine explains the process whereby concupiscence leads to sin in a passage commenting on St. James:

> The Apostle James says: "Everyone is tempted by being drawn away and enticed by his own concupiscence. Then when concupiscence has conceived, it brings forth sin." These words distinguish the thing brought forth from the one giving birth. The one giving birth is concupiscence; the thing brought forth is sin. But concupiscence does not give birth unless it conceives; it does not conceive unless it entices, that is, unless it obtains willing consent to commit evil.[7]

To what practical use St. Thomas puts this dynamic definition, which so clearly discloses the pathology of sin, may be seen later in the *Summa*:

> Now man is placed between the things of this world, and spiritual goods wherein eternal happiness consists: so that the more he cleaves to the one, the more he withdraws from the other, and conversely, wherefore he that cleaves wholly to the things of this world, so as to make them his end, and to look upon them as the reason and rule of all that he does, falls away altogether from spiritual goods.[8]

To this principle St. Thomas returns when he explains the practical duties of the Christian life.[9] He also comes back to it, as shall be seen below, in a vital, related doctrinal matter. Indeed, it may be said that he recurs to it as often as he considers sin in its cause: he thus makes Augustine's doctrine his own.

St. Thomas confirms this teaching at a deeper level when he explains how a turning toward created good can be evil. The turning toward creatures, he says, is the material cause of sin; its formal cause is the turning from God. Created goods cause sin insofar as they turn us from God.[10]

The two texts cited above from St. Augustine are of particular interest. He originally set forth his teaching on concupiscence as the cause of sin in one of his early "Platonic" works, *The Problem of Free Choice,* although he already definitely connected it here with original sin. The other is from *Against Julian,* who was a Pelagian bishop, and was written in 421, in the evening of his life, while the Pelagian heresy was still pressing. Meanwhile, after his treatise *Free Choice* and on the eve of his ordination, he repeated and reinforced this teaching within a fuller theological context in his *True Religion.* He turned it here against the Manichees, although only in passing, as he did more definitely in his commentaries on Genesis. It appears in some form on almost every page of the *Confessions* and over and over in the *City of God* (whose composition occupied twelve years). But the doctrine came to its full growth in his controversy with the Pelagians. He had used it against the Manichees to show that evil is in the will and is not a substantial principle. He used it against the Pelagians to prove that, while nature is good, evil is actual and dangerous and rooted in the sin of Adam. At this very time (the later anti-Pelagian period) when his critics charge him with veering back toward Manichaeism, he was perfecting this principle, which he had been developing from his first years as a Christian, and was putting it in the final form adopted almost verbally, as shall be seen, in the definition of the Council of Trent.[11]

Thus, it is possible to emphasize, even as much as Augustine does, the fierce strength of concupiscence without implying any inherent evil in human nature or created things. In the end what is being "exaggerated" is the intensity of desire in human appetites for their connatural goods—desires which, precisely because of their irrepressible vitality, run so easily out of control, becoming not only vehement but, as we see all around us (not to say within us), every bit as violent as St. Augustine described them.

> For, by concupiscence, the Bishop of Hippo does not understand merely the appetite for bodily pleasures; he understands that general tendency away from the highest good and toward the lower pleasures: "when one turns away from godly things which are truly lasting and turns towards things which are changeable and insecure."[12]

In his anti-Pelagian works, St. Augustine crystallizes this whole teaching with a formula that the Church has made her own. He does this in explaining why St. Paul (Rom 6 and 7) describes concupiscence as *sin*. It is called sin, he says, not because it is *actually* evil, but because it comes from sin and leads to sin.

Besides the places indicated in the note, we quote here as the *locus classicus* one of the frequent gemlike formulas in which Augustine contains the diverse aspects of a complex truth with utmost clarity and brevity. It is from his *Marriage and Concupiscence*,[13] written against the Pelagians:

> Inasmuch, however, as by a certain manner of speech it [concupiscence] is called sin, since it arose from sin, and when it has the upper hand produces sin, the guilt of it prevails in the natural man; but this guilt by Christ's grace through the remission of all sins, is not suffered to prevail in the regenerate man if he does not yield obedience to it whenever it urges him to the commission of evil.

Lest there be any misunderstanding, he adds:

> As arising from sin, it is, I say, called sin, although in the regenerate it is not actually sin; and it has this

The Force of Disintegration 71

designation applied to us, just as speech which the tongue produces is itself called "tongue"; and just as the word "hand" is used in the sense of writing. In the same way; concupiscence is called sin, as producing sin *when it conquers the will.* ...

This passage contains all the elements for a solution of the problem of concupiscence and sin. Concupiscence, as described by St. Paul, is not formally sinful, but it is called sin by the Apostle because it comes from Adam's sin and leads to personal sin. Since in the regenerate the guilt of original sin is remitted, concupiscence has no moral significance for them unless it enters the will and solicits consent to disorderly impulses. It cannot compel this consent but may be brought under control through God's grace. Evil remains exclusively in the moral order, in the will.

This was written at the time when Augustine is supposed by his critics to be reverting to Manichaeism by making evil something substantial!

The Fathers of the Council of Trent decreed:

> This concupiscence, which at times the Apostle calls sin (Rom 6: 12ff.), the holy Synod declares that the Catholic Church has never understood to be called sin, as truly and properly sin in those born again, but because it is from sin and inclines to sin.[14]

Augustine is always thus to be understood when he speaks of concupiscence as "evil," or "sinful": "Because it is from sin and inclines to sin, *quia ex peccato est et ad peccatum inclinat.*"

St. Augustine is to be regarded, not as a pessimist, but as a supreme realist. His witness is urgently needed today. Theology, which has in the recent past been too exclusively speculative, must be balanced by this great Doctor's presentation of the dynamics of concupiscence vis-à-vis remedial grace. Outside the Church (and, alas, within it) the actuality of concupiscence is widely disregarded and denied: it is merged with "the natural" and hence, as with the Pelagians, is considered "good." Yet about us we can see how failure to contend against concupiscence leads to all sorts of disorders and excesses in the personal lives of men and in their society. These excesses cannot be explained as mere mechanical violations of a law abstractly conceived; as Augustine insists, they have a cause, and this cause is concupiscence enticing men away from the divine will.[15]

Daily life also confirms St. Augustine. Does anyone not know from personal experience how ignorance, pride, avarice, and sensuality always inwardly threaten, and often corrode, the noblest actions? This is why even the saints, as Augustine also frequently observes, must pray, and pray truly, "Forgive us our trespasses." The great spiritual masters of the Church who, like Augustine, view man concretely, corroborate his judgment when he says that "we have to struggle in a constant daily conflict against unlawful and unseemly inclinations."[16] Particularly worthy of mention in this respect are St. Francis de Sales, St. Alphonsus Liguori (in his ascetical works), and St. John of the Cross. The last particularly sees the whole course of the developing Christian life, on its negative side, as a purgation accomplished through the painful Nights of Sense and of the Soul. The Council of Trent also holds that concupiscence remains even in the justified *ad agonem*.[17] This word *agon* was used by Augustine in his *De Agone Christiano* (The Christian Combat). His graphic description of concupiscence, *fomes,* a tinder, also appears in the Tridentine definition.[18] The Fathers of the Second Vatican Council corroborate this teaching in language that echoes Augustine:

> Although he was made by God in a state of holiness, from the very outset of his history man abused his liberty, at the urging of the Evil One. Man set himself against God and sought to attain his goal apart from God. . . .
>
> What divine revelation makes known to us agrees with experience. Examining his heart, man finds that he has inclinations toward evil too, and is engulfed by manifold ills which cannot come from his good Creator. Often refusing to acknowledge God as his beginning, man has disrupted also his proper relationship to his own ultimate goal as well as his whole relation-

ship toward himself and others and all created things.[19]

Returning to the idea of struggle (see the text at the head of this chapter), a little later the Fathers write:

> For a monumental struggle against the powers of darkness pervades the whole history of man. The battle was joined from the very origins of the world and will continue until the last day, as the Lord has attested. Caught in this conflict, man is obliged to wrestle constantly if he is to cling to what is good, nor can he achieve his own integrity without great efforts and the help of God's grace.[20]

Concupiscence as human desire, springing from the good of nature, cannot itself be evil and becomes blameworthy only to the extent that its disorderly energies oppose the desires of the human spirit as moved by the divine Spirit. As a defect or disorder, therefore, concupiscence is desire that resists the spirit, says Augustine in a recurrent formula: "Through that concupiscence of the flesh, which Holy Scripture teaches is evil, the flesh wars against the spirit. . . ."[21] Moreover, since it is a disorder arising in desire, it cannot be substantive. Augustine, as we have seen, steadfastly refuses to hypostatize evil.[22] It becomes evil only in deflecting the will from a higher to a lower good. There was concupiscence, in the sense of desire, in Paradise, but not the disorder of desire that man now experiences.[23] Indeed, it is therefore also known to the saints: "That *natural delight* [the Fathers of the Old Testament] derived was by no means given rein up to the point of unreasoning and wicked lust, nor is it to be compared to the debaucheries of lust or the intemperance of the married."[24] The reason is that then "the mind's good will leads the ensuing bodily pleasure, instead of following its lead."[25]

The notion of concupiscence is indispensable to Catholic theology. No other concept casts such a clear, direct, concentrated beam on the cause of sin. Everyone is against "egotism" and "selfishness." Even psychiatrists point out their dangers. But if Christianity can throw no clearer light on the cause of evil, then we do not need Christianity; natural asceticism or psychology will do as well. Little wonder that secular humanists sneer at the doctrine of original sin.

Take concupiscence out of theology and there is no need for detachment, poverty of spirit, or mortification—in a word, for the cross, since mortification is "dying" with Jesus. Only concupiscence reveals why we should mortify natural desires, why we should renounce desires that are in themselves good. Take away concupiscence and there is no need for remedial grace. There is nothing to remedy; enlightened free will, as the Pelagians maintained, and as psychology presupposes, would be sufficient to overcome evil. If carrying the cross merely means avoiding evil, then again natural asceticism will accomplish as much. Only concupiscence lights up those obscure forces that work within our natural desires and that, because they tend to divert us at once from the way of reason and from our true supernatural end, must be crucified. Only concupiscence explains why we do the things we will not and do not the things we will (Rom 7: 15). Only concupiscence shows therefore why we need the remedial power of God's grace and the purifying action of the cross in order to attain restoration and resurrection.[26]

The notion of concupiscence alone makes any sense of the Apostle's "With Christ I am nailed to the cross." Or his "We ... are always bearing about in our body the dying [the mortification] of Jesus, so that the life also of Jesus may be made manifest in our bodily frame" (Gal 2: 19; 2 Cor 4: 10).

In its total meaning concupiscence is a concept that describes and safeguards the psychophysical unity of the human person in his moral activity. For it includes all the desires and powers of men, bodily and spiritual, in themselves and in their combined action. And it has no moral significance whatsoever until it enters the will, whether to divert it from God to created good, thence to evil; or until the exuberant energies of natural desire are disciplined and channeled under the control of grace to life in Christ. "For the inclination of the flesh is death, but the inclination of the Spirit life and peace" (Rom 8: 6).

Obviously the desires themselves, apart from the disorderly tendencies of concupiscence—or rather, with tendencies purified and the desires themselves rightly channeled

—are to be integrated into the total human and Christian life. But this is accomplished through the "lust of the Spirit." For if the "flesh lusts against the Spirit," conversely "the Spirit lusts against the flesh" (Gal 5: 17). Thus, if the desires in their tendency to disorder are a disintegrating force and the explanation of sin, they are also purified and sublimated (but not in the Freudian sense) by the action of the Holy Spirit. As the elements of this integration they are the subject matter of ascetical and mystical theology. In the works of St. John of the Cross the whole ascetical life, and even the mystical life on its underside, is described as a purification of desire. In Augustine's thought also, the highest holiness starts from desire and is realized to the extent that desires are taken up in a total love of God—with the whole mind, the whole heart, the whole soul, and all of one's strength.

At stake here, therefore, is a fundamental theological principle, one deeply involved in the whole Christian life, both in its negative aspect of a struggle against sin and the causes of sin, and in its positive development from minimal conformity to highest holiness.

2. CONCUPISCENCE NOT ORIGINAL SIN

It is commonly asserted, even by Catholic authors[27] and just as commonly without textual proof, that Augustine considered original sin and concupiscence identical. Superficially the matter may seem to be of no great importance, a mere technical refinement. Yet confusion, here beginning with Martin Luther, as shall be seen in a moment, was to have tragic consequences. Catholic authors who hold that Augustine identified concupiscence with original sin have followed the Lutheran understanding of Augustine; this is in line with their acceptance of the Jansenistic interpretation.

Portalié flatly denies that Augustine identifies concupiscence with original sin:

> At first sight and to judge by the apparent wording of certain formulas, one would be tempted to state that Augustine identified original sin with concupiscence. . . . But a comparison of these texts with others leads

to an entirely different conclusion.... He himself warns us that concupiscence is the same as original sin in the same way that ignorance or even death is, in virtue of that metonym which identifies effects with their causes.²⁸

Gilson confirms Portalié, showing how, in Augustine's mind, concupiscence is related to original sin: "These disorders [ignorance and concupiscence] are sins, as was the act from which they flow; they are original sin itself, carried on in the effects it has caused, effects which, in this sense, are still original sin."²⁹

St. Thomas had already correctly interpreted Augustine in this matter. Quoting the latter's words, "Concupiscence is the guilt of original sin, *reatus originalis peccati*," he agrees that concupiscence, an effect of original sin, is also the same as this sin in a limited and secondary sense, i.e., materially, but not formally. To explain this, he recalls the material and formal elements of sin with its definition as a turning toward creatures and a turning from God.

He writes:

> The whole order of original justice consists in man's will being subject to God: which subjection, first and chiefly, was in the will, whose function it is to move all the other parts to the end, as stated above, so that the will being turned away from God, all the other powers of the soul become inordinate. Accordingly the privation of original justice, whereby the will was made subject to God, is the formal element in original sin; while every other disorder of the soul's powers is a kind of material element in respect of original sin. Now the inordinateness of the other powers of the soul consists chiefly in their turning inordinately to mutable good; which inordinateness may be called by the general name of concupiscence. Hence original sin is concupiscence materially, but privation of original justice formally.³⁰

Thus St. Thomas refines the Augustinian teaching. His interpretation, far from being forced, follows at once from the notion of concupiscence—formulated as we have seen above by Augustine and adopted by Aquinas—as the tendency of all the desires of fallen man to seek their respective goods inordinately. With the formal and essential element of sin located in the will, there can be no question of its producing any intrinsic corruption of nature. By concupiscence the appetites of our nature are simply thrown back on themselves, seeking their connatural and particular goods apart from the highest good of the "new man" of grace. Portalié concludes: "Not only is there no contradiction, but rather perfect harmony with Augustine's general theory according to which every sin belongs essentially to the moral order."[31]

This apparently innocent and merely academic distinction between the material and the formal elements of sin is in reality a precise formula by which St. Thomas contained the thought of his master Augustine. Its rupture was to be disastrous. The Scholastics of the decadence, rejecting Aquinas, forgot this distinction or did not understand it. Their shallow rationalism, which Martin Luther rejected, but in which he had received his theological formation, caused him to misunderstand Augustine and misinterpret his own experience of man's sinfulness. Through him concupiscence was to become identified with original sin and thus enter the moral order, corrupting man radically.

> [Luther] retained the old scholastic terms—original sin, infused grace, faith, good works, justification, and so on—but he gave them an entirely different content. For instance, when he defined original sin, he simply repeated the scholastic formula used since the thirteenth century. But what the scholastics considered an effect of original sin—evil desires or concupiscence—he designated as its nature; and what they looked upon as the characteristic expression of concupiscence—sensual lust—appeared to him simply as an accessory symptom. The real nature of concupiscence, and of sin generally was for him the *proprius sensus,* selfishness. Selfishness dominates the whole instinctive and volitional life of natural man.[32]

Transposing this into Catholic terms, a recent biographer of Luther writes that the Reformer was "concerned with the persistence of sin in the believer, not as mere tinder (*fomes peccati*), but as that ferment of egoism for which man is accountable, since his whole personal existence is involved in it, but which in the redeemed is restrained by God until it is finally driven out by grace, a work growingly fulfilled but never perfectly achieved in this present life."[33] This description, written by a writer favorable to Luther, is presumably a fair transposition of the Reformer's thought. The two phrases "not as mere tinder (*fomes peccati*)" and "for which man is held accountable" are critical. They mean that for Luther concupiscence is no longer the merely material element of sin, as it had been for St. Augustine and St. Thomas. Man's hereditary sinfulness is now formally evil. The containing formula has been destroyed.

There is no question of man's sinfulness. Luther's affirmation of this accords with Catholic teaching, and his personal experience of it is akin to that acknowledged by many saints, including saints of completely innocent lives, like St. Teresa. The question is what he means by this sinfulness and how he limits it. Augustine had emphasized man's sinfulness, but he carefully avoids introducing concupiscence into the moral order: it is called sin because it leads to sin, yet is itself not actually sinful. In attributing to man's hereditary sinfulness a moral actuality—in denying that it is a mere tinder and is therefore accountable—Luther introduced into the stream of Christian thought, and for the first time, a strong pessimistic strain, something less than Manichaeism but far more than Augustinian concupiscence, an inherent and irresistible depravity. This stream was to be deepened by Calvin and issue in Puritanism. In its extremist form it infiltrated the Catholics as Jansenism. This is how the Jansenists were able to distort Augustine's teaching.

Thus it was that under the supposed authority of Augustine a dark and pessimistic bias came into modern Christian thought. This is undoubtedly the reason why Augustine has been first misunderstood and then exiled by so many modern Catholics.

3. LOVE OF CREATED GOOD

Attention to concupiscence, the proclivity toward an unruly love of creatures, may still appear negative even with stress laid on the goodness of creation. Taken by itself—and this is where Augustine's critics usually leave the matter—it is negative. But in Augustine's thought it is only half the picture. Positive and negative go together; the purpose of the negative phase of purification in the Christian life, and it is indispensable, is to share in the positive fruits of the Spirit. It is indispensable for the same reason that the Cross precedes the Resurrection; indeed, it is a sharing in the Cross in order to share in the Resurrection.

As "the desires of the flesh," that is, of nature,* are against the spirit, so those of the spirit are against the flesh (Gal 5: 17). And the Spirit is the Spirit of God at work within the human spirit, at once drawing man to God and enabling him to mortify the desires of the flesh. "If by the Spirit you put to death the deeds of the flesh, you shall live" (Rom 8: 13).

Renovation through righteousness, or holiness, is accomplished in us, Augustine holds, recurring many times to a favorite text, "because the charity of God is poured forth in our hearts by the Holy Spirit Who has been given to us" (Rom 5: 5).

> The human will is so divinely aided in the pursuit of righteousness, that (in addition to man's being created with a free will, and in addition to the teaching by which he is instructed how he ought to live) he received the Holy Spirit, by whom there is formed in his mind a delight in, and a love of, that supreme and unchangeable good which is God.... Now in order that such a course may engage our affections, God's "love is shed abroad in our hearts," not through the free will which arises from ourselves, but "through the Holy Spirit, which is given to us."[34]

---

* "By this figurative use of the part for the whole, he [Paul] wants us to interpret the word 'flesh' as meaning the whole of human nature" (*City of God*, XIV, 3).

Caught between opposing desires, for the temporal and the eternal, the critical decision for each man lies in making a choice of end and direction. This is the crossroads. The whole religious (or irreligious) life can be seen in perspective from here. "The general precept is, 'Thou shalt love'; and the general prohibition, 'Thou shalt not covet.'"[35] Each man must make up his own mind. To give in to covetousness is to allow created good to draw us away from God. To respond to the Spirit is to love God and all things in God; seen and embraced in the love of God, creatures also draw us to God.

There are, in other words, two ways of loving creatures. The one way is to love them according to the desires of nature, i.e., under the impulse of concupiscence. This love of created goods draws us away from God. In the end, of course, it is not even a true love for creatures; it proceeds from a disordered selfishness that directs the use of creatures to our own ends and satisfactions rather than orienting their use to God the Supreme Good. Distinguishing the city of God from the city of man, Augustine says: "One city is that of men who live according to the flesh. The other is of men who live according to the spirit. . . . On the one side are those who live *according to man;* on the other, those who live according to God." And further: "The one city began with the love of God; the other had its beginnings in the love of self."[36]

In his *Christian Doctrine,* Augustine describes in some detail a distinction to which he frequently returns, the distinction between use and enjoyment, in explaining how the love of God should envelop and direct the love of creatures. Not for their own sake are creatures to be enjoyed: they are rather to be *used*—not in the narrow modern utilitarian sense—but in the service of God and His divine purposes. So, created goods are caught up in that current of love which, originating in God, is poured into man and draws him back to God. But only God, in any fully satisfactory sense, is to be *enjoyed.*

> When that which is loved is near, it necessarily brings delight with it also. If you pass through this delight and have referred it to that goal where you should remain, you are using it and may *only improperly* be said to enjoy it. But if you cling to that delight and

remain in it, making it the end of your rejoicing, then you may truly and properly be said to be enjoying it. And this kind of enjoyment should not be indulged except with reference to the Trinity, which is the highest good and is immutable.[37]

All things, therefore, should be gathered into the swelling current of God's love:

> When He said, "With thy whole heart and with thy whole soul and with thy whole mind," He did not leave any part of life which should be free and find itself room to desire the enjoyment of something else. But whatever else appeals to the mind as being lovable should be directed into that channel into which the whole current of love flows.[38]

He illustrates:

> Suppose we were wanderers who could not live in blessedness except at home, miserable in our wandering and desiring to end it and return to our native country. We would need vehicles for land and sea which could be used to help us reach our homeland, which is to be enjoyed. But if the amenities of the journey and the motion of the vehicles itself delighted us, and we were led to enjoy those things which we should use, we should not wish to end our journey quickly, and, entangled in a perverse sweetness, we should be alienated from our country, whose sweetness would make us blessed. Thus in this mortal life, wandering from God, if we wish to return to our native country where we can be blessed we should use this world and not enjoy it, so that the "invisible things" of God "being understood by the things that are made" (Rom 1: 20) may be seen, that is, so that by means of corporal and temporal things we may comprehend the eternal and spiritual.[39]

To enjoy something is to cling to it with love for its own sake. To use something, however, is to employ it in obtaining that which you love, provided that it is worthy of love.⁴⁰

Another example may better serve to illustrate the manner in which the love of God "forms" the love of other things—to anticipate the term that St. Thomas was to use to describe the effect of divine love on human activity.

> Let not Satan steal a way into your hearts, saying as he is wont, "Enjoy God's creature: why did He make it but for your enjoyment?" . . . God forbids not the love of these things, but only the finding of our happiness in the love of them: we are to make the love of our Creator the end of our esteem for them. Suppose, brethren, a man should make a ring for his betrothed and she should love the ring given her more than her betrothed who made it for her, would not her heart be convicted of infidelity in respect of the very gift of her betrothed, though what she loved were what he gave? Certainly let her love his gift; but if she should say, "The ring is enough, I do not wish to see his face again," what should we say of her? The pledge is given by the betrothed just that in his pledge he himself may be loved. God, then, has given you all these things; love him Who made them.⁴¹

How far Augustine is ready to take his principle that the use of all creatures is to be directed to the love of God—that it excludes not only mortal sin but governs the whole Christian course of progress in holiness—is shown by his saying, "It is not loving Thee enough to love anything out of Thee, which we do not love for Thee."⁴² To some, despite the beauty of the ideal, this may seem a proof of Augustinian "rigorism." Before making such a judgment, however, it would be well to compare the saint's words to these of St. Francis de Sales, that master of "honeyed" spirituality: "Whoever desires something that he desires not for God, that much less desires God."⁴³ Both saints are obviously describing the fullest growth of holiness.

Some today may find the distinction between use and enjoyment disconcerting. With so much emphasis on this-worldliness, our religion is not as God-centered as Augustine's. His view may not seem to allow sufficiently for the inherent good of creatures. Yet we have already seen (Chapters 1 and 2) how he affirms the goodness of all created natures, regarding them as patterned and formed according to the divine ideas. The order of charity simply brings them to their true and highest fulfillment. "For we know that all creation groans and travails in pain until now. . . . For the eager longing of creation awaits the revelation of the sons of God" (Rom 8: 19, 22). We are here confronted again with Augustine's refusal to regard nature abstractly, as if it were in some sense independent of the overall plan of God. He sees it concretely, as it has been designed, created, and restored by God. His model is mankind before the Fall. Restored by Jesus Christ, man's destiny and duty are to respond to this call and to restore God's universe as He planned it. "The message which the Bishop of Hippo addresses to men is to the effect that the whole world, from its beginning until its final term, has as its unique end the constitution of a holy society, in view of which everything has been made, even the universe itself."[44]

The distinction between the use and enjoyment of creatures, like many of the tools Augustine borrowed from pagan thinkers, is inadequate for his Christian purposes. He himself recognizes this; in studying the love of neighbor, he supplements it with an "order of love." He of course marks the difference between rational and non-rational creatures: "A great thing is man, made in the image and likeness of God, not in that he is encased in a mortal body, but in that he excels the dignity of a rational soul."

He sees the problem arising through this distinction from his teaching on the love of creatures: Are men to be enjoyed or (in his ultimate theological sense) "used"?

> Thus there is a profound question as to whether men should enjoy themselves, use themselves, or do both. For it is commanded to us that we should love one another, but it is to be asked whether man is to be

loved for his own sake or for the sake of something else. If for his own sake, we enjoy him; if for the sake of something else, we use him.

His answer: "But I think that man is to be loved for the sake of something else. In that which is to be loved for its own sake [the Trinity], the blessed life resides."

The same rule applies, not only to one's neighbor, but to oneself:

> But no one ought to enjoy himself either, if you observe the matter clearly, because he should not love himself on account of himself but on account of Him Who is to be enjoyed.[45]

Both our neighbors and ourselves are destined for final and true enjoyment in God: our association receives its highest dignity and value from this common destiny. We are all on pilgrimage together toward the supreme Good; the current of charity carries us all together back to our Source: "The greatest reward is that we enjoy Him and that all of us who enjoy Him may enjoy one another in Him."[46]

Still it may seem, as one scholar puts it, that in this situation there can scarcely be a true love between persons: all love is directed to God.[47] But Augustine does not say that we may not enjoy other persons, merely (see citations above) that such enjoyment is "imperfect" or "improperly so called." He is looking at human relationships within an ultimate scale of values. He says that "he lives in justice and sanctity who is an unprejudiced assessor of the intrinsic value of things." But it is clear from the context that this "intrinsic value" includes man's final relationship to God.[48] Such a viewpoint is understandably not satisfactory to secular humanism; but Augustine, while valuing the excellence of man, sees all human life in relation to its goal in God. It seems a commonplace to say (even to a secular humanist) that there can be no final, fully satisfying, and permanent enjoyment even in the noblest love of human persons. Meanwhile, "not everything which is to be used is to be loved, but only those things which by a certain association pertain to God, like a man or an angel, or pertain to us or require the favor of God, through us, like the body."⁴⁹ According to this formula the only thing that cannot be loved is evil—although it too may be used "to merit God."

If one objects to Augustine discussing the love of neighbor under the category of "things," note that he also discusses the love of self under this same category. Indeed, he places God within this same category:

> The things [res] which are to be enjoyed are the Father, the Son, and the Holy Spirit, a single Trinity, a certain supreme thing common to all who enjoy it, if, indeed, it is a thing and not rather the cause of all things, and both a thing and a cause.⁵⁰

Augustine is here looking at Creator and creature metaphysically, seeking some ultimate common ground for their relationship. And both Creator and creature are *res*, realities: a usage which he finds justified in Scripture: "It is not easy to find a name proper to such excellence, unless it is better to say that this Trinity is one God and that 'of Him, and by Him, and in Him are all things'" (2 Cor 5: 6).

We have already spoken of the value that Augustine placed on the person, and we will return to this subject. The urgency and warmth of the charity that we owe to our neighbors we find best described, not in his doctrinal treatises, but in his sermons, especially, concentrated in his homilies on the First Letter of St. John. Nevertheless, however limited in value the distinction between use and enjoyment, no matter how it needs to be supplemented and explained, in one respect it corresponds to the saint's innermost convictions concerning the absolute majesty of God and the infinite gulf between Him and even His noblest creatures. God alone is supreme good and source of all light. The ultimate value of creatures to man is determined by the degree in which they are bathed in that light. If they lead us away from Him, they draw us into the shadows.

Moreover, St. Thomas would write: "It would be wrong if a man loved his neighbor [and a priori we may add, any creature] as though he were his last end, but not if he loved him for the sake of God; and this is what charity does."⁵¹

Our contemporaries are inclined to seek personal fulfillment in the encounter of "I" and "Thou," realized above all, they think, in the love of the sexes. Augustine, looking deeper than sexuality—whose potentiality he also knew—sees men in their ultimate metaphysical and creaturely limits. He knows that no creature, female or male, can give to any other creature, male or female, final satisfaction and happiness. This can be attained only in God.

"O Lord," wrote Augustine in the *Confessions*,[52] "Thou didst knock at my heart with Thy word, and I have loved Thee." "His whole moral system," writes B. Roland-Gosselin, "is contained in that sentence: 'Lord, I have loved Thee.'"[53] Augustine's moral system is an ethic of love, anchored in Him Who "is love." It would be vain to look in him for any other. But then, are not men today protesting against a mere "code morality" and crying out, precisely, for an ethic of love? Augustine offers a love-ethic in which man's whole life, above all in his encounters with his fellows, but also in his use of the humblest of created goods, is penetrated and permeated by the radiance of Him Who St. John says "is love."

It is sometimes said of Augustine that he is suspicious of all pleasure and even regards it as evil. Such a charge comes from neglecting this positive side of his teaching. If he is consistent with his convictions, as just outlined, it cannot be true; and he is nothing if not consistent. His moral assessment of pleasure, which comes from creatures, is determined by the use made of creatures in relation to God.

> The affection of the upright will, then, is good love and that of a perverse will is evil love. Thus love yearning to possess the object loved is desire and love delighting in the object possessed is joy; its avoidance of what is abhorrent is fear and its sufferance of a present evil is sadness. Further, all such emotions are evil only if a man's love is evil; they are good if a man's love is good.[54]

His own life is marked by abstemiousness; yet we have seen how he rejoices in the goodness and beauty of creatures. The practice he proposed for the religious of his day was moderate, avoiding the excesses of some of the desert monks; and he never attempted a systematic treatment of asceticism, of the kind that was to come later.[55] He is perfectly capable of distinguishing between his own personal practice and the ideal that, as pastor, he should put before his people.

Augustine's idea of pleasure must be placed within the context of his God-centered and theological morality. "God does not forbid you to love these things, but to set your affections on them for blessedness, and rather desires you to approve and praise them to this end, that you may love the Creator."[56] Mere pleasure is swallowed up in rejoicing in the creature's goodness as a reflection of the Creator and a means of attaining Him.

Nor is Augustine's praise of created good perfunctory or made reluctantly. "There is no wholeness in him whom aught of Thy creation displeaseth."[57] "The things of the earth are not merely good; they are undoubtedly gifts from God.... Wherever we turn among the things which He created and conserved so wonderfully, we discover His footprints, whether lightly or plainly impressed.... Citizens of the holy city of God, who live according to God during this earthly pilgrimage, fear and desire, grieve and rejoice, and because their love is rightly ordered, they think it right to have such feelings."[58] "The love of a created thing enjoyed without the love of God is not from God.... Through the love of the Creator, everyone can make a good use even of created things."[59]

Augustine gives his rule for the regulation of pleasure. It is good if taken with measure:

> Lovers of the world lust to eat, drink, cohabit; to use these pleasures. Not, surely, that there is no allowed measure in these things! Or that when it is said, Love not these things, it means that you are not to eat, or not to drink, or not to beget children. This is not the thing said. Only let there be measure because of the Creator, that these things may not bind you by your loving of them: lest you love for enjoyment what you ought to have for use.[60]

However, this is not the measure of mere reason, not the happy mean of Aristotle, not the rule of natural morality. It is derived from redeemed man's special relationship to God: use is determined under the action of grace "because of the Creator." Pleasure of itself, therefore, has no moral significance. It is a good created by God. It indeed presents a risk because, through pleasure, created goods draw us away from God. We exceed measure, and this is the point at which pleasure becomes evil, when it draws us away from God. Love is the rule. Protected by love, one enters God's universe with gladness in the manner of the Psalmist, "I have gone round and offered up in His tabernacle a sacrifice of jubilation."

> Let your mind roam through the whole creation; everywhere the created world will cry out to you: "God made me." Whatever pleases you in a work of art brings to your mind the artist who wrought it; much more when you survey the universe, does the consideration of it evoke praise for its Maker. You look on the heavens; they are God's great work. You behold the earth; God made its numbers of seeds, its varieties of plants, its multitude of animals. Go round the heavens again and back to the earth, leave out nothing; on every side everything calls out to you of its Author; nay the very forms of created things as it were the voices with which they praise their Creator. But who can fathom the whole creation? Who shall set forth its praises? Who shall worthily praise heaven and earth, the sea, and all things that are in them? Now if in considering these creatures of God human language is so at a loss, what is it to do in regard to the Creator? When words fail can aught but triumphant music remain? I have gone round and have offered in His tabernacle a sacrifice of jubilation.[61]

If Augustine seems negative when he speaks of concupiscence of the flesh, so did St. Paul when he said, "Unhappy man that I am! Who will deliver me from the body of this death?" What seems like a cry of despair, however, is really not so; the Apostle immediately answers his own question (and Augustine after him) with a cry of exultation, "The grace of God through Jesus Christ our Lord!" (Rom 7: 24).

Where sin abounded, grace has more abounded (Rom 5: 11). So St. Augustine's conviction that the flesh opposes the spirit is countered and balanced by his teaching that the spirit opposes, heals, and restores the flesh, that is, the whole man.

Part Two

St. Augustine on Sex and Marriage

5. Marriage and Sexuality

> I do not understand what I do. . . . For I do not do the good that I wish, but the evil that I do not wish, that I perform. Now if I do what I do not wish, it is no longer I who do it, but the sin that dwells in me. —Romans 7: 18–20

> Indeed, as a weak and sinful being, man often does what he would not and fails to do what he would. Hence he suffers from internal divisions, and from these flow so many and such great discords in society.
> Vatican Council II, *Gaudium et Spes*, no. 10

> Those who belong to Christ have crucified their flesh with its passions and desires. —Galatians 5: 24

What has been said so far on concupiscence applies in general to all human desires. We come now to apply these principles to a particular area of special sensitivity, namely, to sexuality. In doing this we also become involved in the problem of marriage, with which, in the thought of Augustine, the subject of sexual concupiscence is inextricably bound. This bond may seem evident; yet in modern discussions the two subjects have tended to become dissociated. In fact, concupiscence is now de-emphasized, if not lost altogether; a sexuality, apparently without concupiscence, besides being the instrument of reproduction, is also simply the means of expressing conjugal love. On the other hand, the rules governing marriage are derived from a law of nature that is abstractly conceived in its metaphysical perfection. In a word, advocates of what is nowadays called the more "positive" approach would like to study marriage apart from the background of concupiscence; but in the thought of St. Augustine—and in actual fact, as we shall show—the two aspects, negative and positive, are inseparable.

St. Augustine looks at marriage, as he looks at all human problems, concretely, in the actual historical situation of man fallen, and bearing, even after his restoration, certain consequences of the Fall, including concupiscence. According to Augustine's principles, there would have been no marriage "problem" in the garden of Eden. There the sexual faculty would have been moved by a mind and will themselves governed by divine grace and supported by the gift of integrity. This point is important; it refutes in advance those who assert that for Augustine sexuality is intrinsically evil. It is the loss of integrity, even in man's restored state, that creates the problem: the sexual appetite, like all other human desires, now disturbed by concupiscence, tends to veer from the way marked out for its use by the Creator. Thus, in studying Christian marriage, we must take into account the manner in which it may be deflected by concupiscence from its divinely appointed purpose.

I. SEXUAL DESIRE

St. Augustine's teaching on sexual concupiscence is an extension and application of his general principles on concupiscence, which, as described, is a desire for created goods so strong and disorderly as to divert the will from God.[1]

Sexual union in marriage is a created good: a supreme created good, which Sacred Scripture uses as a type of Christ's union with the Church. No greater honor could be given to marital union than this, except making it a sacrament. Nevertheless, allowing that love, especially when dominated by the human spirit, is exalted, it is still a created good. Its bodily component, also good, is of a lower order, dignified by its union with the soul. Sexual concupiscence, in Augustine's thought, is an inordinate turning toward these goods. The strength of this inclination is most tangible in its bodily appetite, but it does not exist there only; in fact it is harmless as long as it remains in the body; Augustine constantly insists on this. But the will itself, corrupted by pride, turns also to created good, and to none more readily and vehemently than sexual gratification.

Augustine himself applies these principles to sexuality. In

the *Confessions* he writes: "The enemy held *my will;* and of it he made a chain and bound me. Because *my will* was perverse it changed to lust, and lust yielded to became a habit, and habit not resisted became necessity."[2]

The primary emphasis is on the will, not on bodily concupiscence. This emphasis is also strongly brought out on the positive side, seldom adverted to by Augustine's critics, in his teaching on continence and virginity. These virtues, because they reside primarily and essentially in the will, "strike at the root of concupiscence."[3]

He writes:

> This warfare is now going on for as long as this mortal life of ours subject to grace endures, lest sin, that is, the concupiscence of sin (for in this place the Apostle calls this by the name of sin) reign in our mortal body. This is shown to reign, however, when its desires are obeyed. There is, then, a concupiscence of sin within us which must not be obeyed, or it will reign over those who obey it. . . .
>
> For truly, in this war in which the spirit lusts against the flesh, that virtue [continence] is especially powerful, since in a way it crucifies the very concupiscences of the flesh.[4]

Again:

> That virtue of modesty which, in the matter of bridling the genital members of the body, is usually and properly called continence, is violated by no transgression if the higher continence, of which we have just now been speaking, is observed in the heart.[5]

And:

> For just as no one uses the body impurely except through wickedness already conceived in the spirit, so no one preserves purity of body except through chastity already rooted in the spirit.[6]

Sexual concupiscence, then, is a particular manifestation of human desire in its tendency—the result of the Fall—to disorder.

> Bodily pleasure . . . is preceded by a kind of appetite, familiar in the form of hunger and thirst, and commonly called *libido* when connected with sex—although, strictly speaking, lust is a word applicable to any kind of appetite, as in the classical definition of anger as a lust for revenge.[7]

Augustine says the same thing in the manner now familiar, that is, he defines sexual concupiscence in particular, within the general range of concupiscence, as the critical point of choice between different kinds of goods and the consequent preferment of one over the other:

> The will does not fall "into sin"; it falls "sinfully," *deficitur enim non ad mala, sed male*. Defects are not mere relations to natures that are evil; they are evil in themselves because, contrary to the order of natures, there is defection from Being that is supreme *to some lesser being*.
>
> Thus, greed [*avaritia*] is not a defect in the good that is desired but in the man who loves it perversely by falling from justice which he ought to esteem as incomparably superior to gold; nor is lust [*luxuria*] a defect in bodies which are beautiful and pleasing; it is a sin in the soul of the one who loves corporal pleasures perversely, that is, by abandoning that temperance which joins us in spiritual and unblemishable union with realities far more beautiful and pleasing. . . .
>
> In a word, anyone who loves perversely the good of any nature whatsoever and even, perhaps, acquires this good makes himself bad by gaining something good and sad by losing something better.[8]

This text is decisive. Concupiscence rules, not merely through loving that which is good—or beautiful—but rather when, as the result of the primordial sin, the disorder of concupiscence causes us to love that which is good in such wise that we are diverted from a higher good, hence to sin. Sin is in the disorder of the will. St. Augustine affirmed this teaching also in the heat of his controversy with the Pelagian bishop

Julian, even as he labored to demonstrate the evil of concupiscence.[9] Note, too, that concupiscence does not affect sexuality only; allowed to overflow into avarice it corrupts the desire for all created goods.

Of the sexes, Augustine says (he is speaking here in the person of Christ):

> That you may know that no creature of God is bad but that unregulated pleasure perverteth it, when in the beginning I made man, I made them male and female. I do not condemn the creature which I made. Behold, I have been born a man, and was born of a woman. It is therefore not the creature which I made that I condemn, but the sins which I did not make. Let each sex then at once see its honor and confess its iniquity; and let each hope for salvation.[10]

In speaking of marital intercourse he remains faithful to his principle that concupiscence, while the cause of sin, is not itself sinful. Speaking on the critical text, "In sins did my mother conceive me," he says:

> It is not therefore because it is sin to have to do with wives that men are conceived in iniquity, and in sins nourished in the womb by their mother, but because that which is made is surely made of flesh deserving punishment.... This chaste operation [*opus hoc castum*] in a married person hath not sin, but the origin of sin draweth with it condign punishment.[11]

2. SEXUAL DESIRE AND SIN

Nevertheless, Father Louis Bouyer writes:

> In spite of Augustine's assertions to the contrary, he could only see it [marriage] as a kind of permission or toleration of sin.... In his eyes concupiscence was absolutely indistinguishable from a natural desire and enjoyment, an indulgence sinful as such. He did not pursue his ideas to their logical conclusion, and would

probably have declined to accept it, if it had been expressly stated; but it seems impossible, on his own premises, to avoid the conclusion that, if sexual intercourse is not to be sinful, it must cease to be attractive and pleasurable to man.[12]

Since the saint is not to be allowed to speak for himself ("in spite of Augustine's assertions to the contrary . . ."), it would be useless to point out to this author that his own assertion is directly contrary to Augustine's description of conjugal intercourse, in the commentary on Psalm 50 just quoted, as a "chaste operation." Father Bouyer, with his encyclopedic knowledge, is by no means a man of one book. Yet it seems worth remarking that in making this and similar allegations, he cites only Augustine's anti-Pelagian writings and chiefly one book. He neglects the anti-Manichaean writings in which, as we have seen, Augustine had demonstrated the impossibility of substantial evil. Father Bouyer can thus hint of latent Manichaeism in Augustine.[13] Controversy inevitably requires stress on particular points or aspects of a problem. In his anti-Manichaean writings (which the Pelagians tried to use for their purposes) Augustine went as far as possible to demonstrate the goodness of God's creation. In his anti-Pelagian writings, he went in the opposite direction to show the corruption of nature through the Fall and its need of remedial grace. Augustine was a complex man. A few quotations from one of his works do not exhaust his mind. Nevertheless, it is precisely the book quoted by Bouyer, *Marriage and Concupiscence*, in which we found the *locus classicus* where Augustine defines concupiscence so as to affirm on the one hand the actuality of sin and its cause, while safeguarding, on the other, the principle that had guided him from the beginning, namely, that nature is good, and that evil, never substantial, is only in the will.

What we should really like to ask of this author is to explain what he means in saying that, for Augustine, "concupiscence was absolutely indistinguishable from a natural desire and enjoyment, an indulgence sinful as such." Surely this learned man knows that this distinction belongs to the theological order. It is not a real distinction; looking for it *in re* is to be like the lady who, in crossing the equator, kept watching for the line. Concupiscence, materially, *is* "absolutely identical" with natural desire. In its threatening, but not sinful, aspect it is the exuberance of natural desire—an exuberance so strong and "turbulent" in our fallen condition—that constantly threatens the obedience due the divine will. The evil is not in the desire or even in its intensity; the desire is not "an indulgence sinful as such." But the strength of desire, unrestrained by integrity, is a hazard and inclines to sin (*ad peccatum inclinat*) unless it is disciplined by an upright will acting in response to divine grace. Sin—actual evil—occurs only when the will consents to a deflection from virtue, and for this the will is responsible, "since the flesh and the spirit are alike the work of one and the same Creator, and are therefore undoubtedly good because He is good—unless it be that damage which has been inflicted by man's own will."[14]

On Augustine's "own premises," Bouyer said, "it seems impossible to avoid the conclusion that, if sexual intercourse is not to be sinful, it must cease to be attractive and pleasurable to man." What are these premises? Bouyer does not explain. But we have examined the premises, and they lead to no such conclusion. Concupiscence is the desire for some particular created good so strong that unless restrained—"mortified" is the Scriptural word—it inclines a man to disregard his true, total, and ultimate good. Neither the desire nor the strength of desire nor the thing desired is evil; sin occurs only in the choice of a lower good over a higher: "Therefore, as I have said, sin is not the striving after an evil nature [since no nature can be evil], but the desertion of a better, and so the deed itself is evil, not the [good] nature which the sinner uses amiss."[15] Evil exists only in the disorder of the will. And the failure of the will is all the easier since its own desires have been wounded by the Fall.

It therefore "seems impossible," on Augustine's "own premises," to draw the conclusion "that, if sexual intercourse is not to be sinful, it must cease to be attractive and pleasurable to man." The sinfulness is not in the pleasure, which is, however, an alluring created good capable of drawing man away from God, but in the will's acceptance of a wrong or imperfect use of intercourse.

Augustine's concept of pleasure has already been examined. Since the principles he presents are intended to govern the use of all created goods, they also apply here.[16] No doubt he sets a lofty moral and spiritual goal. The use of creatures and the moral worth of the pleasure they afford are to be gauged in relation to man's destined fulfillment in loving God. Created goods are to be "used" in relation to that ultimate good, but only God can be fully and properly "enjoyed." Meanwhile, the "measure" for governing the use of created things is "because of the Creator, that these things may not bind you by your loving of them: lest you love for enjoyment what you ought to have for use."[17] This is not to hold that pleasure is evil; it does indeed point up a high ideal, the norm for a completely God-centered life. But then, what else should a Christian life be?

Observe, too, lest this principle be construed as a one-sided and puritanical attitude toward the body, that it is to be applied to all created goods and pleasures. Speaking of continence, Augustine writes: "Such is the work of continence. There is no doubt therefore that those who limit it to the domination of bodily pleasures alone confine it within limits that are too narrow. Those who do not add the words 'of the body' but who say it is for continence to control pleasure or passion in general, are nearer the truth."[18]

We have heard Augustine acknowledge that the saints derived "natural delight" (*delectatio naturalis*) from marital intercourse, but he distinguished this clearly from the evil effects of unrestrained concupiscence by adding that the delight "they derived was by no means given rein up to the point of unreasoning and wicked lust."[19] Their delight, evidently, was not "an indulgence sinful as such."

St. Thomas was afterward to hold that the pleasure of intercourse in Paradise, because of man's perfection there, would have been greater than after the Fall. This makes it evident that for Aquinas sexual intercourse and pleasure could not be evil in themselves, and he understands Augustine's thoughts on this point as agreeing with his own.[20] Augustine did not pose the problem for himself in exactly this way, but he rejected as absurd the view proposed by some that procreation in Paradise would have been by some means other than marital intercourse.[21]

If he regarded intercourse as evil, how could he entertain the thought of it in man's state of innocence? What we have heard him say about the saints, moreover, indicates that he would not separate intercourse in Paradise from "natural delight" but only from "unreasoning and wicked lust."

For Augustine the right use of sex is regulated by its purpose; when used apart from its rightful purpose it becomes evil. How he limits it in terms of purpose will be the subject of the next chapter. So to limit it by purpose is vastly different from saying that it is intrinsically evil. Only moral disorders resulting from concupiscence are evil; concupiscence itself, according to the usage of St. Paul, is called evil only because it is the principle of sin, because it comes from sin and leads to sin.

That Augustine does not attempt a real distinction between natural desire and concupiscence serves only to confirm the soundness of his analysis.[22] He does, however, mark two other relevant distinctions that show his carefulness.

The first is that between love and the disorders caused by concupiscence. Of himself in his sixteenth year he writes:

> What was it that delighted me, except to love and be loved? But the moderate relation of mind to mind was not maintained according to the bright bond of friendship; rather the mists of slimy concupiscence of the flesh and the bubbling froth of puberty rose like hot breath beclouding and darkening my heart. It thus was not possible to distinguish the serenity of joy from the dark mist of lust. Both [joy and lust] seethed together in hot confusion, and swept foolish youth over the precipice of passions and engulfed it in a whirl of shameful actions.[23]

Again, of himself a little later:

> To Carthage I came and a hissing cauldron of shameful loves seethed round me on all sides. I was not in love, yet I loved to love and in the hidden depths of unsated desire, I hated myself for my partial lack of desire. I sought some object that I might love, loving the very act of love....

> To love and be loved was far sweeter to me if I also succeeded in enjoying my beloved in the flesh. Thus I muddied the waters of friendship with the filth of concupiscence, and I beclouded its brightness with the scum of lust. Yet, though filthy and unsightly, I strove in excessive vanity to appear refined and polished. O my God, my Mercy, with how much bitterness didst Thou, in Thy goodness, sprinkle that which was sweet to me! For I was loved and I both achieved in secret the bond of enjoyment and was joyfully tied down by the entwinements of calamity, to be beaten with iron rods, burning with jealousy, suspicions, and fears, with fits of anger and quarrels.[24]

This description of his adolescence was written almost thirty years later, fifteen years after his conversion, and five after his consecration as bishop. While thus being an account of his youth, it also reflects his mature attitudes. He does not confuse love with concupiscence. It is interesting to note also, since his attitude toward marriage is supposed to be faulty, that in looking back he wished that his desire for love, since it could not then know the final fulfillment of Christian celibacy, could at least have been channeled into lawful marriage.

> If only there had been someone to moderate my wretchedness and turn to use the fleeting beauty of each latest attraction, setting a limit to their delights: so that the flood tide of my youth might have driven me upon the shore of the marriage bond: then in those transient pleasures there might have been found the tranquillity that is content with having the procreation of children as its end.[25]

The other distinction is between natural function and use. To Julian he writes:

> You do not know, or pretend not to know, that the quality, the usefulness, and the necessity of sensation through a sense of the body are not the same as lust

for this sensation.... Necessity for sensation arises when things we do not desire are borne in upon our senses. The lust for sensation with which we are here concerned impels us by the appetite of carnal concupiscence to sense something, *whether we mentally consent to or resist it*.... Our Lord did not say: "Whoever shall look upon a woman," but: "Whoever shall look upon a woman to lust after her has already committed adultery with her in his heart." Consider: He has briefly and clearly distinguished the sense of sight from the lust for sensation . . . .[26]

Citing marriage in Paradise, which was without concupiscence, he says:

> Without this concupiscence it was quite possible to effect the function of the wedded pair in the procreation of children: just as many a laborious work is accomplished by the compliant operation of our other limbs, without any lascivious heat; for they are simply moved by the direction of the will, not excited by the ardor of concupiscence.[27]

Pelagius, in his denial of concupiscence, cites the goodness of the human seed, formed by God, which is sown, he says, as a farmer sows corn. Replied Augustine, "We also assert that God forms man of human seed." He adds drily that there would be no problem if human seed were sown as corn is sown: which is something of the way it was in Paradise.

> For why can we not suppose that God could have granted to man in his happy state in Paradise, the same course with regard to his own seed which we see granted to the seeds of corn, in such wise that the former might be sown without any shameful lust, the members of generation simply obeying the inclination of the will; just as the latter is sown without any shameful lust, the hands of the husbandman merely moving in obedience to his will?[28]

Perhaps the best example that Augustine offers for the difference between natural function and concupiscence, to which he frequently recurs, is the following:

> The case may be illustrated by the example of a lame man. Suppose him to obtain some good object by limping after it: Then, on the other hand, the attainment itself is not evil because of the evil of the man's lameness; nor, on the other hand, is the lameness good because of the goodness of the attainment.[29]

It should be evident from the above citations—which could be multiplied almost indefinitely—that Augustine's norm for measuring the disorder of concupiscence is not a Stoic rule, but the condition in which God originally placed man in Paradise. This condition was one pole in his thought on concupiscence and marriage. He is unpuritanical enough to reject the theory of some early Christian writers that in that happy state there would have been no sexual intercourse at all and that the continuation of the race would have been taken care of by some other (unspecified) means. On the contrary, Augustine maintained that, according to God's plan from the beginning, human reproduction would have been through sexual union. The difference between the Paradisal state and our present condition, he thought, is that the process which is now so likely to be turned awry by concupiscence would then have taken place under the full control of the grace-filled will.

The other pole for Augustine's thinking on this matter is the final condition of men in the Resurrection. Here—and in this case we have the Savior's explicit word for it—there will be neither reproduction nor coitus, yet only then will men attain to their final fulfillment of joy. C. S. Lewis remarks that "The scholastic picture of unfallen sexuality [which may be taken to include Augustine's]—a picture of physical pleasure at the maximum and emotional disturbance at the minimum—may suggest to us something much less like the purity of Adam in Paradise than the cold sensuality of Tiberius in Capri."[30] In any event, modern men, in their sex-saturated atmosphere, may not be much attracted by Augustine's picture of man in Eden. But then, if final fulfillment and beatitude are obtainable only through sexual orgasm, they will not be very happy in heaven after the resurrection of the body. The fault will not be Augustine's. "At the resurrection they will neither marry nor be given in marriage, but are as angels of God in heaven" (Mt 23: 30). Then, indeed, we Christians "are of all men the most to be pitied" (1 Cor 15: 19). Even now: for St. Paul (not, in the first place, Augustine), looking at the resurrection, drew the conclusion for this life: "Brothers, this is what I mean; our time is growing short: those who have wives should live as though they had none" (1 Cor 7: 29). If this prospect seems bleak to the post-Freudian world, it must be added: However important sexuality is now for the development of human love, and it is important, love for the Christian looks beyond sexuality for its fulfillment. This is surely the deepest meaning of Jesus' prophecy: not merely that there will be a depressing absence of sexual and marital love, but that *all* there be united in a love that surpasses any ecstasy that lovers now experience. "Nor has the heart of man conceived what God has prepared for those who love Him" (1 Cor 2: 9).

3. DID AUGUSTINE EXAGGERATE?

Even after we have come to a correct understanding of Augustine's teaching on concupiscence, it may still be wondered if Augustine did not nevertheless exaggerate its force and significance. Certainly the charge is made frequently enough against him. The correct answer to the question should emerge from what has been said. So far, however, we have been looking at his teaching, as it were, in isolation, confining our attention largely to his own books. It remains to consider it in a larger context. To this end we shall submit three considerations or groups of facts. We shall present them neither logically nor chronologically, but as suggested by the development of our theme. Then we shall be better able to answer the question posed. Some remarks by G. K. Chesterton, surely no Puritan, provide a suitable starting point:

> Sex cannot be admitted to a mere equality among elementary emotions or experiences, like eating and

sleeping. The moment sex ceases to be a servant it becomes a tyrant. There is something dangerous and disproportionate in its place in human nature, for whatever reason; and it does really need a special purification and dedication.

He illustrates, recalling the example of the Greeks:

> The wisest men in the world set out to be natural; and the most unnatural thing in the world was the very first thing they did.

And the conclusion:

> There is a bias in man like the bias in the bowl; and Christianity was the discovery of how to correct the bias and therefore to hit the mark. There are many who will smile at the saying; but it is profoundly true to say that the glad good news of the Gospel was the news of original sin.[31]

St. Augustine and Sigmund Freud

It is not within the province of theology to pass judgment on the data of psychology, but it is right to integrate them. In the development of modern psychology none has made a more significant contribution than Sigmund Freud. From the Christian point of view, Jacques Maritain's observation made many years ago still seems valid, namely, that Freud combines the talents of a remarkable observer with an inferior philosophy. Freud's realization of man's psychophysical unity finds its natural context in that conception of the unity of the human person which Augustine affirmed and St. Thomas exactly formulated.[32] A Catholic is disposed to understand and accept this part of Freudianism. But what is relevant in the present discussion is Freud's emphasis on sexuality in the development of human personality. He broke through the curtain of hush-hush to expose the importance of this factor in human life. He was here corroborating Augustine, as in this respect Augustine anticipated Freud. (It has also been observed that

Augustine's discussion of memory, as in the tenth book of the *Confessions*, was a pioneering exploration of what Freud was to call the unconscious.) After Freud it is difficult to understand how anyone could charge Augustine with exaggerating the force of sexuality in human life. Precisely in the area of sexuality "we have been given in our time a reaffirmation of original sin by Freudian psychology."[33]

This is not to say that Augustine corroborates Freud's pansexualism. The excess here is Freud's, and Augustine merely affirms that sexual concupiscence is an element of special importance in the total configuration of concupiscence. Freud confirms Augustine, but Augustine does not fully confirm Freud. Freudianism, in its preoccupation with sex, so acceptable to moderns, goes beyond anything Augustine ever dreamed of.

Nor do we find in Freud, or expect to find in him, the theological concept of concupiscence. Whatever psychology and psychiatry find in man they tend to absorb into their idea of the natural. And concupiscence is basically natural. It is the task of theology, working under revelation, to point out how concupiscence may divert men from their God-appointed supernatural end and, in so doing, violate the truest impulses and inclinations also of nature. Pathological developments of personality may also be, at least in some cases, indirect evidence of such violations. We have noted that Augustine in his inquiries into memory anticipated Freud. He also provides beforehand, in his teaching on concupiscence, an explanation of the Freudian unconscious. The unconscious, if important, is not an absolute; there must also be an explanation of why it becomes a snake pit of festering morbid disorders issuing from perfectly natural impulses and desires.

If by radical surgery it were possible to purge Freud of materialism, if the Freudian "libido" were to be replaced by "love," and "pansexualism" were changed to "panamorism," we would be back in the world of Augustinian and Catholic theology as it reaches down and in to engage the deepest and most intimate aspirations of human nature. For Catholic theology holds that love, the love of God, is the very last end and supreme good of man; and that there is that in man, at the very center of his being, which responds to that love.[34] All human loves are plateaus, rising one above the other like a stairway, with conjugal love at the summit—Jesus is, above all, the Bridegroom—to assist man in his ascent to the God Who "is love." This is why, despite some dissenting voices, there is no impropriety in celibates speaking of sexuality and love. They are also seeking Love. Augustine was indeed overriding, but not condemning, human love—rather he was realizing its innermost meaning—when he cried out in opening his *Confessions*, "Thou hast made our hearts for Thyself, O God, and they will never rest until they rest in Thee!"

The myth of love

Another phenomenon, the myth of erotic love, also confirms Augustine's fear of sexual concupiscence. This myth has come to influence, if not dominate, the practical attitude of almost all modern men, including Catholics, toward marriage and love. Celebrated by troubadours, it originated in the courtly love of Provence in Southern France during the twelfth century. It centers in the cult of a love-goddess who is "adored in adultery." Denis De Rougemont calls this "the psychic revolution of the 12th century"; and J. Langdon-Davies, a critic of De Rougemont, describes it as "the invention of love."

Purified, this new idea of love entered Christian thought and literature through Petrarch and Dante. (It also entered Christian society unpurified. Abélard and Héloïse remind us of this.) It was taken up by St. Bernard (following St. Augustine) and used to illustrate the soul's mystical quest for God. The Spouse of the Canticle and Christ as the Bridegroom, whose symbolism had heretofore been imperfectly realized, now took on new meaning. In time, the purified idea of romantic love would enter Christian conjugal love bringing warmth and new significance. But while women were still regarded as inferior, and as long as marriages were determined by economics, women being merely "peripatetic title deeds to property"—and this means until modern times—conjugal love even after Dante was foredoomed to eke out a meager existence. Even Dante was unable to realize in his life the balance that he achieved in his literary masterwork.

The love-myth in its unpurified strain has also persisted. in our society, down to the apotheosis of Hollywood's latest love-goddess. She is all but omnipresent in literature, drama, films—and advertising. If her affairs, at least in anemic forms of the myth, are not necessarily adulterous, adultery is still no obstacle to her possession. The sovereign rights of "love" are sufficient to justify infidelity, divorce, and the dissolution of homes.

Possibly the love-myth has a more sinister meaning. De Rougemont, at any rate, who has spent a lifetime tracing its intricacies, is convinced that its origin in Provence, the medieval center of the Catharist heresy, is deeply significant. The myth, he contends, is rooted in Catharism, which is to say, in Manichaean theology and metaphysics. This, he argues, explains its antinomianism, its disregard, not to say contempt, for marriage, its invariable preference for adultery, its rejection of procreation—in a word, its anarchistic despoiling of domestic society and of society in general.

It is this Catharist strain, according to De Rougemont, that has created the tension between erotic love and the Christian ideal of marriage. It has established throughout the West, he holds, as Catharism itself did in Christian France, a rival system of religion and morality. This system, "a fusion of sexuality and religion," is largely responsible, he believes, for the modern breakdown of marriage. The future of marriage in our society, hence of our society itself, he concludes, depends on our making a choice between these two conceptions of marriage, the Christian and the Catharist.[35]

If there is any truth in De Rougemont's thesis, and even his critics admit there is some, perhaps Augustine anticipated the danger of Catharism. Although the saint did not live to hear the troubadours, he knew Manichaeism from within, realized its immanent law, and was witness to its orgiastic practices. Who then would be Manichaean? Augustine? Or those who willy-nilly abet its metaphysics? At any rate, with Augustine's experience of Manichaeism, there is little wonder that, meditating on Genesis and convinced of the goodness of all God's creation, he should bind marriage and procreation so tightly to conjugal love and sexuality.

However, we do not argue here for the truth of De Rougemont's thesis, which is undoubtedly pushed too far, nor for the opposing views of his critics. The problem and the controversy, together with the vast materials from which they arise, are cited simply as evidence of the special sensitiveness of sexuality and of the risks it carries. Augustine is by no means alone in his emphasis.

The idolatry of love

The tendency to idolatry in love is no mere poetic invention of the troubadours. Nor a fantasy of the Catharists. Christianity itself carries an inherent risk. It is at least improbable that the Catharist myth, despite its Oriental prehistory, could have arisen anywhere but in a Christian culture. Indeed, without invoking Catharism at all, it is possible to understand the idolatry of love in purely Christian terms. Sexuality is perilous, not only because of the vehemence of bodily concupiscence—if there were only this, it would be no more dangerous than other bodily appetites—but chiefly because of its inner bond with love, thence with divine charity. All men seek happiness, and most seek it in love; the appetite is limitless—"our hearts will never rest"—and love promises to satisfy it. With sexuality thus bound to love, and with human love in turn a ray of the limitless love of God and leading to it, human love may be substituted for God; which is idolatry. On the other hand it is precisely this linkage of human love with the divine that makes possible the mystical ascent of love to God as described by St. Augustine, St. Bernard, and St. John of the Cross.

St. Paul had already called covetousness idolatry (Eph 5: 5; Col 3: 6); and while this covetousness is no doubt narrowly and properly avarice, it may be extended to include all kinds of covetousness and cupidity. St. Augustine makes this extension, and St. Thomas confirms him. In doing this, the Angelic Doctor recalls the choice with which we are now very familiar: "Sin is nothing else than to seek after temporal things to the neglect of divine things."[36] Mortal sin is but man's substitution of a created good for God, the Uncreated Good and true Last End: idolatry. If it is so in the case of wealth, why not in love, which offers the illusion of an infinitely satisfying happiness? This tendency to idolatry is identical with what Von Hildebrand calls the "diabolic" strain in sexuality; for it is the sin of the demon to make his own natural good an absolute, an idol.[37]

Note in passing that the idolatry of love is but one area of a wider idolatry. Concupiscence diverts sexuality from the norm of virtue only because it diverts all human desires. There is no sex-obsession in Catholic (or Augustinian) thought.

Bouyer, while criticizing Augustine's alleged preoccupation with sexuality, whose danger, he says, "however real, is relatively but trivial"—himself errs when he fails to see that this "trivial" sensuality is deeply intertwined with love, hence in what he rightly regards as the real danger and final temptation of married love, i.e., its tendency to idolatry through seeking in itself an earthly paradise.[38] Bouyer himself seems here to move in the direction of a questionable dualism, while Augustine shows his awareness of the bond between sexuality and love by placing the final responsibility for concupiscence in the will, to which love properly belongs.

Leon Bloy wrote in *The Woman Who Was Poor*: "Woman can never believe herself anything but Love personified, and the Earthly Paradise, sought for so many centuries, by Don Juans of every grade, is her Miraculous Image.... All women have one point in common—the preconceived assurance of their dignity and office as Dispensers of Joy.... All women—wittingly or unwittingly—are persuaded that their bodies are Paradise."

To which we may add: men are commonly ready to share that persuasion.

Paul Claudel also takes the nexus between human and divine love as the point and pivot of his dramas *Break of Noon* and *The Satin Slipper*. Here the theology of Augustine and Bernard is confirmed by profound personal experience and artistic vision.

When Juliet said, "Romeo is the god of my idolatry!" she was not indulging in a pretty fancy but was making an act of faith, which she lived up to fully by taking her own life. She was acting out the *symbolum fidei* that Keats would later draw up: "I have now no limits to my love. I have been astonished that men could die martyrs of religion. I have shuddered at it. I shudder no more. I could be martyred for my religion—love is my religion—I could die for you." Juliet, although we have seen her so often that she seems real, is of course a fictional character; yet that we have seen her so often is evidence that she stands for something quite real in all of us.

From real life we have Héloïse: "I would rather be Abelard's whore than mistress of Christendom!" To be sure, there may be discrepancies between profession and practice in the religion of love, as in other religions. The boast of Keats that he would suffer martyrdom for love went untested. Edward Gibbon, when threatened with disinheritance if he would not give up Madam de Stael, "sighed as a lover but obeyed as a son."

Nevertheless, quite apart from heroics, the danger of idolatry ever threatens human love, and idolatry is really if implicitly present in sinful love. When Aucassin, in the medieval tale, is threatened with hell if he takes Nicolette as mistress, he replies that he would rather go to hell with Nicolette than to heaven without her. Minus the poetic touch and operatic gesture perhaps, this declaration is actually carried out in every love that puts creature above Creator—in every grievous sin: and this is idolatry.

Perhaps the most direct and uninhibited expression of the idolatry of love is to be found in the sanctioned prostitution and sexual orgies of pagan religions. Such rituals may seem, on the surface, to be the very negation of religion. Yet they express something real in pagan religion, namely, the tendency to apotheosize sexuality. The devotees at once invoke, imitate, and appropriate divinity to themselves. Their ritualized actions, besides being a fertility cult, are a love rite. Sexual ecstasy apes and replaces divine ecstasy. In examining the meaning of these rites, Mircea Eliade observes:

> Let me point out that this desire [i.e., for eternity and "paradise"] is no spiritual attitude, which depreciates life on earth and all that goes with it in favor of a "spirituality" of detachment from the world. On the contrary, what may be called the nostalgia for eternity proves that man longs for a concrete paradise,

and believes that such a paradise can be won here, on earth, and now, in the present moment.³⁹

As we have just seen, the love cult also takes on more sophisticated forms. It persists right to our own enlightened and unsuperstitious age. D. H. Lawrence has evidently spoken for a large segment of this age, so free of childish idolatries, in his *Lady Chatterley's Lover*. An apologist for the book contends that it is not pornography, on the ground that it is no mere recital of obscenities but has meaning and moral purpose. But modern man has lost his bearings; this very purpose, while it may distinguish Lawrence's book from the purposeless pornography of the newsstands, is precisely what makes it so radically and viciously immoral. For it represents satisfactory sexual orgasm as the summit and *summum bonum* of human life. It substitutes the momentary ecstasy of sex for the eternal ecstasy of the divine embrace. It is the exact opposite of that conception which, as in Augustine, is ready to sacrifice the momentary for the eternal. It would lead men back to a real idolatry even though its sophistication would, perhaps, hinder it from raising actual shrines to Venus or Eros.

In our day, one realizes, even D. H. Lawrence belongs to the prehistory of real moral enlightenment. The idol now is sexual experience—whether lover-related or not, whether other-related or not, and regardless of who the other may be. Thus "progress" has brought us full-circle back to the Greeks and to phallic shrines still deeper in the mists of paganism.⁴⁰

"Enlightened" sexuality

Should such "theoretical" considerations as the above still not seem fully convincing, the doubter might take a practical tour through our world today. He could begin by considering the *Playboy* phenomenon with its appeal to millions. While near the newsstands he might also look over the other varied offerings featuring provocative nudity, salacious fiction, and any available material on sex scandals. Post Office officials claim that half a billion dollars' worth of obscene materials are distributed annually. He might consider the billions that are made by the entrepreneurs who thus cater to a concupiscence in which they have no theological faith but unbounded financial confidence. Let him read the theater page of almost any metropolitan paper for lurid evidence of that combination of sex and violence which goes by the name of entertainment. Let him note the theater marquees that, even in advertising "family" entertainment, are often an embarrassment to the least prudish. Let him, if he will, enter the theaters where current favorites are running, to see how smartly and naughtily they play with sex. As to nudity—here also the theme of peekaboo naughtiness—he might pause to wonder why, if there is no original sin, there is so much bother about it. Augustine is ridiculed for seeing in the shame of Adam and Eve in their nudity evidence that sexuality had been deranged by the Fall. But if not, surely the nudists are right: why so much fuss about nudity even in the post-Christian world? Again, our tourists might inquire how fortunes are made out of something that, for those responsible, does not exist.

The doubter might then go on to reflect that all this literature and entertainment in some way reflects the life and ideals of the society that supports it, otherwise it could not be so popular and lucrative. It also helps to form the ideals of the members of this society. As yet, however, the inquirer has not entered the theaters that feature "adult" shows for the perennially adolescent. Nor into the haunts of the ecdysiasts. These side-trips can be left to his own taste and conscience. But let him at any rate consider how modern man's enlightened quest for liberty has given the entrepreneurs occasion and opportunity to flood the world with moral filth and ransack the archives of the ages for every available specimen of pornography: then to print it cheaply and place it handily in corner stores where adolescents, real or perennial, will be sure of obtaining "enlightenment."

Finally, the doubter should read the statistics and the real-life stories of adulteries, divorces, triangles (often complete with murders), and of what is casually called suburban switcheroo. He could bring his tour to an end by studying the record of sex crimes. Then he should ask whether sexual concupiscence exists, whether perhaps it is not a rather potent force, and whether St. Augustine exaggerated its risks.

Marriage and Sexuality   115

And whether modern man, who considers himself so superior to the fifth-century bishop and has accumulated a vast amount of psychological knowledge, has really brought this force under control in the enlightened manner that he likes to claim as his own. Lastly, he should tell us why the crime rate, instead of being reduced, grows with our enlightenment.

Such tours as the above have indeed been made, at least imaginatively. Voltaire would no doubt be ill at ease in the role of apologist for Christianity, yet his *Candide,* written to ridicule the extreme optimism of Leibnitz, is in fact a vindication of the Christian belief that man is flawed. The innocent Candide, disciple of a Leibnitzian philosopher in his fantastic journey, nowhere finds the perfect man he had been led by his master to expect.

A modern tour, written in obvious imitation of *Candide,* even to the name *Candy,* is concerned only with sex and thus typifies the contemporary preoccupation. Candy—who not insignificantly has become a girl—innocent indeed but still a love-goddess, is pursued on a fantastic journey across the world in a series of sexual misadventures. The story, of course, is a satire on contemporary sexual attitudes and preoccupations; but, characteristic of our day, it exploits sex to the limit in making its point.

This book, and many others like it, indicate the extent to which our generation has reacted against Victorianism and Jansenism. Not only has sexual behavior swung to an extreme of utter license; books and films, obsessed with sex, nudity, and the vicarious enjoyment of intercourse, in all its variations and even perversions, have made voyeurists of a whole generation. Despite claims of having attained maturity in such matters, it is doubtful whether an age of Peeping Toms and sick sex is capable of taking a balanced view of normal sexuality.

There is Jonathan Swift: Gulliver's sorry experiences in his extensive travels may indeed be overdrawn as the result of his creator's pessimistic theological views, yet his acceptance in literature—a "mirror held up to nature"—is some evidence that men have found substantive truth in his adventures.

Newman in his *Apologia* also makes a survey of the world and finds in its omnipresent corruption and evil "a vision to dizzy and appal," a vision that "inflicts upon the mind the sense of a profound mystery, which is absolutely beyond human solution." He adds, "And so I conclude about the world; *if* there be a God, *since* there is a God, the human race is implicated in some terrible aboriginal calamity. It is out of joint with the purposes of its Creator. This is a fact as true as the fact of its existence; and thus the doctrine of what is theologically called original sin becomes to me almost as certain as that the world exists, and as the existence of God."

One is reminded of Chesterton's saying in *Orthodoxy* that original sin is "the only part of Christian theology that can really be proved," since it can be seen "in the street."

Golding's *The Lord of the Flies* gives us a current look at our flawed nature; and if this view, like that of Swift, is distorted by Calvinism, its popularity in the face of the bland optimism and Pelagianism of the day is impressive. On the non-fiction side, Langdon Filkey has described in *Shantung Compound* how, as a doctrinaire secularist, he was driven to an acceptance of original sin through the experience of living in a prison compound in close association with two thousand modern and more or less enlightened Americans and Europeans.

Even Plato, who sublimated eros, was driven to admit, without an assist from St. Paul, that eros may take another, less desirable course. In *Phaedrus* Socrates offers the image of the two horses, one bright and noble, the other dark and ignoble, the one drawing man—the charioteer—to all that is just and beautiful, the other dragging him to the gross and evil. Surely this figure foreshadows St. Paul's "law of the members" that he saw "warring against the law of my mind and making me prisoner to the law of sin that is in my members" (Rom 8: 23).

The phenomena just considered turn up again to complicate and muddy the Christian idea of conjugal love, which we will consider in the next section. Looking back at them, one is led to conclude that it seems almost amusing, and certainly incredible, that Augustine could be charged with exaggerating the dangerous if fruitful potency of human sexuality—unless the exaggeration is measured by a saying of Emerson: Every man is a little wrong-headed in the direction in which he is rightest. In this direction in which he was rightest, St. Augustine, with his teaching on sexual concupiscence, has made a contribution of the most fundamental kind to a dynamic and realistic moral theology.

Augustine, in thinking of original sin and its effects, was measuring disorder in relation to an event that, while modern men speak of it casually or indifferently, not to say unbelievingly, represented to Augustine's burning faith an indescribable disaster for all mankind and the creature's own attempt to sabotage the divine order. The magnitude of the divine redemptive act, by which the ruin was repaired, does not reduce, rather it reveals more clearly, the greatness of the catastrophe.

6. Marriage Thrice Blessed

> God created man in His image. In the image of God He created them. Male and female He created them. Then God blessed them and said to them, "Be fruitful and multiply; fill the earth and subdue it." . . . For this reason a man leaves his father and mother, and clings to his wife, and the two become one flesh. —Genesis 1: 27–28; 2: 24
>
> By their very nature the institution of matrimony and conjugal love are ordained for the procreation and education of children, and find in them their ultimate crown.
> —Vatican Council II, *Gaudium et Spes*, no. 48

St. Augustine does not consider marriage abstractly as an institution or as a sacrament. He studies it in the actual context of a sexuality affected by concupiscence. Here, therefore, according to his critics, the "flavor of Manichaeism" is supposed to be perceptible. We have considered (Chapter 2) the Augustinian principles that should guide us in estimating this charge. It remains to see how these principles affect what he calls "the good of marriage."

In his controversy with the Pelagians, Augustine, though forceful, maintains a fairly academic composure. In his attacks on the Manichees, on the contrary, he is filled with indignation at their "blasphemous madness." Nowhere is he fiercer than in attacking their ideas of marriage—and virginity. (His revulsion against their notion of continence and virginity, which in a Christian sense he so exalted, is an important part of his witness here; to the Manichees, continence was the rejection of an evil.) The Manichees regarded marriage as evil, not only because it involved a joining of bodies, which according to them are evil, but also because through generation the empire of evil matter is extended. Against this teaching, Augustine's *The Good of Marriage* (the title itself is significant) is devoted to enumerating and describing the three goods or blessings—children, mutual faith, and sacrament—which converge in the one comprehensive good of marriage. Since his time, and including the Second Vatican Council, these goods have provided the framework for theological discussion of marriage in the Church.

We may see here why (apart from Scripture and the Hebrew tradition) he bound so absolutely the *good* of generation to the *good* of marriage. For Augustine, Manichaeism was not just a curious and repulsive theory, as it is to us; it had been for him during many years a lived philosophy. His experience of its evil and its dangers was immediate and personal. His revulsion was absolute.

It has ever been the tendency of Catholics not to be influenced by opposing errors, but to overreact against them. A notable instance of this was the reaction against Arianism. We have noted another example in overreaction to Jansenism, which has produced a kind of neo-Pelagianism. In Augustine's time the appearance of the original Pelagianism prevented overreaction to Manichaeism and brought about a balance, which, we have seen, at once affirmed the goodness of nature and the effects of original sin.

Yet it would be a mistake to think that Augustine's theology of marriage was only a response to Manichaeism. This influence, however virulent, was but that of a sect; it was not the mainstream of Roman life. The Empire itself was in decline and would soon come to an ignominious end at the hands of barbarians. This decline, which Augustine was watching and which he was to interpret theologically in the *City of God,* was nowhere more evident than in the decay of sexual morality and the disintegration of Roman family life. The emperors tried, ineffectually, to stem the process by a series of laws regulating marriage and inheritance. Basically, therefore, Augustine, standing on the integrity of Christian doctrine, was trying to halt among Christians the moral and social ruin that he saw spreading all about him. In *Adulterous Marriages* we see him fighting against the corrupt marriage morality of paganism, which he found still influencing his own people. The book answers the ingenious reasons, invoking even Scripture, by which pagan-thinking Christians tried to justify divorce and remarriage; it is a refutation of arguments that, had they been gathered into one volume by an enterprising editor with a twentieth-century public relations flair, might have been entitled *Adultery and Holiness*.

Strictness in the Patristic sexual morality must therefore be seen as a response to pagan laxity. Here again, however, Manichaeism prevented overreaction. Augustine's position, especially, was that of moderate, correcting excessive views, such as those of Tertullian, Jovinian, and Jerome. Of course by Pelagian (or neo-Pelagian) standards, even Augustine's moderate position seems extreme.

Conditions of his own time thus forced Augustine to address himself, simply in the discharge of his pastoral duties, to fundamental questions concerning marriage.[1] In so doing he made the first great contribution to marriage theology in the West. While his teachings on this subject appear in various books and sermons, he has left us in *The Good of Marriage* what has well been called "the best of all treatises on marriage we have from Christian antiquity."[2]

Within the doctrinal outline of this work, Pope Pius XI set forth his teachings on marriage in the encyclical *Casti Connubii* (On Christian Marriage). Further, despite criticisms of both Augustine and Pius XI, the Fathers of the Second Vatican Council followed the same procedure in their treatment of Christian marriage for the twentieth century. After a brief introduction describing the problems of marriage today, the Fathers of the Council cite Augustine's *The Good of Marriage*.[3] They go on to develop their teaching within the framework of the three blessings of marriage that Augustine had described.

St. Augustine laid no claim to omniscience in the solution of the complicated juridical problems involved in particular marriages. His claims were rather modest. Toward the end of the first book of *Adulterous Marriages* he wrote:

> After this rather paltry treatment and discussion of mine, I am not ignorant of the fact that the question of marriage still remains very obscure and involved. Nor dare I say that either in this work or in any other up to the present [*The Good of Marriage* had been

written almost twenty years before] have I explained all its intricacies, or that I can explain them now, even if urged to do so.[4]

Nevertheless, he has provided a body of basic guiding principles that the Church of the twentieth century still finds indispensable in explaining the Christian doctrine of marriage.

1. CHILDREN

Within the encompassing good that Augustine attributes to marriage, therefore, he distinguishes three special convergent and coordinated blessings: children, mutual faith, and the sacramental bond. Children are here considered first among the goods because this is the order given in *The Good of Marriage*, although, as shall be seen, he did not consider this order invariable.

Here is the reason for the modern dislike of Augustine: the inseparable bond he established between marriage and procreation; his assertion that, when not directed to procreation, marital intercourse involves venial sin; in a word, his contention that marital intercourse is not immune from the threat of concupiscence even in the case of faithful Christians and saints.

From this teaching it is inferred that Augustine regarded sex as evil. We have already noted the remark that for Augustine "all sexual desire and pleasure are intrinsically evil."[5] But if all sexual desire and pleasure are intrinsically evil, how could there have been, as Augustine believed, sexual intercourse in Paradise before the Fall? The difference between the state of our first parents and ours is not in the constitution of nature but in their sin, which is continued in us. Carnal concupiscence "is not a good which comes out of the essence of marriage, but an evil that comes out of original sin."[6] The guilt of this sin is remitted in us by baptism. Yet there remains a tendency to disorder in desire—a tendency that is called sin because it comes from sin and leads to sin. In Paradise the desire and the pleasure were kept under the leadings of grace. "Suppose that nature had not been dishonored by sin, God forbid that we should think that marriages in Paradise must have been such that in them the procreative members would be excited by the mere ardor of lust, but not by the command of the will for producing offspring."[7]

A *Life* magazine editorialist wrote that for Augustine, "Sex is bad except as a means of procreation."[8] This is an exact inversion of the truth. In Augustine's mind, sex (although in our present state never free from the threat of concupiscence) is good, but a good limited by its aptitude for procreation and the duty to direct it to this good; used apart from this limiting and defining good, it is still lawful in the married, but, because of concupiscence, does not escape venial fault. His principle is clear, "Therefore the procreation of children is the original [*prima*], natural, and legitimate purpose of marriage."

And the conclusion:

> It is, however, one thing for married persons to have intercourse only for the wish to beget children, which is not sinful; it is another thing for them to desire carnal pleasure in cohabitation, but with the spouse only, which involves venial sin. For although propagation of offspring is not the motive of the intercourse, there is still no attempt to prevent such propagation, either by wrong desire or evil appliance."

The desire for "carnal pleasure" here spoken of is the operation of concupiscence diverting the couple from "the primary, natural, and legitimate purpose of marriage." As he says in *The Good of Marriage,* bringing together both aspects of his teaching:

> In marriage, intercourse for the purpose of procreation has no fault attached to it [*non habet culpam*]; but for the purpose of satisfying concupiscence, provided with a spouse, because of the marriage faith, it is but a venial fault; adultery or fornication, however, is a mortal sin.[9]

These passages, easily misunderstood, are crucial for appreciating Augustine's thought on sex and marriage. One thing, however, should not be misunderstood: he says flatly that intercourse for the purpose of procreation "is not sinful" and is "without blame." We have already heard him call it a "chaste operation." How then does he regard sex as "intrinsically evil"?

On the other hand, how can intercourse between lawful spouses at any time be even venially sinful? Does not such an assertion make intercourse in some sense evil? Does it not bear out Bouyer's statement that, for Augustine, "if sexual intercourse is not to be sinful, it must at least cease to be attractive and pleasurable to man?" Whatever its meaning, which we shall proceed to examine, it is at any rate clear that Augustine does not regard sex as intrinsically evil: any evil that enters the marital act does so extrinsically, *ab extero*, and it is thus a disorder resulting from the activity of concupiscence; the presence of concupiscence is betrayed when intercourse is not open to the procreative good.

It may be noted that St. Thomas's view at this point coincides exactly with Augustine's. There is not a hairsbreadth of difference between their statements.[10] If Augustine is rigoristic, the Angelic Doctor is equally so; and in all fairness "rigorism" should be considered synonymous with "Thomism" as well as "Augustinism."

Actually, this teaching of Augustine and Thomas is rather benign. What they are saying is that, although intercourse outside of marriage is gravely sinful, within lawful marriage, even when passions run out of control and there is no desire of procreation, it cannot exceed venial sin. If we allow that there is such a thing as human weakness, to which the married also may succumb, this does not seem excessive. Especially so when it is remembered that according to Catholic theologians generally there is no parvity of matter (*parvitas materiae*) in sexual sin. Here, say Augustine and Thomas in effect, is an exception: the married, even when they use intercourse apart from its purpose of procreation, and under the influence of concupiscence, do not exceed venial sin.

In explaining his view that the married sin venially when acting under the impulse of concupiscence, Augustine cites the words of the Apostle to the married, "Do not deprive each other, except perhaps by consent, for a time that you may give yourselves to prayer; and return together again lest Satan tempt you because you lack self-control. But this I say by way of concession, not commandment" (1 Cor 7: 5–6). Understanding "concession" as "pardon," Augustine argues that no pardon would be necessary where there is no fault; and the fault is that "you lack self-control."[11] Some modern exegetes reject Augustine's interpretation of this difficult text. Yet, even if deprived on one text, his teaching still rests on the law of nature and on the wider doctrine of the Scriptures and the Church on the effects of original sin.[12]

Augustine has here worked out a natural law teaching for marriage, but concretely for fallen man, not for man in a hypothetical state of pure nature; this is why he introduces concupiscence to explain sexual disorders. He is thinking as a philosopher, but as a Christian philosopher.

We shall return to this matter of venial sin in the married. Let us now consider what Augustine calls the lawful use of marital intercourse. The sole good authorizing this intercourse, he believes, is the desire for offspring. This is the good for which it is naturally designed and intended. Hence, engaged in apart from this good, it is, objectively, a disorder. So long as spouses do not exclude procreation, although not intending it, their yielding to concupiscence does not exceed venial fault. But it is a fault. Not because the pleasure, which is also enjoyed by the saints, is evil. (We have examined this matter in Chapter 4.) But such conduct, at least in desire, is a failure to respect the divinely established purpose. In many places the saint relates intercourse to offspring as the sole fully justifying object. "Is it not a sin in married persons to exact from one another more than this design of 'the procreation of children' renders necessary?"[13] The purpose of procreation "hallows" (in the old Anglican phrase), or sanctifies, marital intercourse. (The word is used also by the Fathers of Vatican II in their discussion of marriage, although in a wider sense.)

The Church's modern acceptance of the natural family planning method for regulating childbirth does not diminish the force of this teaching. Such acceptance was tacit from the beginning in the sanction of permanently sterile marriages and marriages of the elderly. These marriages remain open to procreation; limitations of nature here make it impossible or unlikely. (Of the intention, in a moment.)

Augustine's explanation of the law of nature is simple, lucid, and convincing:

> Surely we must see that God gives us some goods which are to be sought for their own sakes, such as wisdom, health, friendship; others, which are necessary for something else, such as learning, food, drink, sleep, marriage, sexual intercourse. Certain of these are necessary for the sake of wisdom, such as learning; others for the sake of friendship, such as marriage or intercourse, for from these comes the propagation of the human race in which friendly association is a great good.[14]

As a Christian, Augustine, in setting forth his ideas on marriage intercourse, is thinking of Genesis, "Increase and multiply," as fixing the purpose of intercourse and marriage. As a Christian philosopher, he is thinking of the function of sexuality, and he does not see that it has any end independent of procreation. The morality of sex must be judged in relation to its aptitude for this end. Companionship between the sexes, he says, could exist without sexual coitus;[15] indeed, apart from procreation there would be no reason to divide human beings into two sexes.[16] If his former Manichaean experience enters here, it is not to condemn sexuality as inherently evil, but to reinforce his conviction that procreation, or the desire for it, is a good inseparable from marital intercourse.[17] In holding this he was inventing nothing of his own. On the contrary, in frequently quoting the marriage tablets, or contract, of Roman law (as above), which stated that marriage is for the procreation of children, he was appealing, amidst the ruins of Roman morality, to the enlightened conception of Roman law.[18] He was also speaking the conviction and practice of the whole of Christian antiquity; his is the most articulate voice, but not the only voice, from that age. Indeed, he was speaking for the whole of humanity: even the sophisticated evasions of our age cannot obscure the elementary fact, of monumental simplicity, that marriage is a procreative community. The Fathers of the Second Vatican Council expressed this fact in the passage placed at the head of this chapter. To which they shortly added: "Marriage and conjugal love are by their nature ordained toward the begetting and educating of children."

It is false to say, therefore, that for Augustine "all sexual desire and pleasure are intrinsically evil." The question is, rather, "Within what limits is intercourse lawful?" The use of every creature, like a house surrounded by a fence to keep off trespassers, is limited by the divine and natural law: we may obtain property, but not by stealing; and the point of trespass is determined by how close the fence is to the house. For Augustine, conjugal intercourse is limited by the fact that it is designed for procreation; apart from this purpose, even considering the other goods of marriage, it is not without venial fault. To exclude this purpose is of course, by these principles, grievous sin.[19]

According to his critics—and enemies—St. Augustine was far too restrictive in thus limiting fully lawful intercourse to the desire for procreation. Contraceptionists now wish to justify it, independently of the desire for procreation, as an expression of conjugal love and realization of the sacramental sign.[20] He did not see any purpose in the sexual act exclusive of procreation. In his thought, therefore, sexuality is evil only when positively exploited in frustration of this purpose (although but slightly wrong when this purpose is not excluded). This is quite different from holding that sexuality is intrinsically evil. Moreover, if sexuality is taken in the larger sense of the personal communion of the sexes in matrimony—conjugal love—then Augustine did envision other purposes as is clear from his insistence on the threefold blessing of marriage. Indeed, he would agree and affirm, as we shall see (returning to the passage just cited—"intercourse for the sake of friendship"), that there may be marital intercourse out of love, authorized by mutual faith; only for him real love is always open to procreation.

2. MARRIAGE AND HOLINESS

Whatever may be said in praise of the three blessings does not remove from marriage the corrupting influence of unrestrained concupiscence. Modern Catholics tend to ignore this danger. They offer what Bouyer calls an "idyllic view" of sexuality, which, while claiming to be quite modern and enlightened, bears a disconcerting resemblance to the outlook of the old Pelagians. Allowing for the personal needs involved in the marital relationship is not to be confused with the modern exploitation of sex; nor is it to deny the force of concupiscence even in the married.

"Post-Freudian pop psychology" in its view of sexuality tends to regard sex as good in itself, without limitations, and apart from any relation to function, whether procreation or marital love. The sexual experience itself, however procured, is exalted; everyone has a "right," we are told, to satisfactory sexual experience. Well, there is one limitation: the experience should be acceptable to the parties involved. Any distortion of intercourse, even homosexuality—or as the phrase goes, "for consenting adults"—becomes normal for those who wish it that way: *Non disputandum de gustibus*. According to this "enlightened" view, as a current love manual puts it, one thing is to be avoided: "The words 'Thou shalt love thy neighbor as thyself' are the direct progenitors of misplaced consideration in love-making. We believe, on the contrary, that we should love ourselves just a little bit more than the other person. We should show ourselves a little more consideration—think a little more about ourselves."[21]

In this conception of sexuality it is the love of self, of one's own satisfaction, that counts; charity, which in Christian teaching transforms human conjugal love into Christian conjugal love, is the enemy. Written by married doctors to counsel the married, such advice suggests that even in the married concupiscence still exists. Naturally, those who hold such views will regard Augustine as a Puritan or Manichee. To them it will appear that he regards sexuality as evil. But the Fathers of the Second Vatican Council wrote, "Authentic married love is caught up in the divine love and enriched by Christ's redeeming power."[22]

Since Augustine bound intercourse so firmly to the desire for procreation, he saw the intrusion of concupiscence as soon as this purpose was not envisioned. This is why he regarded marital intercourse apart from this purpose as venial sin. The term "venial sin," when applied to an intrinsically legitimate act between married people, seems to the modern mind a scandal. Yet it is preposterous to believe, as many modern Catholics seem to believe, that marriage automatically ends the warfare of the married against concupiscence. In them also it remains, not only after baptism, but also after the sacrament of matrimony, *ad agonem*. Married Christians, no matter how chaste their union or excellent their intentions (and allowing for individual variations), must struggle against concupiscence; if they do not, it may enter to corrupt, perhaps to ruin, their marriage relationship. As the Fathers of the Vatican Council put it, Christian conjugal love "far exceeds mere erotic inclination, which, selfishly pursued, soon enough fades wretchedly away." Indeed, this good "cannot be achieved unless the virtue of conjugal chastity is sincerely practiced."[23]

Secular writers, of course, do not acknowledge concupiscence. For them, concupiscence does not exist. All sexual desire, they believe, is "natural"; they discern its deviations, not in morality, but in psycho-pathology; they are concerned with no disorders except those that are criminal. Short of such extremes, it is rather to be encouraged than feared. In a certain sense they are right; sexuality, even turned awry, is "natural." St. Thomas, commenting on the words of Wisdom (12: 10), "their malice was natural," writes:

> The malice of some men may be called natural, either because of custom which is a second nature; or on account of the natural proclivity on the part of the sensitive nature to some inordinate passion, as some people are said to be naturally wrathful or lustful. . . .[24]

But acceptance of any vagary or even deviation of nature as natural, whereas in fact only those actions which accord with reason are truly natural, gives wide latitude to human weakness and passion. Let it be kept in mind here, too, that for Augustine, "excesses" of sexuality are really defects, a failure to live according to reason and the exigencies of grace. For the married they are but imperfections, akin to all those daily faults of which the Psalmist says, "The just man falls seven times daily."

The Christian is left to struggle against the disorderly inclinations of his nature; and for the faithful Christian, living habitually in grace, this will be his ordinary daily spiritual combat. For this reason there has grown up among theologians what may be called a theology of imperfect actions. For Augustine also, there is an immense difference, indeed a difference in kind, between mortal and venial sin. That both are called sin may, but should not, obscure this difference.

> Although every crime is a sin, every sin is not a crime. And so we say that the life of holy men, as long as they remain in this mortal body, may be found without crime; but, as the Apostle John says, "If we say that we have no sin, we deceive ourselves, and the truth is not in us" (1 Jn 1: 8).[25]

Notice that this passage does not refer to sexuality; all our desires and activities are liable to disorder. While mortal sin is "damnable," venial sin occurs in fallen man even after justification. This venial sin may be forgiven simply by saying the "Our Father"—"Forgive us our trespasses." Augustine frequently uses this text in refuting the Pelagian denial of original sin: the just man must also speak of himself as a sinner. Thus Augustine exhibits both his moderation and his compassion.

Venial sin also is not a fixed quantity. Within this genus there are almost infinite gradations, from *venialissima* to deliberate venial sins, which are an abuse of created goods in the order of means.[26] An imperfection is "a morally good act which can be ordained to the end of charity, but which lacks a certain perfection suitable to spiritual progress."[27] This would include any actions in which some merely natural motive or attachment would hinder or reduce the actual influx of charity. Some writers call these natural actions. Others believe that even such natural actions are not wholly without guilt, because they mark at least some deviation from the order of charity, which binds men to love and seek God with their whole hearts as their final end.[28] Augustine, while warning that they should not be despised, speaks of them as "minor," "light," "minute."

We need not enter the discussion about the precise morality of imperfections. The point for us is that, even in advanced Christians, concupiscence can and does enter their actions to spoil them, as a worm spoils (but does not necessarily ruin) an apple. Speech is a legitimate, elevated, and truly human activity; yet we can hardly enter into conversation without falling into some fault of vanity, exaggeration, or uncharitableness. Perhaps those most interested in this matter of imperfections are religious earnestly seeking perfection as they go through their daily round of eating, sleeping, walking, working. Sexuality is a much fiercer energy; its activity, radically renounced by religious, must be held in control by the married: are these not liable to at least minor deviations of sensuality? Are they exempt, because of the grace of matrimony, from this tendency to fall? St. Augustine (with St. Thomas) thinks not. Temperance, indeed, may be in its own way more difficult than total renunciation.[29]

Moreover, the Church, in permitting natural family planning, does not deny that the married, like all other Christians, are liable to failures. Toleration of natural family planning does not deny, even implicitly, that the married are exposed to the danger of at least venial disorder. The moral and ascetical problem remains even after the sacrament of matrimony as it does after baptism.

Nor does the acknowledgment that coitus may and should express conjugal love free the spouses from concupiscence and the necessity of moral struggle. Love has its own demands, which are not always easy. It does not exclude pleasure, but it certainly forbids the exploitation of sex for mere sensuality: unless one believes, like the "love" manual quoted above, that charity is irrelevant and alien. Those authors who are most positive in asserting that intercourse is intended by God as an expression of love and integral to the sacramental sign are also insistent that it should be so expressive and significative. "Wedded love, however, can perform this function [i.e., of expressing love] only when it is consciously and deliberately anchored in God—is a love in God. Only when the spirit cleaves to God by an express act can it keep its head above the waves of animal life which at this moment [i.e., in intercourse] break violently upon it."[30]

Augustine, as a master of spiritual theology, sees the moral struggle of the married within the context of the whole Christian life. He writes to Julian:

> You think the Apostle's warning against possessing one's vessel in the disease of lust refers only to fornication, not to marriage, and thus you remove from the union of the married all the honesty of temperance, so that none could possess this vessel in the disease of lust no matter what the passion drawing him to this in his wife.[31]

A distinction must be made between the rudimentary demands of morality and the exigencies of that love of God which, as it grows, tends toward the highest holiness. Augustine sees the Christian life, including that of the married, as a development toward holiness, a development in which even minor faults tend to disappear. If Catholic laymen in our day wish to recover their full stature as Christians, they cannot do so merely by gaining certain juridical privileges. Rather, they must accept their vocation to holiness—a vocation that can no longer be dismissed as merely of counsel or as the theory of a school. The Second Vatican Council in *Lumen Gentium* (Dogmatic Constitution on the Church) has supported Augustine's views on this point by devoting a whole section (Chapter 5) to affirming and defining the vocation of all Christians to holiness.

On the other hand, the concrete conception of a nature tending to disorder in its desires is neither Manichaean nor Jansenistic. It is thoroughly and completely Catholic. But this is easily forgotten in the atmosphere of rationalism and of the romantic optimism wafted over the modern world by Rousseau. Through incomprehension of the inward corruption of Jansenist austerity and a failure, or refusal, to accept the Christian law of dying with Jesus in order to live with him, modern Catholics have allowed the Jansenists to steal the cross from them. But those who do not bear the cross of Christ, as St. John of the Cross said, cannot share the glory of Christ.

The Fathers of Vatican Council II wrote:

This [conjugal] love God has judged worthy of special gifts, healing, perfecting, and exalting gifts of grace and charity.[32]

They had already provided the backdrop for this teaching:

Indeed, man finds that by himself he is incapable of battling the assaults of evil successfully, so that everyone feels as though he is bound by chains. But the Lord Himself came to free and strengthen man, renewing him inwardly and casting out the prince of this world.[33]

3. LOVING FAITH AND INDISSOLUBILITY

That Augustine begins his discussion of the three blessings of marriage with children might be evidence to his critics, and the critics of the Church's received position, of what they call biologism, i.e., emphasis on reproduction in marriage rather than on the personalist value of conjugal love.[34] But these critics are themselves guilty of biologism in reducing human procreation to a biological function paralleling the reproduction of animals. Under the good of offspring we are dealing with the origin of human life and human persons; the traditional word, even in canon law (Canon 1013), is procreation, i.e., the sharing by parents in the creative love of God. This is not biologism; it is sacramentalized procreative love.

Moreover, it is understood and desired in the Church's teaching that the procreative act be not a mere response to instinctual drives, but a responsible human act, impelled by love. Even though passion is aroused in lawful marital intercourse and the pleasure is intense, "it does not go beyond the bounds previously appointed by reason before the commencement of the act, although reason is unable to regulate it during the act itself."[35] Biological function and instinct are to be controlled by the rational will moved by grace.[36] Such insistence on rational control by the will has led to the opposite charge of "angelism." But you cannot have it both ways. The truth is that the Church in her teaching, like St. Augustine, stands for the integrity and unity of the human person.

Augustine's critics, reducing procreation to animal reproduction and separating it from conjugal love, are guilty of biologism not to be found in the saint's thought. "By conjugal faith," he says, "it is provided that there should be no carnal intercourse outside the marriage bond with another man or woman; with regard to offspring, that children be begotten of love, tenderly cared for, and educated in a religious atmosphere."[37]

Since mutual faith is one of the blessings of marriage, it is urged that conjugal love is also sufficient reason for intercourse.[38] As evident from the above quotation, Augustine would agree—but not to the extent of considering it sufficient to the exclusion of procreation. Mutual faith, indeed, makes intercourse a *duty* where one or both parties desire it, as St. Paul teaches; although Augustine, while assenting to this, regards it even then as an imperfection if not open to procreation. Moreover, considering faith in relation to conjugal love, Augustine says, in a passage already noted, that marital intercourse is *necessary* "for the sake of friendship," although again not to the exclusion of procreation. He distinguishes between goods that are to be sought for their own sakes—"wisdom, health, friendship"—from others "which are *necessary* for something else, such as learning, food, drink, sleep, marriage, sexual intercourse." He goes on: "Certain of these are *necessary* for the sake of wisdom, such as learning; others for the sake of friendship (*propter amicitiam*), such as marriage or intercourse, for from these comes the propagation of the human race in which friendly association is a great good."[39]

This statement is important; it refutes in advance those who say that only in modern times has marital intercourse been seen in relation to conjugal love and the interpersonal relationship of spouses.

While some dismiss the Church's concern with marital faith as mere legalism, designed only to protect mutual "rights," for Augustine (and the Church) marital faith has a much deeper meaning. (Nor should it be forgotten that the concern for mutual rights originates with St. Paul.) This faith is substantially identical with conjugal love, is the expression and safeguard of this love. When Pope Pius XI developed the theme of conjugal love in *Casti Connubii,* he did so under the Augustinian heading of marital faith, one of the three goods of marriage. This faith, he said, is *rooted* in love; in other words, love opens up into faith. The love he speaks of here is human love transformed by divine charity and leading to the perfection of love, which is identical with the "summit of holiness." In this the Pope's teaching not only harmonizes with Augustine but also anticipates Vatican II.

Chesterton, attacking free love and trial marriage, noted that if the law does not demand faith, lovers themselves will give it, as when they carve their interlinking hearts on a tree trunk. Canonical or legal safeguards merely institutionalize what lovers spontaneously, freely, and inevitably give each other. Can faith and loyalty be imagined without love? Can love be imagined without mutual faith? Fidelity as a legal or canonical requirement merely recognizes the deep and abiding human desire for faithful love. Augustine indicated this in his persistent distinction between *concubitus* and *connubium.* Faith, for him, is loyalty to that love which pervades all the duties and goods of *connubium.* Marital "friendship" has the special quality of mutual, exclusive, and lifelong faith.

Accordingly, the importance of the procreative blessing does not mean that when for any reason there are no children, conjugal love loses its value. "In a good marriage, although one of many years, even if the ardor of youth has cooled between man and woman, the order of charity still flourishes between husband and wife." Nor is childlessness a reason for divorce and remarriage. "That bond of fellowship between married couples is so strong that, although it is tied for the purpose of procreation, it is not loosed for the purpose of procreation," i.e., to seek divorce and remarriage under pretext of desiring children.[40] Critics of Augustine are clearly in error when they assert that this teaching is inconsistent with his emphasis on procreation. The obligation—and the privileges—come from mutual loving faith. What is required is that the three blessings be not arbitrarily separated.

Conjugal love is also bound within the blessing conferred by the sacrament. However, for Augustine, the blessing of the sacrament is largely identified with indissolubility, signified for Christians by the union of Christ and the Church.[41] In

Augustine's time the theology of the marriage sacrament was as yet undeveloped. Here, as elsewhere, he took a first step; and later development took off from his beginnings. Meanwhile, although he regarded mutual fidelity as belonging to all marriages, he could not but observe the lack of such fidelity, despite the natural obligation and bond, among the pagans (here also the disintegrating effects of concupiscence). He thus saw indissolubility as the divinely given bond—the sacrament—for permanently preserving marital fidelity and conjugal love according to the pattern of Christ's union with the Church as described by St. Paul in his letter to the Ephesians (5: 25).

The greatest compliment that the Church could confer on the marriage relationship, whatever the difficulties experienced by her individual members in rising to this conception, was drawing marriage into her sacramental system. No greater exaltation is possible. It is an objective fact, long preceding the modern interest in conjugal love and more splendid than any praise that could be written or spoken. What is perhaps more remarkable, in view of strictures leveled at former theologians for their reserved attitude toward sex, is that they came to believe that the sacred symbolism is fully present only in consummated marriage, which alone is absolutely indissoluble. It is true that Augustine did not yet fully understand the meaning of this sacramentalism. He did not realize that matrimony confers grace directly through the action of Christ, although he affirmed that the marriage relationship is elevated by the grace and charity of Christ. He did see that the marriage is the symbol of the indissoluble union of Christ with His Church and that, conversely, this union is the pattern for the marriage of Christians.

Indissolubility, like a loving mutual faith, is thus no mere legalistic obligation but necessary to conjugal love: it is the bulwark of such love, bestowing permanence on the union of two equal persons. Without such permanence and equality, conjugal love could not exist. Thus Augustine, seeing marriage as originating in conjugal love, which then extends itself to embrace children, also adumbrated the basic conditions needed to protect and preserve this love. His doctrine of the threefold blessing reveals marriage as a fruitful, faithful, and undying love between one man and one woman.

In the mind of Augustine, therefore, the three goods of Christian marriage are coordinated to realize the total good of marriage. He never envisioned their separation; and marital intercourse, like every manifestation of conjugal love, thus serves all the goods of marriage. It is the moderns demanding revision who separate these goods. They thereby create a false issue. It was not that Augustine did not see that intercourse serves the other goods besides procreation; it was simply that he did not envision the separation of these goods.

There is no issue concerning the value of any of the goods of marriage. Nor does anyone doubt that marital coitus is multifunctional. Labor expended to prove this point is labor lost. The question is simply whether conjugal love and the sacrament may be arbitrarily and artificially separated from the good of procreation.

Not only is marital intercourse, according to Augustine, justified by love; it is justified *only* by love. We have just heard him state that "children should be begotten of love."

It is precisely this—marital intercourse should express love—that the saint is also saying in the celebrated text in which he condemns contraception. If intercourse does not proceed from love, he believes it comes from lust:

> Well, if both parties alike are so flagitious, they are not husband and wife; and if such were their character from the beginning, they have not come together by wedlock but by debauchery. But if the two are not alike in such sin, I boldly declare either that the woman is so to say, the husband's harlot; or the man, the wife's adulterer.

True, according to Augustine—and here we come around again to the heart of the problem—conjugal love reaches out to embrace the child, or at least should not exclude him. The saint does not see how love can be claimed when there is such an exclusion "by wrong desire or evil appliance":

> They who resort to these, although called by the name of spouses are really not such; they retain no vestige of true matrimony, but pretend the honorable

designation as a cloak for criminal conduct. Having also proceeded so far, they expose their children, who are born against their will. They hate to nourish and retain those whom they were afraid they would beget. This infliction of cruelty on their offspring so reluctantly begotten, unmasks the sin which they had practiced in darkness, and drags it clearly in the light of day. The open cruelty reproves the concealed sin. Sometimes, indeed, this lustful cruelty, or, if you please, cruel lust, resorts to such extravagant methods as to use poisonous drugs to secure barrenness; or else, if unsuccessful in this, to destroy the conceived seed, by some means, previous to birth, preferring that their offspring should rather perish than receive vitality; or if it was advancing to life within the womb, should be slain before it was born.[42]

Harsh words, these, for the supporters of Planned Parenthood and advocates of legalized abortion on demand. But for Augustine these practices, "cruel" and "criminal," are opposed to love. Divine love, of which human love is the derivative and image, is diffusive of itself, creative. How can there be love in the embrace that suppresses the creativity of love? The definition of marriage as "love in the service of life" accords with Augustinian teaching—in fact accurately expresses that teaching.

Contraceptionists find an opposition, or at least a tension, between conjugal love and procreation. But in Augustine's teaching, as in the Church's, there is not, and cannot be, any such opposition. Human conjugal love, impregnated through Christ with the divine, inevitably finds its pattern in Him Who "is love," and it is therefore procreative as His love is creative. The "community of love" between spouses normally widens creatively to embrace children. Conjugal love grows to include parental love. "The Church issues the reminder that a true contradiction cannot exist between the divine laws pertaining to the transmission of life and those pertaining to the fostering of authentic conjugal love."[43]

St. Augustine and the Second Vatican Council

The Fathers of the Second Vatican Council, while speaking appreciatively of conjugal love, no more envision it apart from procreation than does Augustine. At least five times in the chapter on marriage they explicitly make this point:

> By their very nature the institution of matrimony itself and conjugal love are ordained for the procreation and education of children, and find in them their ultimate crown.

> Marriage and conjugal love are by their nature ordained toward the begetting and educating of children. Children are really the supreme gift of marriage.

> Parents should regard as their proper mission the task of transmitting human life and educating those to whom it is transmitted.

> Hence, while not making the other purposes of matrimony of less account, the true practice of conjugal love and the whole meaning of *the family life which results from it,* have this aim: that the couple be ready with stout hearts to cooperate with the love of the Creator and the Savior Who through them will enlarge and enrich His own family day by day [emphasis added].

> Thus trusting in divine Providence and refining the spirit of sacrifice, married Christians glorify the Creator and strive towards fulfillment in Christ when with a generous human and Christian sense of responsibility they acquit themselves of the duty to procreate.

Even when directly praising conjugal love, the Fathers several times imply the fruitfulness of this love:

> This [witnessing to Christ] the family will do by the mutual love of the spouses, by their generous fruitfulness, their solidarity and faithfulness, and by the liv-

ing way in which *all members of the family* assist one another.

Authentic married love is caught up into divine love and is governed and enriched by Christ's redeeming power and the saving activity of the Church, so that this love may lead the spouses to God with powerful effect and may aid and strengthen them in the sublime office of being a *father* or *mother*.

In describing marriage as "community of love," the Fathers are praising ways "of perfecting its life," and assisting "parents in their lofty calling." The spouses in the community of love are also parents.[44]

The Council Fathers scarcely seem to approve separation of the other goods of marriage from procreation. They have rather reaffirmed the Augustinian teaching of the three coordinating goods within the one good of Christian marriage.

Three in one

The Council Fathers, it is true, do not assert the priority of procreation over conjugal love. But then—some may be surprised to learn—neither did Augustine. In his thought the three goods of marriage are concomitant; all are to be realized simultaneously in Christian marriage. If in *The Good of Marriage* he listed offspring first, this does not mean that he intended to give procreation any absolute priority. In the first chapter he had already affirmed that "the first natural tie of human society is man and wife." Elsewhere, in enumerating the goods of marriage, he places mutual fidelity first, describing the one comprehensive good of marriage as "tripartite."[45] The Fathers of the Council are faithful to the thought of Augustine in considering these goods as realized together when, after citing "the various benefits and purposes" that Augustine attributes to marriage, they go on:

> All of these have a very decisive bearing on the continuation of the human race, on the personal development and eternal destiny of the individual members

of the family, and on the dignity, stability, peace, and prosperity of the family itself and of human society as a whole.[46]

The importance of the discussion on the priority of ends has been both misunderstood and exaggerated. The problem seems to have arisen from canon law, which states, "The primary purpose of marriage is the procreation and education of children. The secondary purpose is to furnish mutual aid and a remedy for concupiscence" (Canon 1013). But the canon does not say that conjugal love is the secondary purpose. It does not mention conjugal love. The secondary purpose is to furnish mutual aid and a remedy for concupiscence: something quite different. All of these purposes presuppose conjugal love and would be meaningless without it. The need for a "remedy for concupiscence," a phrase so offensive to modern ears, is but an implicit acknowledgment of the effects of original sin in all the activities of all men, not a derogation of marriage. The "remedy" is itself a form of mutual aid intended to restore conjugal love to its divinely intended purposes. Although the Second Vatican Council bypasses the question of the priority of ends in marriage, it clearly affirms the effects of original sin.

Marriage begins as a personal relationship between man and woman: "The first natural tie of human society is man and wife." This tie arises from a mutual commitment and is bound in a vow consecrating a reciprocal, total, and exclusive sharing of two lives and hearts until death. The marriage ritual, long before Vatican II, made this love until death quite explicit. Pope Pius XI, inspired by Augustine, describes it in *Casti Connubii* as "the mutual familiar intercourse between spouses."

Moreover, in Augustine, as in all Christian thought, all personal ties—all human loves—are subsumed under the higher bond of divine love. Conjugal love, for the Christian—and explicitly in Augustine—becomes conjugal charity. "Christ the Lord abundantly blessed this many-faceted love, welling up from the fountain of divine love and structured as it is on the model of His union with the Church."[47]

But marriage, once it is contracted, gives a new dimension

to the personal relationship. It is assimilated to the marriage institution. As such it becomes subject to the legislation of Church and State, both of which in different but complementary ways are concerned with the future of the race. As the Fathers of the Council put it, "For the good of the spouses and their offspring as well as of society, the existence of the sacred bond no longer depends on human decisions alone."[48] Canon law is not a marriage manual or pastoral instruction but legislation governing the marriage institution for Catholics. Its omission of conjugal love does not imply depreciation of this love; it is concerned only with the juridical relations of spouses, hence with their external acts only.

The idea of hierarchy of ends comes from St. Thomas. In him also it involves no devaluation of conjugal love. In fact, although we like to think the concern for conjugal love is modern, St. Thomas in developing his teaching is responding to an objection that is common today.

Peter Lombard had listed the goods of marriage as faith, children, and the sacrament. The Angelic Doctor deliberately changed this order to children, faith, and the sacrament. The objection proposed to this change states:

> The object of matrimony among men is not only the procreation and education of children, but also the partnership of a common life [*consortium communis vitae*], because of a communion of works [*communicatio operum*]. Therefore, just as offspring is considered a good of marriage, so should the communion of works.

To this Aquinas responds (in harmony with Augustine) that this partnership with its communion of works is already involved in the blessing of children. For the end of marriage is not only the procreation of children but their procreation and education. To this education, "as to an end," St. Thomas explains, "is directed the entire communion of works between man and wife as united in marriage, since parents naturally *lay up* for their children (2 Cor 12: 14); so the offspring, like a principal end, includes another, as it were, secondary end."[49] Procreation, in other words, introduces a child into a human community of "man and wife united in marriage." Conjugal love is contained in the original purpose of marriage, established by mutual faith. The "community of love" issued from *parents* carrying out their "lofty calling."

The word "communion" in the above statement of St. Thomas is significant. "Communion" is the heart of friendship in his thought: "All friendship is based on some fellowship in life *[super aliqua communicatione vitae]*."[50] Here it is the fellowship of "husband and wife as united in marriage." Procreation and education take place in a community of love. Marital intercourse, while including the marital act, extends to the entire relationship of husband and wife. (Although St. Thomas places procreation first among the goods of marriage, it is not without significance that he considers the marriage-sacrament, because it confers divine grace, first in dignity. Also, since the sacrament guards the indissolubility of marriage, it is, he believes, more essential (*essentialus*) than the other goods (without whose realization a true marriage remains).[51] If placing matrimony among the sacraments is the Church's unique way of honoring it—and the sacramental teaching is found fully developed in Aquinas—it is hard to see how his belief in a hierarchy of ends, with sacrament first in dignity, in any way derogates from conjugal love, which he thus so effectively protects. Nor is it easy to see how such a conviction is compatible with biologism. If the saint analyzes as a philosopher, he does not forget the inspired lesson of the Ephesians.

In view of the clear teaching of St. Thomas, it is astonishing to hear the linkage between education and procreation spoken of as a "development" of Vatican II. The same linkage appears in St. Augustine. He wrote, "Marriage is a good in which the married are better in proportion as they fear God more chastely and more faithfully, especially if they also nourish spiritually the children whom they desire carnally." Again, "Let spouses have their blessing, not because they beget children, but because they beget them honorably and lawfully and chastely and for society, and bring up their offspring rightly, wholesomely, and with perseverance...." To the widow Juliana he wrote: "Moreover, you have children while [Anna the prophetess] perhaps had none; yet you are deserving of merit, not because you have them, but because you are zealous in rearing them in the ways of piety."[52] Marriage is thus a community of love between spouses, but of a creative love that reaches out to embrace the persons of children.

St. Augustine, then, does not distinguish a hierarchy of ends within marriage: the one good of marriage is three-faceted. If procreation is for him "the first—or original—natural, and legitimate purpose of marriage," the other goods are not secondary but concomitant and coordinate. To put it differently, there is only one *purpose* of marriage, but there are *three* goods: these goods, realized together, serve to justify and ennoble marriage. They provide stability and permanence to domestic society, sanctify conjugal love, incorporate the family into the larger society, and draw it also into the Church and into the divine pattern of living in Christ. Augustine knows nothing of a hierarchy of ends within marriage. For him "the remedy for concupiscence" is not a *purpose*: rather, marriage "in Christ" hallows the sexual drive by restoring it to its proper good, thus freeing it also from disorders that might otherwise occur. Conjugal love is also not subordinate, but concomitant and integral to marriage. If there is no need for a division of the sexes, as Augustine says, except for the sake of children, then spouses, if they value their mutual love and its privileged character, must thank their children for it.

The unity and coordination of the three goods into the one good of marriage, as described by St. Augustine, explain the apparent contradiction that has been alleged to exist in *Casti Connubii,* where Pope Pius XI, so deeply indebted to Augustine, speaks both of conjugal love and the procreation and education of children as primary in marriage. The Pope, after saying that "the child holds first place among the blessings of matrimony," goes on to state, when treating of marital faith, that "conjugal love pervades all duties of the married life and holds a kind of primacy of nobility [*principatum nobilitatis*] in Christian marriage."

The contradiction is only apparent. Both goods, procreation and conjugal love, converge in the one comprehensive good of marriage. Which is placed first depends on the standpoint from which we view marriage: as a personal relationship beginning with the spouses and sanctified by the sacrament, or as an institution established for the continuance of society and the Church. The difference is relative, as when a person, facing one way, says that an object is to his left, while turning the other way, he says that it is to his right. And so Pius XI adds (in a passage omitted from some translations): "This mutual formation of husband and wife, this constant zeal for bringing each other to perfection, in a very true sense, as the Roman Catechism teaches, can be said to be the very first cause and reason of matrimony [*primaria matrimonii causa et ratio*]; if, however, matrimony be not accepted too narrowly as instituted for the proper procreation and education of children, but more broadly as the mutual participation in all life, companionship, and association."[53]

Although Pope Pius XI is sometimes credited with the Church's modern emphasis on conjugal love, and on its primacy in the sense just explained, he derived this teaching, as he himself has indicated, from the Roman Catechism. Authorized by the Council of Trent, this Catechism says in its treatment of the sacrament of matrimony, "The *first* reason for its institution is because nature instinctively tends to such a union. . . . *Another* is the desire for a family. . . ." A little later, however, the Catechism says that "The *first* advantage [of matrimony] is that of legitimate offspring. . . . The next advantage is [marital] faith. . . ." Of course, these *advantages* are the goods that Augustine distinguished within the one overreaching good of matrimony. The order of their listing may be varied; they are realized together.

Accordingly, if there is any significance in the fact that the Fathers of the Second Vatican Council were silent about the hierarchy of ends—that is, if they did not merely intend to bypass this issue—it marks a return to the three concomitant and coordinated goods, which, according to St. Augustine, constitute the good of marriage. Those who interpret the omission of this discussion as an abandonment of the traditional doctrine are letting their desires run away with their judgment. The Council has in fact returned to a deeper stratum of doctrinal teaching.[54]

If the Second Vatican Council makes the latest affirmation of these goods and their unity, the first statement was by no means made by Augustine. St. Paul, who praised conjugal love so beautifully in his letter to the Ephesians, relating it to the union of Christ and His Church, was afterward to say—perhaps now thinking of the Gnostic or Manichaean threat to marriage—"Woman will be saved through bearing children, if she continues in faith and love and holiness, with modesty" (1 Tim 2: 15). Long before this, Genesis, in the passages placed at the head of this chapter, had brought these goods together. "The God Himself Who said, 'It is not good for man to be alone . . . wished to share with man a certain participation in His own creative work. Thus He blessed male and female, saying: 'Increase and multiply.' "[55]

7. Free and Equal Persons

> There is, therefore, in Christ and in the Church no inequality on the basis of race or nationality, social condition or sex, because "there is neither Jew nor Greek; there is neither bond nor free; there is neither male nor female. For you are all one in Christ Jesus."
> —Vatican Council II, *Lumen Gentium*, no. 32

> Firmly established in the Lord, the unity of marriage will radiate from the equal personal dignity of wife and husband, a dignity acknowledged by equal and total love.
> —Vatican Council II, *Gaudium et Spes*, no. 49

I. CONJUGAL LOVE AND CHARITY

The Fathers of the Second Vatican Council have stressed the personal and sacramental character of the Christian marriage union. In doing this they extolled conjugal love, which is "caught up by the divine love and enriched by Christ's redeeming power and the saving activity of the Church...."[1] While the Council decree went further than any previous document of the Magisterium in treating of this subject, its authors were nevertheless following the precedent of Pope Pius XI, who had in his *Casti Connubii* enlarged on the value of conjugal love. In turn, both the Pope and the Fathers of the Council were working within the Augustinian framework and elucidating the saint's original insights into the personal relationship of husband and wife. The "natural companionship" that Augustine said belongs to the purpose of marriage, the "bond of fellowship" between the spouses, and their loving mutual faith are quickly raised in his thought to "the order of charity" and become "conjugal charity."[2]

The Bishop of Hippo thus introduced the notion of conjugal love into the theology of the West. Whatever is said on this score by the Second Vatican Council is a development of his treatment.

This conjugal love, although primarily personal and influencing the will, involves the whole person:

> This love is an eminently human one since it is directed from one person to another through an affection of the will; it involves the good of the whole person, and therefore can enrich the expressions of body and mind with a unique dignity, ennobling these expressions as special ingredients and signs of the friendship distinctive of marriage.[3]

While thus holding that conjugal love enriches its bodily expressions, the Fathers give short shrift to the modern preoccupation with eroticism. Christian conjugal love "far excels mere erotic inclination, which, selfishly pursued, soon enough fades wretchedly away."[4]

The companionship of husband and wife "produces the primary form of interpersonal communion."[5] Augustine had also written, introducing his *The Good of Marriage:*

> Since every man is part of the human race, and human nature is social and possesses the capacity for friendship as a great and natural good, for this reason God wished to create all men from one, so that they might be held together in their society, not only by similarity of race, but also by the bond of blood relationship. And so it is that the first natural tie of human society is man and wife.[6]

We have already considered in Chapter 2 how St. Augustine brought a keen sense of the unique value and dignity of the human person into Western thought for the first time. The second part of the present chapter will be concerned with how he understood and illustrated the personalist relationship of the sexes.

Meanwhile, it may be asked whether Augustine accepted as part of marriage those "bodily expressions" of love, of which we have just heard the Fathers of the Council speak.

Or in his mind was conjugal charity a kind of disembodied love? Without doubt, conjugal charity, for Augustine, includes sex. "That no one would perchance suppose that the Creator of sex despised sex, He became a man born of a woman."[7] The birth here referred to is of course virginal. But the statement shows at least that even in speaking of the sacred person of Jesus, Augustine did not feel the slightest Neoplatonic distaste in contemplating the bodily and sexual process by which Jesus had been born. Nor did he ever experience the Docetic temptation to question the reality of the Savior's body. It would be preposterous, in fact, to expect to find him dallying with such temptations; if he had, he could not have believed in the Incarnation. The ultimate implication of some statements by Augustine's critics is that he did not. If he laid great stress on the virginal birth of Jesus, this was not through any puritanical suspicion of the reproductive process, but at once to remove the Savior from the transmission of original sin and protect His identity as the Son of God.[8]

The conception and birth of Mary, which were humanly normal, did not lessen Augustine's esteem for her or prevent him from providing later ages with a model of sound Mariology. He seems even to have arrived at a realization of the Immaculate Conception.[9]

Conjugal charity should include the marital embrace of Christians. Does Augustine think so? He speaks of the delight of the marital embrace as lawful—*"Delectant conjugales amplexus"*—distinguishing it from the pleasure of unlawful intercourse. Yet even this remark has been made the occasion for a slur; it is represented as concession reluctantly made, perhaps under prodding from the Pelagian bishop Julian.[10] Yet nothing in the text of the sermon supports—or suggests—such an inference. The preacher is merely saying that holiness is preferable to earthly delights, and he shows the manner in which these pleasures are compatible with holiness. (The whole passage should be read by those who contend that the saint regards pleasure as evil.)[11] The marital embrace is included in what might almost be called a routine sermon listing of instances—although made with characteristic grace. The sermon in which the passage appears is just that, a sermon or homily to his people, not a polemic. Its theme is the love of justice (holiness), which, he urged, is to be preferred to all other goods and pleasures.

Long before the Pelagian controversy we have found Augustine speaking of the "natural delight" of the saints in their marital relationship and saying that sexual intercourse between spouses "is necessary . . . for the sake of friendship."[12] Here again the Second Vatican Council is developing his thought.

The idea that supernatural charity operates in a void independently of our human condition reveals a deep misunderstanding of the nature of charity. The theological virtues, although supernatural, accommodate themselves to our human mode of existence. As iron plunged into fire is rendered malleable and then molded to serve many uses, so the will is transformed by charity to prepare it for the various tasks of Christian living:

> It is God that worketh in us both to will and to do for His good pleasure. We therefore will, but God worketh in us to will also. We therefore work, but God worketh in us also for His good pleasure.[13]

> Men are unwilling to do what is right, either because what is right is unknown to them, or because it is unpleasant to them. For we desire a thing more ardently in proportion to our certainty of our knowledge of its goodness, and the warmth of our delight in it. Ignorance, therefore, and infirmity are faults which impede the will from moving either for doing a good work, or for refraining from an evil one. But that what was hidden may come to light, and what was unpleasant may be made agreeable, is of the grace of God which helps the wills of men.[14]

> Someone says to me: Then we are acted upon but do not act ourselves. I answer: In truth you at once act and are acted upon: and we act well if we are impelled by the Good. The Spirit of God Who acts upon you is your helper in acting. The very name of this Helper

prescribes that you yourself do something. . . . No one is helped except under His action.[15]

St. Augustine's situation ethic

St. Augustine is fond of tracing in detail how charity moves the will.[16] However, the manner in which he sees the activities of nature mesh in practice with the movements of grace is to be found chiefly in his theology of the intention. His well-known "Love God and do what you will!"[17]—although presented in a limited context—accurately expresses his thought on assessing the moral worth of actions.

Love, active love, is the final determinant of morality, and this love takes hold of our actions concretely through motivation. Subjectively the motive or intention impels action, because the motive reaches out to obtain a desired good and directs our actions toward its possession, indeed presses us to seek it. "The love of Christ impels us . . ." (2 Cor 5: 14). Thus charity, although "poured forth in our hearts by the Holy Spirit" (Rom 5: 5), is not a gift to be preserved in aloof dignity but is an active, dynamic principle.

Love, therefore, penetrates and inwardly determines the moral value of actions by means of the intention. The Christian's intention, induced by the love first given to us, should arise from love and press toward love. Augustine remarks that the one word *tradere*, "to give over," was used in Scripture of Judas who betrayed our Lord and of the Father Who delivered His Son for our redemption. There is, however, a difference. "The Father and Son did it in love, but Judas in treacherous betrayal." Therefore, "You see that not what the man does is the thing to be considered; but with what mind and will he does it."

> The diverse intention therefore makes the things done diverse. Though the thing done be one, yet if we measure it by the diverse intentions, we find the one thing to be loved, the other to be detested. Such is the force of charity. See that it alone discriminates, it alone distinguishes the doings of men. . . .
> See what we are insisting upon: that the deeds of men are only discerned by the root of charity. For

many things may be done that have a good appearance, and yet proceed not from the root of charity.[18]

The love that one has in one's heart, fanned into activity, determines the moral significance and character of actions that would otherwise be neutral; it gives the real moral meaning to actions that are outwardly good in themselves yet need this interior formative principle. Augustine develops this thought in his exposition of the Sermon on the Mount, where, using the examples of good works mentioned by Jesus—prayer, almsgiving, fasting—he shows that the "single eye" with which we are to direct our actions and the "secret chamber" in which we are enjoined to carry them out is nothing other than the intention.

> The "eye," therefore, we ought to take as meaning in this place the intention by which we do whatever we do.... Therefore, not what one does, but with what intention he does it, is the thing to consider. For this is the "light" within us because it is by this that we are certain of doing with a good intent what we are doing; *"for all* that is made manifest is light." ... Even though what you do with an intention that is not upright and pure may turn out well for someone, it is how you have done it, not how it has turned out for him, that is imputed to you.[19]

Clearly we are dealing here with what is now called situation ethics, in the only sense that it can be acceptable to Christians. For Augustine, morality could never be mechanical or legalistic, a mere outward conformity to rules. It is the expression of a living, active love. Had his lead been followed, Christian morality would never have hardened into that legalism and rigidity against which modern situation ethics is reacting.[20]

This does not mean that Augustine did not believe in objective moral standards, that his ethic of love slips into antinomianism, subjectivism, or mere self-delusion. It means rather that for him, natural law and the Mosaic code are a realization of love; further, they set minimum standards that love cannot violate and survive. Love is the inner principle of morality, it offers also the highest goal of morality, but it is not a release from morality. Accordingly, "to have charity and be a bad man is not possible." Contrariwise, "Love: it is impossible to do this without doing good."[21] Love is, truly, "the fulfillment of the law" (Rom 13: 10).

Love does not replace the other virtues; it demands them and rules for them, for virtue is simply "the ordering of love."[22]

> There is as it were the army of an emperor seated within your mind. For as an emperor by his army does what he wills, so the Lord Jesus Christ, once beginning to dwell in our inner man (i.e., in the mind through faith) uses these virtues as his ministers. And by these virtues which cannot be seen with the eyes ... the members are visibly put to motion, the feet to walk, but whither they are moved by the good emperor: the hands to work; but what? that which is bidden by charity which is inspired by the Holy Spirit.[23]

Rather than excusing from obedience, the genuineness of love is proved by obedience. Jesus said, "If you keep My commandments, you shall abide in My love" (Jn 15: 10). Augustine comments:

> He shows not the source from which love springs, but the means whereby it is manifested. As if he said, "Think not that you abide in My love if you keep not My commandments; for it is only if you have kept them that you shall abide.... So that no one need deceive himself by saying that he loves Him, if he keeps not His commandments. For we love Him just in the same measure as we keep His commandments; and the less we keep them, the less we love."[24]

And now we come full circle, for the commandment that above all others must be kept to prove our love for God is the commandment to love thy brethren:

What are His commandments? Must we always be repeating? It is charity itself that he speaks of, it is this that he enforces. Whoso then shall have brotherly charity and have it before God, where God sees, and his heart being interrogated under righteous examination make him none other answer than that the genuine root of charity is there for good fruits to come from....²⁵

The ethical control of action, in Augustine's situation ethics, is therefore not lost in the obscure mists of subjectivism. Love has standards and responsibility. In the matter of sex, the "new" morality agrees that any behavior is acceptable that is agreeable to those involved: "Love" is the arbiter, but it is a love without norms and subject to the individual's almost infinite capacity for self-delusion. But for Augustine the love desired is from the Holy Spirit; the love of neighbor, drawn into this divine love, must be as for one's self. Now, "to love one's self is nothing but to wish to be happy, and the standard is union with God. When therefore a person who knows how to love himself is bidden to love his neighbor as himself, is he not, in effect, commanded to persuade others, as far as he can, to love God?"²⁶ The love of neighbor (or partner) must seek also his union with God; a "love" that excludes this ultimate good and is satisfied merely with what is here and now judged acceptable cannot be the norm of morality; it has itself fallen away from the norm. There can even be evil love. "The affection of the upright will, then, is good love, and that of a perverse will is evil love...."²⁷

Human love also has its rules, and they can be exacting. An unfaithful husband, protesting that he loves his wife, is not likely to be believed. So with divine love and divinely impelled conjugal love. Children, we have heard from Augustine, are to be "born of love," but it is an undeluded love that excludes adultery, fornication, and contraception.

> Hence when there is question of harmonizing conjugal love with the responsible transmission of life, the moral aspect of any procedure does not depend solely on sincere intentions or an evaluation of motives, but

must be determined by objective standards. These, based on the nature of the human person and his acts, preserve the full sense of mutual self-giving and human procreation in the context of true love.[28]

The perfection of love

Charity enters our faculties at once to heal, elevate, and sustain them. It establishes a kind of ontological bond between God and ourselves—a connaturality, St. Thomas was to say, enabling us to love Him intimately and familiarly in a kind of equality—personal love demands equality—as Father and Spouse. This bond embraces also our neighbors, making them our brethren, relating us to them, not "according to the flesh," but in the blood of Jesus Christ.

But charity shares also the remedial character of grace. It sustains us in love; it heals our weakness and failure in love. "Love is a sweet word," said Augustine, "but sweeter the deed. To be always speaking of it is not in our power.... But though we may not always be speaking of it, we may always keep it."[29] Nowadays, however, we are almost always speaking and singing of love. But marital discord, triangles, adulteries, and divorces (to attend only to the present problem) would indicate that the difficulty of keeping it remains. Rather than being opposed to conjugal love, supernatural charity works to preserve and increase it. Grace perfects nature even in its own order.

> Catholics say that human nature was created by the good Creator; but, having been corrupted by sin, it needs the Physician Christ.... Inasmuch as [Adam's] pure nature was corrupted in him, it has run on in this condition by natural descent through all, and still is running; so that there is no deliverance for it from this ruin, except by the grace of God through our Lord Jesus Christ.[30]

Augustine as a youth, we have seen, sought love and was carried away by concupiscence. But the desires of the flesh are opposed by the desires of the spirit. Nature is healed in being elevated by grace and charity. Conjugal love, in being transformed from "natural companionship" to "conjugal charity," binds the partners together also "in the mutual service of sustaining each other's weakness."[31]

Of the divine life of grace the Second Vatican Council has this to say:

> Pursuing the saving purpose which is proper to her, the Church does not only communicate divine life to men but in some way casts the reflection of that life over the entire earth, most of all by its healing and elevating impact on the dignity of the person. . . .[32]

Accordingly, "The call to grandeur and the depths of misery, both of which are a part of human experience, find their ultimate and simultaneous explanation in the light of revelation."[33]

The Fathers apply this to conjugal love: "This love God has judged worthy of special gifts, healing, perfecting, and exalting gifts of grace and of charity."[34]

But grace, besides being "healing," is also "perfecting and exalting." Conjugal love, caught up in the order of divine love, follows the law of growth that governs this love. In *Casti Connubii* Pope Pius XI wrote:

> This outward expression of love in the home demands not only mutual help but must go further; must have as its primary purpose that man and wife help each other day by day in forming and perfecting themselves in the interior life, so that through their partnership in life they may advance ever more in virtue, and above all that they may grow in true love towards God and their neighbor, on which "indeed dependeth the whole law and the prophets." For all men of every condition, in whatever honorable walk of life they may be, can and ought to imitate that most perfect example of holiness placed before man by God, namely Christ our Lord, and by God's grace arrive at the summit of perfection. . . .

In speaking thus (also in his encyclical on St. Francis de Sales), the Holy Father was anticipating the teaching of the Second Vatican Council:

> All the faithful, whatever their condition or state, are called by the Lord, each in his own way, to that perfect holiness whereby the Father Himself is perfect.[35]

To the married the Fathers say:

> Married couples and Christian parents should follow their own path [to holiness] by faithful love.[36]

St. Augustine's moral teaching is an ethic of love; this is what he taught tirelessly for more than forty years to the men, women, and children of Carthage:

> Begin to love: you will be perfected. Have you begun to love? God has begun to dwell in you. Love Him Who has begun to dwell in you, that by more perfect indwelling He may make you perfect.[37]

> Inchoate love, therefore, is inchoate holiness; advanced love is advanced holiness; great love is great holiness; perfect love is perfect holiness.[38]

St. Augustine was not a casuist seeking minimal rules accommodated to the imperfections of his flock. He was a saint trying to lead his flock to sanctity. Modern Catholics say they are weary of casuistry and "code ethics"; they desire the fullness and perfection of their Christian vocation. Well, St. Augustine is an ideal guide. None has excelled him.

2. ST. AUGUSTINE AS PERSONALIST

St. Augustine, in trying to bring the light of the Gospel to bear on conjugal love, was working against great odds in a still-pagan society little able to understand such an ideal. We have already noticed, in speaking of his book *Adulterous Marriages*, the kind of pastoral problem that he was daily confronted with. Apparently not a few of his flock, influenced by paganism but cleverly citing the Christian Scripture, were trying to dissolve their marriages in order to remarry. The bishop firmly closed the door on divorce and abuse of the Pauline privilege. He rejected the double standard for men and women despite male pressure in that man's world; he insisted on the equality of women with men under the laws of marriage. This was groundwork that had to be done in order that marriage might "radiate from the equal personal dignity of wife and husband."[39] He sought to protect conjugal fidelity by invoking lifelong indissolubility.

It all seems clear enough to us today—thanks largely to St. Augustine.

St. Paul, revealing a "mystery," had written: "Husbands, love your wives as Christ loved the Church." Yet it may be doubted whether St. Paul himself grasped, as a man, all the implications of his own inspired teaching. Integral to the understanding of Christian marriage is the realization of the dignity of women as human persons. In this matter the Jews had come a long way, in comparison with their pagan neighbors. Yet theirs, too, was a patriarchal and male-dominated society. Women were regarded as inferior, at least socially, and conjugal love as we think of it now, which involves the personal equality of husband and wife, was but imperfectly realized. Even Sarah, Rebecca, and Rachel, still held up as models for Catholic brides in the nuptial blessing, had to live with polygamy and concubinage. Christ firmly reestablished monogamy. It would take many generations, however, to realize the meaning of St. Paul's teaching.

Slavery affords a parallel. When Paul sent the slave Onesimus back to his master, Philemon, instructing the latter to treat Onesimus "as a brother," he was for the first time applying the doctrine of evangelic love to slavery (Philemon 16). Thereby, without realizing it, he initiated the process that was to make slavery impossible in a Christian society. A slave loses his economic value in becoming a brother; he can no longer be a slave. Yet Paul himself (and Augustine) took slavery for granted as an unquestioned part of the social and economic structure of his time.

Similarly, it may be doubted whether the Apostle realized

fully and concretely the meaning of what he was inspired to write on the sacramentality of marriage. The Hebraic and Christian insights were further obscured as Christianity parted from Judaism and had to fan its light amid the darkness of paganism. It was within this darkness, or semi-darkness, that Augustine propounded the ideal of Christian marriage.

Romantic love, we have seen,[40] did not enter Europe until the Middle Ages, and then from a tainted source that brought more dangers and a new threat to Christian marriage. Moreover, until quite recent times—and still, in some places—marriage revolved around the transmission of property rather than around personal love.

Meanwhile, Augustine was busy with the problems of his own day and diocese. The inferior and degraded position of women in paganism hindered the idea of friendship between man and woman. Among pagans, friendship with the predictable results, was between men: love in the sense of friendship can exist only between equals. Women were useful for reproduction and pleasure. They were treated not only as inferiors but brutally. They were more accustomed to beatings than to caresses, except perhaps in bed.[41] Without making a lengthy excursion into Roman history, we can see something of the nature of family life at the time from Augustine's own relatively enlightened household. Augustine credits it to the discretion of his own mother, Monica, quite different in this respect from other women of her acquaintance, that while her husband, his father, Patricius, was "violent in anger," she never showed the marks of beatings:

> In short, while many matrons, whose husbands were more gentle, carried the marks of blows on their dishonored faces, and would in private conversation blame the lives of their husbands, she would blame their tongues, admonishing them gravely, as if in jest that from the time they heard what are called the matrimonial tablets read to them, they should think of them as instruments whereby they were made servants; so, being always mindful of their condition, they ought not to set themselves in opposition to their

lords. And they, knowing what a furious husband she endured, marveled. . . . .[42]

This offers a rather bleak picture of domestic bliss in that day! Moreover, concubinage was common, as was resort to prostitutes; although chastity was demanded of women. Augustine's father can serve as an example here, too; for Monica "sore bore the wronging of her bed as never to have any dissension with her husband on account of it." As bishop, Augustine was to incur the resentment of men for condemning such evils, especially for calling their concubines prostitutes. (It should be noted that there was something more than a moral lapse here; it was a moral lapse involving complete disregard of the dignity, equality, and rights of woman.) Naturally, to continue in such lives, men would remain catechumens, postponing baptism; a custom also exemplified by Patricius. Yet the gentle and saintly—but determined—Monica had the last word with him as she was to have with Augustine.

> Finally, her own husband, now towards the end of his earthly existence, did she gain over unto Thee; and she had not to complain of that in him, as one of the faithful, which, before he became so, she had endured.[43]

Augustine, the bishop, worried about his friend Marcellinus, a nobleman unjustly condemned to death, sought him out in prison. "Having in mind some secret impropriety, he asked Marcellinus directly whether there was yet anything for which he ought to undergo the great ecclesiastical penance. Hereupon this man, who was usually so reserved, took the bishop's right hand in both his own, and said with a rather nervous smile: 'I declare by the sacraments that have been administered by these hands that I have never known any other woman than my wife, either before marriage or afterwards.' It is the bishop himself who has given us an account of this little scene. . . ."[44] "This little scene" also discloses the pastoral worries of a bishop in those times, and the expected rarity of chastity even among "devout" Christians.

Friendship between a man and woman, intercourse at all levels of life—all but unheard of among the Greeks and Romans, and but imperfectly realized among the Hebrews—became for Augustine the core of Christian marriage; a friendship further transformed by divine charity. His contribution to marriage theology in this respect, and to civilization, was thus twofold. He demanded equality in marriage for women, and he showed that they are to be loved as human persons in an exalted charity—faithfully unto death in indissoluble wedlock. These are implications of Christianity still imperfectly realized in the twentieth century; in the circumstances of Augustine's times their affirmation was a truly remarkable achievement.

Cicero in his celebrated essay on friendship thought of it only between men; he spoke but passingly and contemptuously of friendship with a woman. Plato, living in a world in which friendship also existed only between men, and familiar with the abuses of this friendship, yet reacted against these abuses and turned erotic love into a passionate quest for wisdom and the good. (Curiously, in the *Symposium,* Socrates confesses that he had learned of this enlightened (or sublimated) erotic love from a woman, the prophetess Diotima—indicating Plato's glimpse of the truth that men and women are essentially equal.) It remained for Christianity to point the way to a genuine human and personal love between man and woman. And Augustine was the one to "discover" it; while muting the undertones of sexuality and failing to perceive the overtones of romantic love, which came into our culture only later, he firmly established conjugal love as the bond between two persons equal before God; and he held that this love is sanctified by the divine love itself. Whatever psychology may nowadays disclose about the importance of sexuality in the total personality, the core of marriage, still the primary interest of the Church, is this sanctified personal relationship. And if the teaching of Pius XI and Vatican II on marital love is a development, it is a development of Augustinian doctrine.

Meanwhile, the men of our age, praising the love of the sexes, claiming to be personalistic, and deploring the alleged biologism of the Church's teaching, have rather widely identified love between the sexes with anatomical conjunction.

3. THE FIRST FEMINIST

Modern feminists deplore the manner in which Eve's part in the Fall has been used, especially in antiquity, to hold women in subjection. Augustine, sometimes reputed a misogynist, may be said to be the first Christian feminist. While he could not change the record of the Fall in Genesis, he showed how this history was completed, and in a sense reversed, by the New Testament. Thus:

> The women came to the sepulchre; they found not the body in the sepulchre; they heard from the Angels that the Lord was risen, and they told these things to the men. And . . . "these words seemed to them as idle tales" (Lk 24: 1–12). But when Eve told what the serpent had said, she was at once listened to. To the lying woman credence was given, that we should die; to the woman speaking true words, that we should live, no credence was given. If women ought not to be believed, why did Adam believe Eve? If woman ought to be believed, why did not the disciples believe the holy women? And therefore in this fact the benign dispensation of Our Lord is to be carefully noticed. For it is this which the Lord Jesus Christ did, that the feminine sex should be the first to proclaim that He was risen. Since through the feminine sex man fell, through the feminine sex man was reinstated, for Christ was born of a Virgin, a woman proclaimed that He was risen. Death through the woman, through the woman life.[45]

Augustine regarded man and woman as equal persons. We have seen (Chapter 2) how through the study of the Trinity he arrived at a unique conception at once of God as Person and of the human person. Seeking analogies of the Trinity in creation, modeled as it is after the divine ideas, he found the supreme created likeness of the Trinity, and therefore his chief means for studying this mystery, in man himself, in his personal unity expressing itself in mind and will. Thereby are we given a created type of the Word reflecting the Father, and the Holy Spirit joining them in love. Augustine had no trouble tracing this analogy in men, but when he turned to women he ran into a difficulty, not merely from his pagan environment, but from the teaching of no less an authority than St. Paul himself, at least as the Apostle was interpreted by men wishing to bolster their own presumed superiority. The Apostle had said, "A man indeed ought not to cover his head, because he is the image and glory of God. But the woman is the glory of the man" (1 Cor 2: 7). This seemed to prove that only man is made in the image of God and that woman is therefore inferior. Augustine rejected such an interpretation, insisting that woman also bears the image of the Trinity. Man, indeed, in his highest powers, contemplates, and thus, in his pursuit of wisdom, clearly bears the image of the divine Word. Woman on the other hand, as man's helpmate, is immersed in temporal tasks and in this sense she is inferior to the man. For this reason she is to wear the veil, signifying that we must check the concern for temporal matters. She is thus like Martha, "worried about much serving." But she is also, as a human being redeemed by Christ, called like Mary to the contemplation and love of God. So she also carries within her person the image of the Trinity.

> But according to this renewal we are also made the sons of God through the Baptism of Christ, and when we put on the new man, we certainly put on Christ through faith. Who is it, then, that would exclude women from this fellowship, since they are with us co-heirs of grace, and since the same Apostle says in another place: "For you are all children of God through faith in Christ Jesus. For whoever have been baptized in Christ have put on Christ. There is neither Jew nor Greek, there is neither slave nor freeman, there is neither male nor female. For you are all one in Christ Jesus." Have believing women, therefore, lost their bodily sex?[46]

At first blush we might be disappointed in Augustine's apparent failure, in the very act of making his supreme contribution to theology—his exposition of the Trinity—to see in marriage itself the markings of the Trinity as he wandered through the universe looking for such evidences. He did note the trinity of father, mother, and child, but he did not pause long over it.[47] Augustine was looking for an analogue of the Trinity in each person; he felt it should be in Adam even before the creation of Eve. Finding it in Adam led him to finding it also in Eve. In discovering the supreme analogue of the three divine Persons in woman as well as in man, Augustine laid bare the basis for regarding marriage as a union of two human persons equal in dignity. This is the foundation stone of Christian conjugal love, a major breakthrough in the male-dominated Roman world.

Nor are women, according to Augustine, merely second-grade human beings because of their sex (a still-surviving ethnic and cultural prejudice).[48] Women's sex, for Augustine, however, is not a temporary disadvantage, but part of their humanity. It will be retained even in the resurrection:

> There are some who think that in the resurrection all will be men, and that women will lose their sex. . . . The interpretation is based on the fact that the man alone was made by God out of "the slime of the earth," whereas the woman was made from the man. For myself, I think that those others are more sensible who have no doubt that both sexes will remain in the resurrection. After all, there will be none of that lust which is the cause of shame in connection with sex, and so, all will be as before the first sin, when the man and woman were naked and felt no shame. In the resurrection, the blemishes of the body will be gone, but the nature of the body will remain. And certainly, a woman's body is her nature and no blemish; only, in the resurrection, there will be no conception or child-bearing associated with her nature. Her members will remain as before, with the former purpose sublimated to a newer beauty. There will be no concupiscence to arouse and none will be aroused, but her womanhood will be a hymn to the wisdom of God, and to the clemency of God, Who freed her from the corruption into which she fell.

Therefore, woman is as much the creation of God as man is. If she was made from the man, this was to show her oneness with him; and if she was made in the way she was, this was to prefigure the oneness of Christ and the Church.[49]

4. MONICA

Augustine illustrated this new attitude toward women—only subsequent to his conversion, it is worth noticing—in the life that he shared with his mother, Monica, at Cassiciacum, near Milan, where he prepared for baptism. "Fair, reverent, amiable, and admirable to her husband," he describes her; and although he had not long since escaped her presence and influence by stratagem, he now calls their common life "a most sweet and dear habit of living together." While she is mistress of the house, she is no mere housekeeper. She is included in the circle of friends and disciples in their dialogues in search of wisdom. Monica was herself surprised at this; it was not the treatment usually accorded women. "What are you doing?" she asked. "In those books which you read, have I ever heard that women were even introduced into this sort of disputation?" Her son explained that he was now in search of a higher wisdom, which is often given to the lowly rather than to those proud in their learning.

"Moreover, in olden times, women, too, have worked on the problems of philosophy." Then, directly to Monica, "And your philosophy is very pleasing to me!" He goes on:

> Now if you had no love whatever for wisdom, I would utterly disregard you in my writings; if, however, you had just ordinary love for it, I would not entirely disregard you; and much less if you were to love wisdom as I love it. And now, seeing that you love it even more than you love me, and knowing your great love for me, and seeing that you have made such advance in it that you are not frightened by the dread of any chance discomfort or even death itself—a most difficult attainment for even the most learned, and a position which all acknowledge to be the stoutest stronghold of

philosophy—in view of all this, shall I not gladly entrust myself to you as a disciple?[50]

Monica demurred, embarrassed, protesting that her son had "never uttered so much that is untrue." But Augustine, the master of this little school, meant what he was saying, and he listened to her discourse with attention and respect: "She voiced things in such manner that we, unmindful of her sex, would feel that some great man was seated beside us. Meanwhile I became aware, as far as I could, from what source—yes, from how divine a source—those things flowed."[51]

What we are watching here for the first time in our civilization—and we do not see it very commonly even yet—is a woman being treated, not as a source of gratification, not as a love-goddess, not only as the mother of desired children, but simply as a human person, beloved of God.

After his baptism, Augustine started back to Africa, stopping at Ostia near Rome; and here Monica died. But not before they had shared together what was perhaps the supreme moment of Augustine's spiritual Odyssey. One day they stood together at the window of the house where they were staying, gazing out upon the garden and conversing "very pleasantly" about the life of the saints.

> And our conversation had brought us to this point, that any pleasure whatsoever of the bodily senses, in any brightness whatsoever of corporeal light, seemed to us not worthy of comparison with the pleasure of that eternal Light, not even worthy of mention. Rising, our love flamed upwards at that Selfsame, we passed in review the various levels of bodily things, up to the heavens themselves, whence sun and moon and stars shine upon this earth. And higher still we soared and speaking and marveling at Your works: and so we came to our own souls and went beyond them to come at last to that region of richness unending, from which you feed Israel forever with the food of truth; and there life is wisdom....
> But this wisdom is not made.... And while we were thus talking of His Wisdom and panting for it,

with all the effort of our heart we did for one instant attain to touch it; then sighing, and leaving the firstfruits of our spirit bound to it, we returned to the sound of our own tongue....[52]

The decisive moment is shared with a woman—"our heart, our spirit." It is true that the woman is not his wife, but his mother. But the point is his recognition of her as a *person*. He saw in this woman, his mother, not merely human loveliness, not just the capacity to receive and return the love of a mere man, not only the fruitfulness of motherhood, but the capacity, shared with man, to receive and return the love of the divine Lover. He had already learned the lesson taught by Jesus when, rejecting the praise of his earthly mother, He said, "Who is My mother and who are My brethren? ... Whoever does the will of My Father in heaven, he is My brother and sister and mother" (Mt 12: 48–50).

In all literature there is no more beautiful or heartfelt tribute to a woman than that which Augustine in his *Confessions* (IX, 8–12) pays to Monica. It was no Mother's Day oration. It was a tribute to a fellow searcher, one who had already largely attained that wisdom and happiness which Augustine himself so passionately desired and regarded as the ultimate fulfillment of human life.

8. To Marry or Not to Marry

If anyone serve Me, let him follow Me.   —John 12: 26

Whoever follows after Christ, the perfect man, becomes himself more of a man.
—Vatican Council II, *Gaudium et Spes*, no. 41

1. MARRIAGE AND CELIBACY

The Church's teaching on marriage is at once complicated and balanced by her esteem for celibacy. Our Lord's counsel of celibacy runs like a cross-current against His elevation of marriage to the sacramental order. Yet there can be no contradiction once we accept Him as the supreme teacher of divine wisdom; and it is the task of Christian reflection to learn how these two apparently conflicting ideals may be held at once, if in tension, also in unity.[1]

In the first place it is necessary to bear in mind that the ideal of celibacy does come from Jesus. Not the Blessed Mother, but our Lord Himself, as Augustine said, was the supreme example of virginal integrity. And he invited His followers, or at least some of them, to follow Him in this also: "Let him accept it who can" (Mt 19: 12).

All this is obvious enough. Yet it is seemingly forgotten at times in current discussions. Whether all priests should be required to accept the celibate vocation is indeed a matter of disciplinary regulation. There is nothing incompatible between marriage and sacred orders, as Oriental priests remind us. Nevertheless, the ideal of celibacy is itself of divine origin. And surely no group more appropriately assumes this special imitation of Christ than those who share ministerially in his priesthood.[2]

While we are currently learning much from our Protestant brethren, this is one matter in which they have seriously compromised the fullness of Christian truth. They have retained little or no admiration for the ideal of celibacy; their acceptance of it has been slight and belated.

Despite modern attacks on the celibate vocation, the Church has reaffirmed its value in our age. "The evangelical counsels of chastity dedicated to God, poverty and obedience are based upon the words and example of the Lord." The religious state, in which these counsels are professed, "whose purpose is to free its members from earthly cares, more fully manifests to all believers the presence of heavenly goods already possessed here below."[3]

Of chastity in particular the Fathers say: "That chastity which is practiced 'on behalf of the heavenly kingdom' (Mt 19: 12), and which religious profess, deserves to be esteemed as a surpassing gift of grace. For it liberates the human heart in a unique way (cf. 1 Cor 7: 32–35) and causes it to burn with greater love of God and all mankind."[4]

The celibate or virginal state, while by no means diminishing the good of marriage, is a reminder of its limits as a temporary state. The religious life based on the counsels "not only witnesses to the fact of a new and eternal life acquired by the redemption of Christ, but it foretells the future resurrection and the glory of the heavenly kingdom."[5] "At the resurrection they will neither marry nor be given in marriage, but are as angels of God in heaven" (Mt 22: 30).

Not only does the counseled ideal of celibacy balance Christian thought on marriage by offering an alternate vocation in the pursuit of holiness: it also enters marriage itself. A pivotal point is the marriage of Mary and Joseph, which, although a true marriage, was virginal. Naturally, this marriage was prominent and formative in Augustine's thought. Although coitus consummates marriage, there can be true marriage without it.

Nowadays, coitus is described in popular literature as the "act of love"—as if there could be no other or no higher act of love. Yet sexual intercourse may be an act of sensuality; in houses of prostitution it takes place without love; in the *Playboy* philosophy it is a gesture of contempt, an act that excludes love by fleeing "involvement" and regarding sexual conquest as a status symbol. Coitus may be, and should be, an act of love, as we have heard Augustine strongly affirm. Even so, it is not the highest act of love. Here also the axiom obtains: where possible and permissible, the best use of the best of creatures is to return it to God unused. St. Paul indicates the possibility of applying this principle to marriage—and its limits: "Do not deprive each other, except perhaps by consent, for a time, that you may give yourselves to prayer; and return together lest Satan tempt you because you lack self-control" (1 Cor 7: 5).[6]

Of course this attitude, whether in St. Paul or St. Augustine, will seem strange and unacceptable to the biologism that reduces love to a union of bodies.

The Scripture—not only Augustine—teaches the value of continence. St. Paul reflects the spirit of the Gospel, as well as the example of Jesus (and Mary), when he writes: "I would that you were all as myself, but each one has his own gift from God" (1 Cor 7: 7). Applying this he continues, "But I say to the unmarried and widows, it is good if they so remain, even as I" (1 Cor 7: 8), Further, "Not I but the Lord commands, that a wife is not to depart from her husband, and if she departs, she is to remain unmarried" (1 Cor 7: 10–11). If spouses separate, they lose their "right" to a sexual life: they are to remain celibate. If they remain together, as noted, they are counseled—or permitted—to practice continence, by consent and for a time, to give themselves to prayer (1 Cor 7: 29). For Christian spouses, obviously, sexual orgasm will not be the *summum bonum*, not a substitute for the eternal ecstasy of union with God.

Augustine is thus not responsible for this praise of continence and virginity. The blame, if blame there is to be, must go higher. Those who consider even temporary continence an intolerable and inhuman burden—instead of a need requiring God's help—should lodge their complaints at the proper place. "Let him accept it who can" (Mt 19: 12).

Incidentally, Augustine held that married chastity, like continence, is a gift of God and therefore possible only when spouses are sustained by divine grace.[7] He also showed his balance and his ability to keep the several elements of the situation in perspective by refusing to allow the married, especially women, to use continence as a pretext for getting rid of unwanted spouses.[8]

All that Augustine had to do with the Christian doctrine on celibacy was to "preach the word, urgent in season and out of season" (2 Tim 4: 2).

We come to a direct confrontation: Christ or Freud (or pseudo-Freud). Is sexual experience necessary for maturity, for human completeness, for fulfillment? Under the influence of pansexualism, the contemporary faith that pretends to explain everything in man, many, even Catholics perhaps, would answer these questions affirmatively. Yet even among contemporaries there are dissenting voices. "Sex leads to nothing," wrote Albert Camus, who is scarcely an apologist for Christianity. "It is not immoral but is unproductive. One can indulge in it so long as one does not want to produce. But only chastity is linked to personal progress."[9] As to the Church, there is no doubt where she stands. "Whoever follows after Christ the perfect man becomes himself more of a man."[10] The mode of this perfection: "He Himself revealed to us that 'God is love' and at the same time taught us that the new commandment of love was the basic law of human perfection...."[11] The evangelic counsels, including chastity of course, aid in the pursuit of this perfection:

> All men should take note that the profession of the evangelical counsels, though entailing the renunciation of certain values which are undoubtedly to be esteemed, does not detract from a genuine development of the human person, but rather by its very nature is beneficial to that development. Indeed, the counsels, voluntarily undertaken according to each one's vocation, contribute a great deal to purification of heart and spiritual liberty.[12]

The counsels also bring those who follow them into conformity with Christ's own example: "Christ proposed to His disciples this form of life, which He as the Son of God accepted in entering this world to do the will of His Father. This same state of life is accurately exemplified and perpetually made present in the Church."[13]

The Fathers of the Council look to a deeper cause than sexuality to explain man's lack of fulfillment. "Sin has diminished man, blocking his fulfillment."[14] How then shall fulfillment be attained? In answering this, the Fathers quote St. Augustine, inevitably: "Apart from this message [of the Church] nothing will avail to fill up the heart of man: 'Thou hast made us for Thyself, O Lord, and our hearts are restless till they rest in Thee.' "[15]

2. CELIBACY AND CHASTITY

The celibate life, offered as an ideal for the few by our Lord Himself, is a "hard saying" for the natural man. It reminds him all too plainly of his legacy from Adam. Apart from the sin of Adam and its consequences, there would be neither occasion nor need for celibacy.[16] If all man's desires were integrated under the control of reason and grace, as in Paradise, what would be the purpose of such a vocation?

The celibate is thus a witness to man's past, his elevation and fall, as well as of his future resurrection. He is also witness, in the present, to the continued effects of original sin. He is evidence of the threat of concupiscence. His vow of chastity indicates that concupiscence, ever ready to distort all our natural desires, is likely to intrude here also. If such statements seem only to confirm a celibate obsession with sex, the reader is referred again to what has already been said on this score (Chapter 5, section 3) by noncelibates.

In recent debates a persistent criticism made of the Church's theology of marriage is that, having been largely formulated by celibates, it is inevitably one-sided and therefore faulty. The premise itself is dubious.[17] Nevertheless, celibacy, because of the disorder in human desires to which it testifies, gives the celibate's witness a special value and relevance. Apart from the realization of concupiscence and the need to combat it—of which the celibate vocation is a constant reminder—there would be grave danger of slipping into the idyllic view of sex once entertained by the Pelagians and now again in vogue, allegedly supported this time by the findings of depth-psychology.

The married, while claiming that experience gives their testimony special value, may be likely, because of this very experience, to be influenced by the idyllic view of sex. This is shown in the sexual and marital tragedies that frequently overtake their children, to whom even the devout at times fail to give adequate guidance and protection.

The danger of lapsing into this idyllic view, really a kind of neo-Pelagianism, is particularly great today as a consequence of two currents of thought that have flooded the modern world. The one is a roseate optimism about man's natural state—at least a *de facto* denial of concupiscence and original sin—which stems from Jean Jacques Rousseau. This may have happened apart from the intention of Rousseau,[18] but the influence is here, and its pervasiveness may be seen, without even reading Rousseau, by viewing *South Pacific* or *Mutiny on the Bounty* or joining in the contemporary quest for *Islands in the Sun*.

The other current is Freudianism, if not the hypotheses of the master, at least in their popular extension and distortions. All sense of danger from sex is lost: sexuality becomes the supreme means of human completeness, of personal maturity, of fulfillment.

In such an atmosphere even the "elect" may be "deceived" (Mt 24: 24) and carried away. Consequently, as Father Bouyer observes, much recent Catholic writing on marriage and sexuality less resembles the ideas of Augustine than those of his Pelagian opponents. Little wonder that these writers find the ideas of the Bishop of Hippo repugnant.[19]

Canon 1013 gives as one of the purposes of marriage that it is a "remedy for concupiscence." "Horrible phrase," comments one writer.[20] It would doubtless be unfair to attach too much importance to a parenthetical remark, a mere straw, yet even straws show which way the wind is blowing.

To speak of marriage as a "remedy for concupiscence" is not to depreciate marriage or conjugal love. It is simply to place marriage in its total human setting, accepting nature as it comes to us, fallen and restored yet still bearing the wounds of the Fall. It is the Church's teaching that Christ through the action of His grace on men at once heals and elevates them, making them "partakers of the divine nature" (2 Pet 1: 4). "Pursuing the saving purpose which is proper to her, the Church does not only communicate divine life to men but in some way casts the reflected light of that life over the entire earth, most of all by its *healing and elevating* impact on the dignity of the person...."[21] In order to perfect men, Christ must heal them: He is Physician in becoming Savior. "How can a thing be healed," asks Augustine, "if it is not wounded nor hurt nor weakened and corrupted?"[22]

Or shall we say, to please our married friends, that human nature is wounded indeed in all areas except sexuality? That the area of their moral combat includes every other sector except this? That, although baptism itself has not the power to remove the consequences of original sin, the sacrament of matrimony accomplishes this completely and once for all?

Or shall we not rather ask them to accept their place "with Adam and all mankind?"

In the present economy, since the Fall, Christ through His grace elevates us but not without healing us. That is what is now meant by justification. Adam before the Fall could enjoy grace that elevates without healing; but we cannot. Sanctification for us involves a cure; to reject the cure is to forfeit the restoration.

"The role of grace is understood only in terms of the evils it is to cure."[23] Remove concupiscence from theology and there is no need for remedial grace (except, as even the Pelagians admitted, for forgiveness). With the *agon* removed from the Christian life, there is no need for help and healing.

Augustine demonstrated against the Pelagians not only the necessity for salvation of a grace "beyond the constitution of nature"; he also showed, and it was an integral part of the first demonstration, that men also need the medicinal property of grace in their daily struggle against darkness and evil if they are to enjoy the benefits of life in Christ. By discarding Augustine's teaching on concupiscence, therefore, we lose not only his theology of remedial grace, but really his whole theology of grace. For the grace of Christ is one, and we cannot enjoy the elevation it effects if we do not submit to the purification it demands. Without grace that heals (and response to it), the grace that elevates to share the divine life becomes an abstraction, a beautiful superstructure, with no way of rising to its possession. By neglecting the one, we also, in practice, lose the other.

This brings us to the difference between the old Pelagianism and its modern reincarnation. The old Pelagianism denied the need for both elevating and remedial grace: man could be saved by his own powers. But the new Pelagianism, not wishing to be preoccupied with the negative, denies (in practice) only the need for remedial grace by neglecting the need of response to it. It readily admits that incorporation into Christ is a supernatural gift. Indeed, it may be said that there has never been a clearer grasp than in the modern Church of the supernatural character of grace and salvation in Christ. But with concupiscence unacknowledged and purification through remedial grace considered unnecessary, one cannot enter this supernatural world, so beautifully described; entrance is possible only through the purification effected by healing grace in ascesis, renunciation, warfare against concupiscence, suffering—in a word, through the cross. In man's present state, the healing and transforming qualities of Christ's grace are not detachable from each other. Both are involved in our restoration. Loss of one is loss of the other. We must always bear about in our bodies the dying of Jesus if the life of Jesus is to be made manifest in our bodily frame (2 Cor 4: 10).

3. DYING WE LIVE

In some religious orders profession is made in a simulated funeral ceremony signifying Christian renunciation as explained by St. Paul, "You have died and your life is hidden with Christ in God" (Col 1: 3). He had just given the reason for this: "Since you are risen with Christ, seek the things that are above, where Christ is seated at the right hand of God." This is the law of the cross, the "foolishness" of the cross: death and resurrection, resurrection through death. It was exemplified by the redemptive act of Jesus Himself: "Did not the Christ have to suffer these things before entering into His glory?" (Lk 24: 26). Since the "disciple is not above His master," all those who claim Jesus as Savior are drawn into this law: "Through many tribulations we must enter the Kingdom of God" (Acts 14: 22). "Dying, behold we live" (2 Cor 6: 9).

The law obviously is not limited to professed religious. St. Paul was speaking to all his converts at Colossae. The Church in her liturgy for Holy Saturday (and throughout Easter week) uses his words to them to explain to her children the personal meaning and application of Christ's death and resurrection for them.

In order to share in the resurrection of Jesus, the celibate (and the religious taking the three vows) plunges into this mystical death, as it were, all at once. But again, its necessity follows in the first place from baptism, not from acceptance of the counsels. "Do you not know that all who are baptized in Christ Jesus are baptized in His death? If we have been united with him in the likeness of His death, we shall be so in the likeness of His resurrection also" (Rom 5: 3–5). Those who take the vows make their renunciation—"share in the dying" of Jesus—radically and at once. But there may be an equal or greater difficulty in the prolongation of this dying throughout the normal Christian life. As Newman says: "Men who make such sacrifices [as Abraham's and Lot's] often evidence much strength in making them. . . . But it is an even greater thing, it requires a clearer, steadier, nobler faith, to be surrounded by worldly goods, yet to be self-denying; to consider ourselves but stewards of God's bounty, and to be 'faithful in all things' committed to us."[24]

Augustine, while appreciative of the value of the virginal life, was not unaware of its risks and dangers. Fully the last third of his *Holy Virginity* is occupied with warnings against these dangers; it is a treatise on the need for humility in consecrated virgins, lest they lose the fruit of their virginity. The "death" of religious profession is not final; it must be carried on throughout life. It may happen that the "corpses" rise from their funeral service to become *bon vivants*.

Human life is a series of deaths ending in death. Christian life is a series of deaths and resurrections, ending in a final death and resurrection. The cycle is the same for all, celibate or married. "Human activity, constantly deranged by self-love, must be purified by the powers of Christ's cross and resurrection."[25]

A psychologist writes, "The great problem at the present stage of the development of the human consciousness is one of integrating marriage into eroticism or eroticism into marriage."[26] No doubt. Yet there are obstacles, as this writer also points out, among which are "the banalities" of domestic life. Moreover, too much weight should not be placed on this erotic element; as the Council has said, conjugal love "excels mere erotic inclination which, selfishly pursued, soon enough fades wretchedly away."[27]

Meanwhile, the process of maturing—and aging—is merged with the cycle of life and death. The love manual says—and for a love manual this seems like a confession of defeat: "The sexual urges of the woman possibly increase a little with the years, while those of the man dwindle slowly after his twentieth year."[28] F. J. Sheed writes:

> Too many men who have reached middle life must admit that for them sex has not lived up to its promise—that on balance their life has been rather more begloomed by sex than delighted by it. . . . First, it cannot continue to satisfy even at its own unambitious level: it follows the law of diminishing returns that governs the merely physical pleasures. . . .[29]

As eroticism follows its law of diminishing returns, there is need, if the marriage is to survive—and much more, if there is to be growth in love—that there be an increase of the divine love that comes of grace and draws human love into itself, thus developing within the latter the new principle of divine life. Only in this way can death be followed by resurrection.

This is why the Church—from Augustine to Vatican II—is right in stressing the personal, rather than the sexual, bond between spouses and the divine love that seals it. "Authentic married love is caught up into the divine love and is governed and enriched by Christ's redeeming power and the saving activity of the Church, so that this love may lead the spouses to God with powerful effect. . . ."[30]

4. ST. AUGUSTINE—"CONVERTED RAKE"?

Augustine had learned of the cross, though not yet its meaning, long before his conversion. The untimely death of a friend after a painful estrangement was perhaps "the great emotional experience" of his life.³¹ It happened after his return from school at Carthage to begin his teaching career at his native Tagaste. Five chapters of the *Confessions* (Book IV) are filled with his grieving: but also with reflections on the meaning of this bitter event and on the transience and incompleteness of human love. It was here that he learned by anticipation the negative side of the law of the cross, that all things human must die.³² It conditioned all his subsequent response to human love and prepared him to learn the positive lesson of resurrection through divine love. His own subsequent, almost inevitable, embracing of the celibate life was an acceptance of death to obtain the perfect fulfillment of life and love and happiness.

Margaret Sanger contemptuously dismissed the encyclical of Pope Pius XI on marriage with the remark, "He therefore instructs the faithful how to regulate their conjugal life without the benefit of science and according to theories written by St. Augustine, also a bachelor, who died fifteen centuries ago."³³ It might be added now that the convocation of "bachelors" meeting as the Second Vatican Council has also followed the guidelines of the "bachelor" who lived fifteen centuries ago.

The Christian idea of celibacy is here drained of all spiritual meaning and value. It is used as a reproach and evidence of an alleged antimarriage attitude on the part of the Church.

Catholics, in assessing Margaret Sanger's view, might well recall that all Christians take their guidance from One who lived even more than fifteen hundred years ago and was also a "bachelor." A bachelor may be one who refuses responsibility and shirks maturity; but the bachelorhood taught and exemplified by Jesus is of a kind altogether different.

Final fulfillment, Augustine held, is attainable only in God. Only in Him is rest, true enjoyment. Human loves, of which married love is the especially privileged type of the love between God and man, are steps of a ladder to divine love. The celibate, in renouncing this love, is not renouncing love. His human nature forbids this. He is voluntarily dying to one kind of love to possess the fullness of love. His renunciation does not depreciate human love. The paradox of Christian renunciation is that it gives up a *good*; and St. John of the Cross was to say that the higher the good we renounce for love, the greater is the proof of love.[34] Besides, domestic love, although intended by God to lead to a wider embrace of one's fellows, tends, as St. Paul says, to be absorbing: "He who is married is concerned about the things of the world, how he may please his wife; and he is divided" (1 Cor 7: 33). The celibate, although running the risk of selfishness peculiar to his own life, is at any rate freer to love God in all his fellows: "I would have you free from care. He who is unmarried is concerned about the things of the Lord, how he may please God" (1 Cor 7: 32).

Augustine's whole life as bishop beautifully illustrates this celibate love. At a time when the Church is reemphasizing the pastoral office, he stands as an unexcelled example of pastoral love. His apostolate was a constant daily immolation of love for his people.[35] He might have claimed with St. Paul that his whole life was a sacrifice of love: "I am dead all the day long, I am accounted as sheep for the slaughter" (Rom 9: 36).

St. Augustine has also been described as a "converted rake"; his theology of marriage may then be rejected as merely the rationalization of his violent personal recoil. Even Bouyer says, "We must remember, above all, that his experience of sexuality was that of a libertine. Conversion, so far from cancelling out that kind of experience, has the effect of deepening its shadows."[36] But Vernon Bourke writes:

> It is perfectly clear that Augustine was never a complete sensualist, a libertine who valued only bodily pleasure. His interest in what he conceived to be the Epicurean doctrine of happiness, as corporal pleasure, was but momentary. His will did not close up his mind to the infiltration of spiritual truth when he was reading Plotinus. Nor, on the other hand, was his moral reform independent of his advance in knowledge of the spirit.[37]

And Van der Meer:

> The *continens* [Augustine believed] has chosen the better part. Fortunately, however, he never repeated

the angry words of the *Soliloquies*, and instead of providing modern psychoanalysis with symptoms from which to diagnose fears and resistances, he confined himself to singing in simple and beautiful terms the praises of virginity.[38]

These are the "angry words" of the *Soliloquies*:

However much thou please to portray her and adorn her with all manner of gifts, I have determined that nothing is so much to be avoided by me as such a bedfellow. I perceive that nothing more saps the citadel of manly strength, whether of mind or body, than female blandishments and familiarities. Therefore, if (which I have not yet discovered) it appertains to the office of a wise man to desire offspring, whoever for this reason only comes into this connection, may appear to me worthy of admiration, but in no wise a model for imitation: for there is more peril in the essay, than felicity in the accomplishment. Wherefore, I believe, I am contradicting neither justice nor utility in providing for the liberty of my mind by neither desiring nor seeking, nor taking a wife.[39]

It is fallacious as well as unfair to pin any permanent importance to these words, spoken at a time of personal crisis and change. At the worst they mean only that for himself he rejected marriage as a vocation. Neither feminine companionship (which he had valued highly enough) nor children (although he had one son whom he loved) seemed to him sufficient reason to give up his singlehearted quest for "wisdom." Perhaps his thinking was still too human; yet apart from pagan philosophers, there had been Solomon to teach him that "female blandishments and familiarities" may indeed "sap manly strength."

To use these words of the *Soliloquies*, as has been done, as a decisive norm for estimating the mature Augustine is like judging the whole output of a scholar or litterateur by a college composition. True, Augustine was no collegian when he wrote this. He was a rising young professor in the Roman schools. Most of his previous life, however, had been lived in inward turmoil. He had just reached, in the climax of his conversion, a resolution of his problem and the beginning of tranquillity. The *Soliloquies* are the record of his inward stress and argument as he tried to put his life in order. What he says here represents but a temporary phase in his thinking, not a final or mature statement. When he wrote it, he was not yet a fully instructed Christian. He was preparing for baptism. And he "never repeated these angry words." His ideas on marriage and celibacy would now be completely transformed as he plunged more and more deeply into the study of Scripture.

C. S. Lewis, a benign enough figure, has written much more drastically than Augustine of the difference between any kind of human happiness and divine beatitude:

> The letter and spirit of Scripture, and of all Christianity, forbid us to suppose that life in the New Creation will be a sexual life; and this reduces our imagination to the withering alternative either of bodies that are hardly recognizable as human bodies at all or else of a perpetual fast. As regards the fast, I think our present outlook might be like that of a small boy who, on being told that the sexual act was the highest bodily pleasure, should immediately ask whether you ate chocolates at the same time. On receiving the answer no, he might regard the absence of chocolates as the chief characteristic of sexuality. In vain would you tell him that the reason why lovers in their carnal raptures don't bother about chocolates is that they have something better to think of. The boy knows chocolate; he does not know the positive thing that excludes it. We are in the same position. We know the sexual life; we do not know, except in glimpses, the other thing which, in Heaven, will leave no room for it.[40]

If Augustine was a rake, he was a rake with a difference. No Don Juan with a long record of amorous adventures and conquests, he was faithful to one woman for twelve years, and this while a Manichee whose tenets condoned license, before he understood the Christian ideal of marriage.

Before his conversion, Augustine had moreover decided to marry. But the marriage proposed to him seems to have been one of mere convenience. He had to wait two years until the girl would come of age. Meanwhile, he dismissed his mistress—but took another. He blames this further lapse on his sensuality; but it has been suggested that it was perhaps also an assertion of independence against the persistent influence of Monica (from whom, in going from Carthage to Rome, he had fled). The apparently harsh dismissal and subsequent relapse, however, do not erase the poignancy of his separation, recalled years later, from his first mistress, the woman with whom he had lived so long.

> Meanwhile my sins were being multiplied, and my mistress being torn from my side as an impediment to my marriage, my heart, which clung to her, was racked and wounded and bleeding. And she went back to Africa, making a vow unto Thee never to know another man, leaving me with my natural son by her.[41]

Is this the cynicism of a Don Juan? Was there no affection? Even after taking the second mistress, an interim consolation while awaiting marriage, he still remembered the first:

> Nor was that wound of mine as yet cured which had been caused by the separation from my former mistress, but after inflammation and most acute anguish it mortified, and the pain became numbed, but more desperate.[42]

There can be no doubt about the affection of Augustine for the son of this union, who, surprisingly in the circumstances and fittingly as it turned out, was called Adeodatus. A youth of rare nobility, he moves in and out of the early dialogues and the *Confessions,* taking the center of the stage just once before his early death, in his father's book *The Teacher,* which, Augustine assures us, accurately reflects the youth's elevated thought.

Why, then, as Augustine consented to marry, did he not plan to take as his wife this mistress with whom he had lived for twelve years, from whom separation caused him such pain, who bore him this beloved son? Why was not this mistress a suitable partner for marriage? Why this abrupt, if painful, repudiation? It was not, at any rate, the result of his conversion, which came only later. It was done under the influence of Monica when, confused and miserable, he was trying to put some order into his life. The girl he had picked up on the streets of Carthage was not considered a suitable partner for this rising university professor. And Monica was a woman, and a devout woman. Yet evidently she was not without faults—her sanctity was also a growth—and she still had worldly ambitions for her brilliant son; but she was presumably no misogynist.

It has been pointed out that a decisive experience in Augustine's life had been the loss of his young friend at Tagaste. His subsequent attitude toward love cannot be appreciated without considering this experience. It impressed on his mind that no human love would fill the void in his heart or bring the total fulfillment he desired.

Without doubt Augustine, despite his self-depreciation, did love the unnamed woman so long his mistress, although his love seems to have been seriously marred by sensuality. His reaction was against lust: not against love, which he had learned of from her, as also from his youthful friend; he was henceforth to seek love in the final beatitude of loving God, as this possibility now opened up to his eager gaze.

The idea of celibacy, as it had first reached him in the imperfect view of the pagan sages, had attracted him even before his conversion. He had thought that an association of celibates would provide the best opportunity for gaining the wisdom he desired. His friend Alypius, who was in time to be his fellow convert and fellow bishop, sought to dissuade him from marrying "with his unvarying argument that if I did we could not live together with untroubled leisure in the pursuit of wisdom."[43] But the learned society of celibates broke up— through marriage.

Again, the stories that moved him most as he approached the climax of conversion were those of St. Antony and three young contemporaries who, being converted, embraced celibacy.[44] It was almost inevitable that he should himself desire to embrace the celibate life upon encountering Christ, Whom he was shortly to describe as the "supreme example of virginal integrity."[45]

When fully instructed and formed as Christian, Augustine himself directly repudiated his earlier statement in the *Soliloquies*.

> They rather discourage than encourage virgins who compel them to persevere in their state by condemning marriage. How will they rely on the truth of what is written: "And he who does not give her does better," if they consider false that which is just as surely written: "and he who gives his virgin in marriage does well" (1 Cor 7: 38)?[46]

The saint reveals his true estimate of marriage, as a Christian, when he places the value of virginity next to that of martyrdom.[47] He is here certainly not downgrading marriage; he is rather saying, in effect, that its goodness is such that its renunciation is exceeded in merit only by the surrendering of life itself for the sake of Christ. "The more and the greater things a man despises for the sake of another, the more does he esteem and exalt that other."

Already in the *Confessions* we find an attitude at once more mellow, more mature, and more Christian. The love of God is not so much a renunciation as the fulfillment of the deepest aspirations of love. Note the italicized phrases:

> What is it that I love when I love You? Not the beauty of any bodily thing, nor the order of seasons, not the brightness of light that rejoices the eye, nor the sweet melodies of all songs, nor the sweet fragrances of flowers and ointments and spices; nor manna nor honey, *not the limbs that carnal love embraces*. None of these things do I love in loving my God. Yet in a sense I do love light and melody and fragrance and food *and embrace* when I love my God—the light and the voice and the fragrance and food and embrace in the soul,

when that light shines upon my soul which no place can contain, that voice sounds which no time can take from me. I breathe that fragrance which no wind scatters. I eat the food which is not lessened by eating, and *I lie in the embrace which satiety never comes to sunder.* That is what I love when I love my God.[48]

Still later, in praising virginity, he has almost forgotten the renunciation altogether. True, he compares consecrated virgins to the martyrs, but as witnesses to love, which the martyrs certainly were. The value of holy virginity, he says, after having completed his book on *The Good of Marriage,* is in total dedication and consecration. In what may be called a canticle to virginity, he said:

> Press on, then, saints of God, youths and maidens, men and women, celibates and virgins, press on unflaggingly towards the goal! Praise the Lord more sweetly, to whom your thoughts are more fully devoted; hope in Him more eagerly, whom you serve more eagerly; love him more ardently, whom you please more carefully. With loins girt, and lamps lit, await the Lord when He returns from the wedding.[49]

The youthful reader of Hortensius has come to the end of his quest. Obscure and amateur psychoanalysis does not explain him. The explanation of Augustine—and of his theology—is his finding fulfillment in renunciation through continence, his experience of resurrection and life in "dying." Only God can satisfy the restless, aching heart. And now God has broken through the darkness of his mind:

> Late have I loved Thee, O Beauty ever ancient and ever new, late have I loved Thee! . . . Now I pant for Thee; I have tasted and now I hunger and thirst; Thou didst touch me, and I was inflamed with desire for Thy peace.[50]

Now that the journey's end had been reached, now with true wisdom and supreme good attained, would he do other than follow to the end his inspired mentor: "The things that were gain to me, these, for the sake of Christ, I have counted loss. Nay more: I count everything loss for the excellent knowledge of Jesus Christ my Lord. For His sake I have suffered the loss of all things, and count them as dung that I may gain Christ" (Phil 3: 7–9).

In Christian art Augustine is sometimes depicted holding a heart in his hand. The symbol is a telling one and really captures the essence of the man. Not only did he himself love and place his life under the authority of love; not only did he attempt to make love the determining element of existence in general and of Christian existence in particular—he *thought from the heart,* and he created an image of existence which only the heart can understand.[51]

"Age upon age had no power to shake the design He formed in His heart to rescue our souls from death and to feed them in their hunger." These words of the Psalmist (32: 11) have been appropriately placed by the Church in the liturgy for the feast of the Sacred Heart, celebrated in honor of the divine love. They describe the kind of love for which Augustine hungered. His entire life, especially after his conversion, exemplifies that conviction, shared by many and perhaps obscurely experienced by all, but never so beautifully expressed outside of Scriptures as by Augustine himself: "You have made our hearts for yourself, O God, and they will never rest until they rest in You."[52]

5. SUMMARY AND CONCLUSION—
DOCTOR OF LOVE HUMAN AND DIVINE

The strands of thought that we have followed throughout these pages may be brought together and summarized as follows:
1. St. Augustine's invariable habit of studying man, not in his metaphysical essence, but in his concrete historical situation, in his place in the divine economy, has received corroboration, as remarkable as unexpected, from this statement of the Second Vatican Council:

The root reason for human dignity lies in man's call to communion with God. From the very circumstances of his origin man is already invited to converse with God.[53]

The divorce between nature and grace is over. This distinction is not to be misunderstood as separation. Nature is restored to its setting in the divine plan, and an impoverished rationalism cannot parade itself as Catholic theology.

2. Integral to Augustine's concrete view of man is his realistic assessment of the effects of original sin. The Second Vatican Council, far from muffling this doctrine, so humiliating to the natural man, speaks of these effects repeatedly and emphatically. "Although he was made by God in a state of holiness, from the very onset of his history man abused his liberty and sought to attain his good apart from God.... Therefore man is split within himself. As a result, all of human life, whether individual or collective, shows itself to be a dramatic struggle between good and evil, between light and darkness."[54]

3. St. Augustine's teaching on man, we have seen, is personalist. He insisted on the unique dignity of the person, both in his general teaching and his teaching on marriage. It is unnecessary to repeat (or multiply) texts to show how completely this teaching harmonizes with that of the Second Vatican Council.

4. St. Augustine's moral teaching is an ethic of love that derives, not merely from the law of nature or reason, but from man's destiny to love God intimately in the order of grace. He attaches great weight to the law of nature, but he is not satisfied with viewing this law abstractly, but concretely, as threatened by concupiscence, while concupiscence in turn is balanced—and overbalanced—by grace expressing itself in love. He respects reason—who has respected it more?—but for him reason is ever illuminated by faith.

He taught a morality that is based on love, pivots on love, and thus anticipated all that is valuable in situation ethics. Legalism and code morality are utterly foreign to his thought.

5. Finally, in distinguishing within the one good of marriage a threefold division of coordinated and inseparable

goods, Augustine has provided a basic framework for the theology of marriage, which the Church has found indispensable down to the present day.

A bitter critic of Augustine's marriage theology recently said that the saint's "views paralyzed thinking in this area for roughly a thousand years."[55] The statement should be corrected to read, "for roughly two thousand years"—down to and including the Second Vatican Council. Then for complete accuracy the word "paralyzed" should be changed to "inspired."

Notes

INTRODUCTION
1. The National Catholic Welfare Conference translation is used in all references to the conciliar decrees. References are to paragraph numbers.
2. John Henry Newman, *An Essay on the Development of Christian Doctrine*, chap. 5.
3. *Jubilee*, vol. 13, no. 10, p. 38.
4. "Professor Janssens, of the Theological Faculty of the University of Louvain, has shown how St. Augustine's false interpretation of the doctrine of Marriage contained in Genesis and the Epistles of St. Paul has been the root of a matrimonial ethic imbued with neo Platonism and agnosticism of a Manichaean type" (Gustavo Pérez Ramirez, "Family Planning and Latin American Problems," *The Human Reality of Sacred Scripture*, p. 159). John T. Noonan, however, sees Augustine's marriage teaching as characteristically Stoic (*Contraception*, p. 130). One might well wonder whether this Doctor of the Church was even a Christian!
5. "The Pope's Position on Birth Control," *The Nation* 134 (Jan. 27, 1932).
6. John T. Noonan, *Contraception*, p. 447.
7. Philip Hughes, *A History of the Church*, vol. 2, p. 22.
8. Étienne Gilson, *The Christian Philosophy of St. Augustine*, p. 364, note 49.
9. John Baptist Reeves, O.P., "St. Augustine and Humanism." in *St. Augustine: His Age, Life, and Thought*, p. 126.
10. St. Augustine, *Adulterous Marriages*, I, 25–32.
11. J. Tixeront, *History of Dogma*, vol. 2, p. 505.
12. St. Augustine, *Retractations*, Preface.
13. Whitney Oakes in *The Basic Writings of St. Augustine*, p. xi.
14. Étienne Gilson, "The Future of Augustinian Metaphysics," in *St. Augustine: His Age, Life, and Thought*, p. 300.

CHAPTER 1
1. "The influence, therefore, came from the Neoplatonists rather than from Plato, but a closer examination will show that the imprint left on Augustine's soul derives from the fundamental Platonic doctrine rather than from Neoplatonic variations" (Eugène Portalié, S.J., *A Guide to the Thought of St. Augustine*, p. 96).
2. Étienne Gilson, *The Christian Philosophy of St. Augustine*, p. 234. There has been some debate as to whether and how far St.

Augustine knew Plato directly or through the latter's disciple Plotinus. The discussion does not concern us here.

3. Jacques Maritain, "St. Augustine and St. Thomas," in *St. Augustine: His Age, Life, and Thought*, chap 3.
4. Portalié, *A Guide*, p. 16. The quotation from Augustine is from *Against the Academics*, II, 2–5.
5. F. Van der Meer, *Augustine the Bishop*, p. 7.
6. Ibid., p. 4.
7. Gilson, *The Christian Philosophy*, pp. 75, 200.
8. "The dispositions of his mind, then, are unconditionally those of a believer. He is not ready to condemn the Gospel in the name of Plato, but rather to explain it by his philosophy. Grandgeorge puts the case well: 'Therefore, insofar as his philosophy is in agreement with his religious doctrines, St. Augustine is unreservedly Neoplatonic, but wherever a contradiction presents itself, he does not hesitate for a moment to subordinate his philosophy to his religion, reason to faith.... He was above all a Christian. Philosophical questions in his mind are found relegated to the background, the more so as he grew older'" (Portalié, *A Guide*, p. 97). Portalié also provides a useful summary of Augustine's use of Platonic teachings: Christian theories wrongly considered Platonic; Platonic theories always approved for use in dogma; Neoplatonic theories always rejected; Neoplatonic theories first adopted, then rejected.
9. St. Augustine, *City of God*, XI, 23. "He rejected with abhorrence the hypothesis of a humanity in which the body would be only a prison.... Everything God made is good. Therefore the body was created for its intrinsic goodness, not as a consequence of our punishment for sin" (Gilson, *The Philosophy*, p. 51).
10. St. Augustine, *City of God*, XXII, 24.
11. St. Augustine, *Confessions*, X, 20.
12. St. Augustine, *City of God*, XIV, 5.
13. Ibid., 3.
14. Gilson, *The Christian Philosophy*, pp. 56ff.
15. Ibid., p. 47; and p. 271, note 5.
16. Ibid., pp. 44, 55.
17. St. Augustine, *City of God*, XIII, 24.
18. Paul Henry, S.J., *St. Augustine on Personality*, pp. 12, 3.
19. Ibid.
20. St. Augustine, *Continence*, 5.
21. Ibid., 4.
22. Actually Augustine does later advert to this opposition—but only to reject it—in his controversy with the Pelagians. Pelagius, noting the Pauline texts on the opposition between flesh and spirit, affirms the goodness of both flesh and [human] spirit in man, since both were created by God. He then asks, "If, therefore, both the spirit is good, and the flesh is good, as made by the good Creator, how can it be that the two good things can be contrary to one another?" His implication is that, contrary to Augustine, there can be no such

defect as concupiscence. For Pelagius, as he interprets the Apostle, the opposition is solely between good works and evil works; and the evil works, like the good works, are purely the products of man's freedom, without any push from "concupiscence." To say otherwise, he contends, would be to imply an inner disharmony in the works of the Creator. Augustine replies:

"I need not say that the whole of this reasoning would be upset if one were to ask him, 'Who made heat and cold?' and he were to say in answer, 'God, without a doubt.' I do not ask the string of questions. Let him determine himself whether these conditions of climate may either be said to be not good, or else whether they do not seem to be contrary to each other. Here he will probably object, 'These are not substances, but the qualities of substances.' Very true, it is so. But still they are natural qualities, and undoubtedly belong to God's creation; and substances, indeed, are not said to be contrary to each other in themselves, but in their qualities, as water and fire. What if it be so with flesh and spirit? We do not affirm it to be so; but to show that his argument terminates in a conclusion which does not necessarily follow, we have said so much as this. For it is possible for contraries not to be mutually opposed to each other, but rather by mutual action to temper health and render it good; just as, in our body, dryness and moisture, cold and heat—in the tempering of which altogether consists our bodily health" (*Nature and Grace*, 63).

Two things are clear from this passage:

First, even if it is granted that there is a natural opposition between flesh and spirit because of their diverse natures, this need not imply any split or division or discord in God's handiwork; it means only the mutual "tempering" of diverse elements, as with heat and cold.

Second, however, Augustine does not wish even to discuss this matter. It is not, for him, to the point: "I do not affirm it to be so." The opposition for him is not philosophical, but theological; it derives from Adam's sin. Hence his conclusion: "The fact, however, that the flesh is contrary to the spirit, so that we cannot do the things that we would, is a defect, not nature." He thus also rejects in advance the position of philosophically minded theologians—who, however, did not hesitate to claim his authority—who would later explain concupiscence merely in terms of the diverse elements in the human composite. (See also Chapter 3, note 1, below.)

A significant thing about the above passage, in which Augustine refuses to consider any evil in nature, locating it always in the will, is that it was written at the height of the Pelagian controversy, when his critics see him swinging back toward Manichaeism.

23. St. Augustine, *Continence*, 7.
24. Fernand Prat, S.J., *The Theology of St. Paul*, vol. 2, pp. 52–57, 69–76. Karl Rahner, "The Theological Concept of *Concupiscentia*," *Theological Investigations*, p. 354 and note. The latter charges Augustine "definitely" with Neoplatonic dualism.

192   St. Augustine on Nature, Sex, and Marriage

    25. Gilson, *The Christian Philosophy*, p. 13.
    26. See Chapter 2, note 10, below.
    27. "Augustinian thought tends to be existential, the word taken in its strictest (Kierkegaardian) sense" (Romano Guardini, *The Conversion of St. Augustine*, p. 70). Guardini also says: "His thinking is existential, not only in the sense that it is grounded in earnestness and passionate participation, not only because it aims at seizing and forming the fulness of reality, but in the last analysis precisely because the thinker sees and understands himself in his existence: himself in the world (world as setting for and stuff of his life); because he sees his own acts and existence as the process by which it becomes evident what this life is" (p. 136).
    28. St. Augustine, *Enchiridion of Faith, Hope, and Charity*, 34.
    29. Vernon J. Bourke, *Augustine's Quest for Wisdom*, p. 111.
    30. Gilson discusses this subject in "The Future of Augustinian Metaphysics," in *St. Augustine: His Age, Life, and Thought*, chap 9.
    31. See Michael Novak, "The Break with Platonic Religion," in *Eyes on the Modern World*, ed. John Deedy, chap. 2. But John T. Noonan thinks it was Stoicism that, entering Christianity with (among others) St. Augustine, deflected at least Christian moral thought (*Contraception*, chaps. 3–4). He omits to mention, however, that Augustine spent the last twenty-five years of his life warring against Stoicism newly resurgent in Pelagianism. These writers, and others, seem to doubt, not only the perceptiveness, not to say orthodoxy, of the great Doctor, but also the assimilative powers of Christianity. It sometimes happens that the very ones who criticize Catholic thinkers of the past for trying to assimilate truth wherever they found it, in a truly catholic spirit, also criticize modern Catholic theologians for allegedly failing to absorb the positive contributions of modern thought. The truth is that Catholic thought must strive to incorporate, from every age and any source, whatever can be assimilated into the living and growing unity of Christian truth. "For the rest, brethren, . . . think on these things" (Phil 4: 8). Augustine is faulted with having adopted the viewpoint, presumably from the Stoics, that sexuality should be governed by reason. But perhaps one need not be a Stoic to be convinced of this.

    CLEOPATRA: Is Antony or we in fault for this?
    ENOBARBUS: Antony only, that would make his will lord of his
        reason.
                        —*Antony and Cleopatra*, III, 13

    32. Vatican Council II, *Gaudium et Spes* (Pastoral Constitution on the Church in the Modern World), no. 15.
    33. Ibid., no. 14. Derrick Sherwin Bailey charges Augustine with dualism, but at least traces it back to Scripture (*Sexual Relations in Christian Thought*, pp. 10, 14). Some seem to imagine that the affirmation of man's psychophysical unity demands a denial of all variety and hierarchical order, thus reducing the whole universe to

homogeneity in a sort of metaphysical egalitarianism. But Teilhard de Chardin, so often invoked by such writers, states: "In any domain—whether it be the cells of a body, the members of a society or the elements of a spiritual synthesis—*union differentiates*" (*The Phenomenon of Man*, p. 262, emphasis in original).

34. Harvey Cox, for example, treats metaphysics, like primitive religion, as a means of "control" rather than as an instrument for exploring ultimate truth (*The Secular City*, pp. 2, 19, 20, 31, and passim).

35. *Gaudium et Spes*, no. 10.

CHAPTER 2
1. St. Augustine, *Confessions*, III, 7.
2. St. Augustine, *The Nature of Good*, 3–17.
3. St. Augustine, *Marriage and Concupiscence*, I, 1.
4. St. Augustine, *Continence*, 2.
5. St. Augustine, *Holy Virginity*, 8.
6. Afterward, when the barbarians were spreading havoc in the Empire, Augustine demonstrated his belief in this principle by forbidding Christians to commit suicide in order to preserve virginity. "The virtue which governs a good life controls from the seat of the soul every member of the body, and the body is rendered holy by the act of a holy will. Thus as long as the will remains unyielding, no crime, beyond the victim's power to prevent it without sin, and which is perpetrated on the body or in the body, lays any guilt on the soul. An attack on the body may inflict not merely physical pain, but may also excite carnal pleasure. If such an act is perpetrated, it does not compromise the virtue of chastity, to which the sufferer clings with an iron will; it merely outrages the sense of shame. We must not consider as committed with the will what could not, by the very constitution of nature, occur without some fleshly satisfaction" (*City of God*, I, 16).

These words, written after the anti-Manichaean and -Pelagian battles, show how constant he was in denying that there could be any evil in the flesh. His teaching provides no rationale to modern theologians who hold that nuns may protect themselves in rape by means of contraceptives.

7. Étienne Gilson, *The Christian Philosophy of St. Augustine*, p. 65.
8. St. Augustine, *Against Faustus the Manichee*, 18.
9. "It is commonly held that Augustine's ontology, in which evil is treated as a privation, a nonentity, does no more than evade the problem which it professed to solve; and that his deeply Christian sense of the reality of moral evil caused him to relapse into Manichaeism with his doctrine of original sin, in which the Non-Being, the Nothing out of which man was created, is transformed into a Something with fatal power. In fact the originality of Augustine appears just in *his steady refusal to hypostatize evil*. It is Plotinus

194   St. Augustine on Nature, Sex, and Marriage

who identifies evil with 'Matter'—not indeed with material existence, but with the potentiality in which material existence originates. For Augustine, creation *de nihilo* is simply creation, and creatureliness means a being which is not God and therefore not unchangeable. His whole conception of moral good and evil is dynamic: man's soul is in the making and cannot stand still. Righteousness is its movement towards integration, sin its movement towards disintegration—a verging *ad nihilum*, an 'unmaking.' Change is the rule of temporal existence, changelessness is the quality of the eternal, the limit towards which the creature may approximate" (John Burnaby, *Amor Dei: A Study of the Religion of St. Augustine*, p. 37, emphasis added).

10. In his *Two Souls, Against the Manichees*, Augustine had said, "Sin is nowhere but in the will." Commenting on this in the *Retractations* (I, 15, 2), he writes, "The Pelagians may think that this was said in their interest, on account of young children whose sin which is remitted to them in baptism they deny on the ground that they do not yet use the power of the will. As if indeed the sin, which we say they derive originally from Adam, that is, that they are implicated in his guilt and on this account are held subject to punishment, *could ever be otherwise than in the will*, by which will it was committed when the transgression of the divine precept was accomplished. Our statement, 'that there is never sin but in the will,' may be thought false, for the reason that the Apostle says: 'If what I will not this I do, it is no longer that I do it, but sin that dwelleth in me.' For this sin is to such an extent involuntary, that he says: 'What I will not this I do.' How, therefore, is there never sin but in the will? But this sin concerning which the Apostle has spoken is called sin because by sin it was done and it is the penalty of sin; since this was said concerning carnal concupiscence."

This is precisely the concept of concupiscence—i.e., that it comes from sin and leads to sin, but is itself not sinful—which is found in his early books, such as *The Problem of Free Choice* and *True Religion*, as also in his later works against the Pelagians. See Chapter 4.

11. St. Augustine, *Reply to Faustus*, XXII, 21.
12. St. Augustine, *Against Julian*, III, 18.
13. St. Augustine, *Confessions*, V, 8.
14. Ibid., 6, 7, 10.
15. St. Augustine, *The Nature of Good*, 3.
16. St. Augustine, *True Religion*, 21.
17. St. Augustine, *The Nature of Good*, 6.
18. Ibid., 7.
19. Louis O. Mink, in his Introduction to a translation by J. H. S. Burleigh of St. Augustine's *Of True Religion* (Chicago: Henry Regnery, 1959).
20. St. Augustine, *City of God*, XI, 22.
21. St. Augustine, *Against Julian*, V, 13.
22. Hugh Pope, O.P., has brought together many of these observa-

tions on nature in "St. Augustine and the World of Nature," in his *St. Augustine of Hippo*, chap. 6.
23. St. Augustine, *City of God*, XXII, 24.
24. Ibid.
25. F. Van der Meer, *Augustine the Bishop*, p. 245.

CHAPTER 3

1. Concupiscence is here called theological because it diverts man from his final supernatural end of loving God. It may also be defined philosophically as the tension resulting from the different components of human nature. Thus: "Modern theologians teach that original sin consists in being deprived of sanctifying grace, which is the state in which, before his baptism, a child is found to be through the Fall. Concupiscence is, in fact, a consequence of the Fall. But in itself it is not an evil, but a danger; it is natural to man made as he is of flesh and spirit. Had not God raised man to the supernatural state, had He created him in a state of pure nature as theologians say, He would have created him as he now is—minus original sin—and with concupiscence. This theological teaching will enable us to avoid all rigorism in spirituality" (Pierre Pourrat, *Christian Spirituality*, vol. 1, p. 181).

This definition does enable us to avoid all rigorism, but it also removes man from his actual condition and views him abstractly. This was the manner of definition of later theologians. But Augustine always viewed man concretely in his actual supernatural condition as ordained by God, then lost and restored. Thus his concept of concupiscence was theological rather than philosophical. This was illustrated in Chapter 2 by the manner in which he dealt with the conflict of flesh and spirit.

2. H. J. Denzinger, *Echiridion Symbolorum*, ed. A. Schönmetzer, 32d ed. (1953), 1515.
3. St. Thomas Aquinas, *Summa theologiae*, I-II, 85, 3. Concupiscence exists in the senses only materially or instrumentally. Only the will gives it moral significance. "Now in this transmission [of original sin] it is to be observed that whatever accrued from the motion of the will consenting to sin, to any part of man that can in any way share in that guilt either as its subject or as its instrument, has the character of sin. Thus from the will consenting to gluttony, concupiscence of food accrues to the concupiscible faculty . . ." (I-II, 83, 1).
4. Vatican Council II, *Gaudium et Spes* (Pastoral Constitution on the Church in the Modern World), no. 11, emphasis added.
5. Ibid., no. 40, emphasis added.
6. For an example of a crude oversimplification of Augustine's struggle and conversion, see John Marshall, M.D., *Catholics, Marriage, and Contraception* (Baltimore: Helicon Press, 1966), pp. 10ff.
7. Étienne Gilson, *The Christian Philosophy of St. Augustine*, p. 151.
8. St. Augustine, *Nature and Grace*, 52.

9. Concupiscence is therefore not to be limited to sexual concupiscence, which as we see in Chapter 5 is but a particular manifestation of it. Although Augustine in his Pelagian polemic was chiefly occupied with sexual concupiscence, he reminded his opponent Julian that it is not to be confined to this meaning: "You speak as though we say that the concupiscence of the flesh is solely in the excessive pleasure of the genitals. However, it is also to be recognized in any of the senses whose desires oppose [*concupiscit*] the spirit; and if the spirit does not oppose it more strongly, it draws towards evil and evil is committed" (*Against Julian*, o.i. IV, 28).

Again: "Bodily pleasure, however, is preceded by a kind of appetite, a sensation in the flesh corresponding to desire in the soul, familiar in the form of hunger and thirst, and commonly called *libido*, when connected with sex—although, strictly speaking, lust is a word applicable to any kind of appetite, as in the classical definition of anger as lust for revenge" (*City of God*, XIV, 15).

After speaking of the desirable kinds of concupiscence (e.g., for wisdom, holiness), Augustine remarks, "Nevertheless the custom has always prevailed of interpreting *cupiditas* and *concupiscentia* in a bad sense unless a specific object has been indicated" (ibid, 7). The same is true of the word "lust."

Karl Rahner offers a notion of concupiscence that combines all these elements: which, however, if not fully coordinated, were already present in the teaching of Augustine (see *Theological Investigations*, vol. 1, pp. 345ff). But Rahner follows the Jansenistic interpretation of Augustine in saying that, for the saint, man's "primal constitution" is perverted "in *its very depths* by the sin of the first man" (ibid., p. 375, emphasis added).

10. Although we do not usually associate desire with the mind, there is in the mind a natural desire for knowledge and truth. It is this desire that is frustrated and diverted by the wound of ignorance. Augustine speaks of a "concupiscence of wisdom," quoting Wisdom 6: 21, "The desire of wisdom bringeth to the everlasting kingdom" (*Marriage and Concupiscence*, II, 3–10).

11. St. Augustine, *City of God*, XIV, 6.

12. St. Thomas Aquinas, *Summa theologiae*, I-II, 85, 3.

13. According to St. Thomas, the summary of the effects of original sin under the heading of the four wounds came into usage with Bede (ibid.).

14. J. Tixeront, *History of Dogma*, vol. II, p. 457.

15. Jacques Maritain, "St. Augustine and St. Thomas," in *St. Augustine: His Age, Life and Thought*, chap. 6. The references to St. Augustine's works given by Maritain are: *Grace and Free Will*, XIII, 25; *The Predestination of the Saints*, V, 10; *Exposition of the Psalms*, XLIX, 2; *Rebuke and Grace*, XI, 29; *The Trinity*, XIV, 15; *City of God*, XII, 9.

Perhaps the simplest way to establish the fact that St. Augustine clearly saw the supernatural character of grace is in his handling of the argument that Pelagius put forth as his *pièce de résistance*, intended to handle all contingencies. In developing this argument, Pelagius distinguished three elements in human action: the ability to act, volition, and the act itself. According to Pelagius, the last two are within man's own powers; only the first, he allows, the ability to act, is a "grace."

Against this, Augustine shows that by "grace," as the word is here used, Pelagius meant only man's natural endowments, which, in their own order are of course a gift of God but not a gratuitous grace in the Catholic sense. Then the saint demonstrates, from St. Paul, that man, to merit redemption, needs, beyond his natural endowments, an "ability" that is entirely gratuitous and is supplied only by the grace of Christ. He goes on to show that the grace of Christ is also necessary (and not only useful) for "volition" and the "act." Hence, the whole course of Christian conduct, for Augustine, moves in the supernatural order (*The Grace of Christ and Original Sin*).

Moreover, since Christ's grace is a "restoration" (*The Spirit and the Letter*, 47), Adam's pristine state being the type and norm, it is evident that Adam's state was also supernatural.

Augustine's own full account may be read in *City of God*, books X to XIV.

Part of the difficulty of understanding him correctly comes from his failure to distinguish clearly (i.e., conceptually) between the natural and supernatural orders. This distinction was to be perfected later, especially by St. Thomas. Although all the elements for the distinction are present in St. Augustine, he does not make it formally or analytically. Nor does he use the word "supernatural," also of later vintage; yet his modern translators have sometimes used it, so appropriately does it render his thought. See also Eugène Portalié's article "Augustine" in the *Catholic Encyclopedia*.

"The former immortality man lost through the exercise of his free will; the latter he shall obtain through grace, whereas if he had not sinned, he should have obtained it by desert. Even in that case, however, there could have been no merit without grace; because, although the mere exercise of man's free will was sufficient to bring in sin, his free will would not have sufficed for his maintenance in righteousness, unless God had assisted it by imparting a portion of His unchangeable goodness" (St. Augustine, *Enchiridion of Faith, Hope, and Charity*, 106).

16. J. Fargot, "Jansenius," *Catholic Encyclopedia*. Karl Rahner has written: "In theology the Jansenist doctrine of grace was wholly erroneous: grace was due to Adam by right, the virtues of pagans are only vices, mankind is enslaved to sinful concupiscence and even the justified remain subject to it, at least interiorly; sin is possible even without interior freedom of choice; Jesus died for the elect only and the mass of men are damned" (*Theological Dictionary*, s.v. "Jansenism").

17. H. J. Denzinger, *Echiridion Symbolorum*, ed. A. Schönmetzer,

32d ed. (1953), 2459. The Jansenists in their interpretation of Augustine erred for two reasons: First, they attributed "naturalism" to St. Augustine, that is, they did not (or would not) realize that in Augustine's thought as in Catholic teaching the Fall was from the order of grace. Second, following the purely rationalist procedure of a decadent Scholasticism, they transposed without correction what he said of nature in the concrete order into the abstract order with which they were preoccupied; thereby they attributed a taint to nature itself.

18. Étienne Gilson, "The Future of Augustinian Metaphysics," in *St. Augustine: His Age, Life, and Thought*, chap. 9.

19. A breathtaking example of this is provided by John T. Noonan when he describes Jansenism (*Contraception*, p. 317) as the transporting of Augustinism "from the fifth century to the seventeenth and restored without allowance for the growth that had occurred in the Church." This is historicism with a vengeance. Actually things are not so simple. Jansenism was an internal distortion of Augustinism—in Gilson's word, a "deviation." But Noonan obviously reads Augustine through the eyes of Jansenius, a fact that suggests the need for a reexamination of his analysis of the saint's teaching, particularly on concupiscence.

20. Felix Klein, *Americanism: A Phantom Heresy*.

21. Gilson, *The Christian Philosophy*, p. 143.

22. St. Thomas Aquinas, *Summa theologiae*, III, 71, 1.

23. While the harmful influence of Jansenism was deep and widespread enough in Catholic life, it should not be exaggerated. Certain areas were unaffected. St. Vincent de Paul opposed Jansenism, and his influence was great on laity and clergy alike. The Jesuits, not without influence, were the arch-enemies of Jansenism, as the *Provincial Letters* remain to remind us. One can read the great Jesuit spiritual masters of the 17th century, such as Louis Lallemant and Jean Nicolas Grou, without suspecting the existence of Jansenism. In the case of Grou this is particularly remarkable since he was deeply indebted to St. Augustine, whom the Jansenists claimed as their authority. Grou's *Morality from St. Augustine*, a perennial favorite, reprinted in English as late as 1934, is simply a reflection of Augustine's ethic of love. Augustine's critics would have difficulty finding any trace of Jansenism in Grou. Unfortunately, Jansenism did infiltrate the Oratorians and Sulpicians, along with their colleges and seminaries.

Nor, in assessing the influence of Jansenism, may we forget the quite opposite and more extensive influence that later came from France through Jean Jacques Rousseau: a roseate optimism about nature, stemming from a denial of original sin.

CHAPTER 4

1. St. Augustine, *Marriage and Concupiscence*, II, 22.
2. See St. Thomas Aquinas, *Summa theologiae*, II, 113, 1 ad 1:

"Through free will man can to some extent avoid evil, but not sufficiently."
   3. Étienne Gilson, *The Christian Philosophy of St. Augustine*, p. 149.
   4. See Chapter 3. In *Nature and Grace* (70), Augustine approaches the problem in the abstract terms in which it was later to appear but dismisses it as speculative; for him, whatever the goodness of nature, justification is only through the grace of Christ. Nevertheless he says elsewhere: "Charity may be divine or human; human charity may be either licit or illicit. Charity towards a wife is licit; it is illicit when given to a prostitute or another's wife. . . . It is lawful for you to love with a human charity your spouses, your children, your friends. Yet observe that this kind of charity is possible also to the impious" (*Sermon* 349, 1).
   5. St. Thomas Aquinas, *Summa theologiae*, I-II, 71, 6.
   6. St. Augustine, *The Problem of Free Choice*, I, 15.
   7. St. Augustine, *Against Julian*, VI, 15.
   8. St. Thomas Aquinas, *Summa theologiae*, I-II, 108, 4.
   9. See St. Thomas Aquinas, *De Perfectione Vitae Spiritualis* and *De Duobus Praeceptis Caritatis* (opuscula 29 and 35).
   10. St. Thomas Aquinas, *Summa theologiae*, II-II, 20, 3.
   11. Relevant passages in the works mentioned are as follows: *True Religion*, 20, 38. *On Genesis, Against the Manichees*, II, 15–21. *Genesis, Literally Interpreted*, VIII, 14–31; *Confessions*, X, 27; IV, 12. *City of God*, XII, 6; XV, 22. *Against Two Letters of the Pelagians*, I, 27–13. *Against Julian*, II, 3–5; II, 9–32; VI, 23–73.
   12. J. Tixeront, *History of Dogma*, vol 2, p. 467, quoting and commenting on St. Augustine's words in *The Problem of Free Choice*, I, 35.
   13. St. Augustine, *Marriage and Concupiscence*, I, 25.
   14. H. J. Denzinger, *Echiridion Symbolorum*, ed. A. Schönmetzer, 32d ed. (1953), 1515.
   15. St. Augustine, *Against Julian*, IV, 13.
   16. St. Augustine, *Nature and Grace*, 45.
   17. Ibid.
   18. St. Augustine, *Marriage and Concupiscence*, II, 22.
   19. Vatican Council II, *Gaudium et Spes* (Pastoral Constitution on the Church in the Modern World), no. 13. The whole paragraph should be read in this connection.
   20. Ibid, no. 37.
   21. St. Augustine, *Against Julian*, o.e. III, 202: also *City of God*, XV, 20; see also Chapter 3, note 6, above. In Paradise, things were different: "Now in the Garden, before the Fall, these 'two parts' of the soul [the passions of anger and lust] were not 'defective.' This means that these passions were never so aroused counter to the commands of the rational will that reason was forced, so to speak, to put them in harness" (*City of God*, XIV, 19).
   22. See Chapter 2, note 9, above.

23. St. Augustine, *Against Julian*, o.e. VI, 9. Augustine admits that this is hard to understand since we have no experience of it. See *City of God*, XIV, 26.

24. St. Augustine, *The Good of Marriage*, 16.

25. St. Augustine, *Marriage and Concupiscence*, I, 13.

26. Concerning *Man and Sin* by Piet Shoonenberg, S.J., a reviewer states: "One of the commendable aspects of Father Shoonenberg's treatment is the way in which he gives centrality to the mystery of Christ. So often the treatment of sin, particularly of original sin, has dealt with human culpability as if somehow it exists apart from the providence of God and the mystery of redemption. Seen in this abstract and unreal context, sin becomes utterly enigmatic and inexplicable" (Bernard Cooke, S.J., in *The Critic*, February–March 1966, p. 84).

St. Augustine knew of no other way to speak of sin than in the context of the mystery of Christ. He explained sin, especially original sin, in relation to the grace of Christ and the mystery of redemption.

Here as in other matters the "new" insight of modern theology is essentially a recovery of what is very old after a period of overly rationalistic and legalistic theology. Cardinal Manning said in his funeral oration over Newman that the latter had "found" the key to the Fathers of the Church. Perhaps one of Newman's contributions to modern theology was thus to open the door to the treasures of the Fathers.

27. For example, Louis Dupré, *Contraception and Catholics*, pp. 26–27: "Augustine's entire theory of original sin has been tainted by this strange sexual pessimism. *For him the essence of original sin is concupiscence,* and it is transmitted to further generations through the sexual desire in the act of conception" (emphasis added).

Naturally, then, this author believes that for St. Augustine "sexual pleasure and desire are intrinsically evil." He makes these statements without offering text or authority, thus affording a good example of the cavalier manner in which modern Catholics treat the saint. Augustine's notion of sexual concupiscence, here distorted, is taken up in Chapter 5.

And Karl Rahner: "Modern theology has abandoned an interpretation of concupiscence deriving from St. Augustine which materially identifies it with original sin." Yet the guilt of original sin is remitted with baptism, while concupiscence remains as its effect and punishment. Only in this way (with St. Thomas) can the Augustinian formula be rightly understood. Rahner's own definition of concupiscence is entirely Augustinian: "The Church teaches that concupiscence is something natural (D. 1079f.); but as compared with the life of God originally bestowed on man, it is also, especially as we experience it, a lack of that power of decision that God originally bestowed. To this extent, then, concupiscence is a result of original sin and an inducement to personal sin, but as the latter it can be

overcome by the grace of God" (*Theological Dictionary*, s.v. "Concupiscence").
28. Eugène Portalié, *A Guide to the Thought of St. Augustine*, p. 208.
29. Gilson, *The Christian Philosophy*, p. 151.
30. St. Thomas Aquinas, *Summa theologiae,* I-II, 82, 3.
31. Portalié, *A Guide*, p. 210.
32. Heinrich Boehmer, *Martin Luther: Road to Reformation*, p. 128. "In Luther's eyes sin is never simply an 'absence of being.' Nor in so far as it exists was it for him, like everything that is or participates in being, good. But evil is always the absolute opposite of good, and consequently never simply *a longe a Deo esse* but always *a contra Deum esse*. This is why it was never possible for Luther to agree with Augustine that there is something in evil or in sin which does not destroy the order or beauty of the world, but rather, like dark shadows in a painting, belongs to its inherent order and beauty and, in fact, sets them off effectively. Luther always saw in sin something which should not be, something which must by all means be removed" (p. 149).
This distinguishes Luther's thought sufficiently from Augustine's.
33. John M. Todd, *Martin Luther*, p. 91. It is worth observing that on this point Todd confirms Jacques Maritain, although the latter's account of Luther has now been largely discredited. Maritain said: "Concupiscence Luther identifies with original sin and the consequences of this: 'Original sin is always in us, ineffaceable; it has made us radically bad, corrupt in the very essence of our nature'" (*Three Reformers*, p. 9). Maritain wrote in the pre-ecumenical age when these questions were still fogged with prejudice. This should not blind us in our turn to some real merit in the book, including his central contention that Luther was an authentic mystic who was not able to find his way through the Dark Night (no one can) and had no one at hand to help him. A Protestant writer states: "The mystics knew this [sense of alienation] too. They called it the dark night of the soul, the dryness, the withdrawing of the fire from under the pot until it no longer bubbles. They counselled waiting until exaltation would return. For Luther it did not return because the enmity between man and God was too great. For all his impotence, man is a rebel against his Maker" (Roland H. Bainton, *Here I Stand*, p. 43).
The difference between the Catholic and Protestant views of man's sinfulness is a matter for ecumenical dialogue. Meanwhile, it seems already that the matter no longer has the importance attached to it in post-Tridentine polemics. The tendency now for both Protestants and Catholics is to attend more carefully to the positive content of Luther's theology on justification. Louis Bouyer, for example, distinguishes between the positive teaching of Luther—substantially identical with Catholic doctrine—and negative elements that Luther drew from decadent Scholasticism. These negative elements, he

202 St. Augustine on Nature, Sex, and Marriage

says, were intended to buttress and support the positive doctrine, but they really have no necessary connection with it: "The Reformers no more invented their strange and despairing universe than they found it in Scripture. It is simply the universe of the theology they had been brought up in, scholasticism in its decadence.... The structure they raised on their own principles is inacceptable only because they used uncritically material drawn from that decaying Catholicism they desired to elude, but whose prisoners they remained to a degree they never suspected. No phrase reveals so clearly the hidden evil that was to spoil the fruit of the Reformation as Luther's saying that Occam was the only scholastic who was any good" (L. Bouyer, *The Spirit and Forms of Protestantism*, New York: Meridian Book, 1964, p. 153).

See also *Luther and Aquinas on Salvation*, by Stephen Pfurtner, O.P. (Sheed & Ward, 1965). Hans Kung also finds substantial agreement between Catholics and Protestants (*Justification: The Doctrine of Karl Barth with a Catholic Reflection*).

Bainton also writes: "The center about which all the petals clustered was the affirmation of the forgiveness of sins through the unmerited grace of God made possible by the cross of Christ, which reconciled wrath and mercy, routed the hosts of hell, triumphed over sin and death, and by the resurrection manifested that power which enables man to die to sin and rise to newness of life. This of course the theology of Paul heightened, intensified, and clarified. Beyond these cardinal tenets Luther was never to go" (*Here I Stand*, p. 51).

34. St. Augustine, *The Spirit and the Letter*, 5.
35. St. Augustine, *Man's Perfection in Righteousness*, 5.
36. St. Augustine, *City of God*, XIV, 1; XV, 1; XIV, 13.
37. St. Augustine, *Christian Doctrine*, I, 33.
38. Ibid., 22.
39. Ibid., 4.
40. Ibid.
41. St. Augustine, *On the Letters of St. John*, II, 11.
42. St. Augustine, *Confessions*, X, 29.
43. St. Francis de Sales, *Treatise on the Love of God*, XII, 3.
44. Étienne Gilson, "Foreword," *City of God*, Fathers of the Church series.
45. St. Augustine, *Christian Doctrine*, I, 22.
46. Ibid., 27.
47. Cf. Irving Stone, *The Nature of Love: Plato to Luther*, pp. 354ff.
48. St. Augustine, *Christian Doctrine*, I, 27.
49. Ibid., 23.
50. Ibid., 5.
51. St. Thomas Aquinas, *Summa theologiae*, II-II, 25, 1 ad 3.
52. St. Augustine, *Confessions*, X, 6.
53. B. Roland-Gosselin, "St. Augustine's System of Morals," in *St. Augustine: His Age, Life, and Thought*.
54. St. Augustine, *City of God*, XIV, 7.

55. F. Van der Meer, *Augustine the Bishop*, pp. 199ff.
56. St. Augustine, *On the Letters of St. John*, II, 12.
57. St. Augustine, *Confessions*, VII, 14.
58. St. Augustine, *City of God*, XV, 4; XI, 25; XIV, 9.
59. St. Augustine, *Against Julian*, IV, 3, 33.
60. St. Augustine, *On the Letters of St. John*, II, 12.
61. St. Augustine, *On Psalm 26*, II, 12.

CHAPTER 5
1. Throughout this chapter we shall speak of "sexual concupiscence" rather than of "lust." The latter term is ambiguous. It may refer, as shall be seen, simply to sexual concupiscence—not sinful in itself but the principle of sin. Or it may refer to the capital sin of lust. In the capital sin concupiscence has already been actualized. It is a definite disposition. As such it cannot itself bear actual guilt, but it nevertheless results from guilty actions. Since the word is used in both senses, we must carefully distinguish them.
   On the subject matter of this chapter, as well as of the preceding, see Hans Staffner, "St. Augustine on Original Sin," *Theology Digest*, vol. 9, no. 2 (spring 1961). William H. Van der Marck, O.P., *Toward a Christian Ethic*, pp. 94ff., also confirms Augustine's teaching on the results of original sin and relates it to current speculation on the subject.
2. St. Augustine, *Confessions*, VII, 5.
3. St. Augustine, *Holy Virginity*, 24.
4. St. Augustine, *Continence*, 3.
5. Ibid., 2.
6. St. Augustine, *Holy Virginity*, 8.
7. St. Augustine, *City of God*, XIV, 15.
8. Ibid., XII, 8.
9. St. Augustine, *Against Julian*, IV, 14.
10. St. Augustine, *Sermon 51*, 2.
11. St. Augustine, *On the Psalms*, L, 10, v. 7. In view of what has been said of Luther (Chapter 4, section 2), it is interesting to contrast Luther's understanding of this text with that of Augustine. One of Luther's hymns reads:

> In devil's dungeon chained I lay
> The pangs of death swept over me.
> My sin devoured me night and day
> In which my mother bore me.
> My anguish ever grew more rife
> I took no pleasure in my life
> And sin had made me crazy.
> —from R. H. Bainton, *Here I Stand*, p. 50

12. Louis Bouyer, *Seat of Wisdom*, p. 73.
13. Ibid., p. 55. Of the charge of Manichaeism made against Augustine, Stanislas de Lestapis, S.J., says, "This accusation errs by its

204   St. Augustine on Nature, Sex, and Marriage

excess and has its origin in bad feeling" (*Birth Regulation*, p. 75, note 5).
  14. St. Augustine, *Nature and Grace*, 60.
  15. St. Augustine, *The Nature of Good*, 36.
  16. See Chapter 4, section 3.
  17. St. Augustine, *On the Letters of St. John*, II, 12. See also Chapter 4, pp. 70–71.
  18. St. Augustine, *Continence*, 13.
  19. St. Augustine, *The Good of Marriage*, 16. See also Chapter 4, pp. 75, 77.
  20. St. Thomas Aquinas, *Summa theologiae*, I, 98, 2, c. He reconciles his view with Augustine's in the answer to the fourth objection, citing a passage in which the latter says, "How in the world, then, can anyone believe that, in a life so happy and with men so blessed [as in Eden], parenthood was impossible without the passion of lust? Surely, every member of the body was equally submissive to the mind and, surely, a man and his wife could play their active and passive roles in the drama of conception without the lecherous promptings of lust, with perfect serenity of soul and with no sense of disintegration between the body and soul. . . . So could connection and conception have occurred by a mutually deliberate union unhurried by the hunger of lust" (*City of God*, XIV, 26).
  21. St. Augustine, *City of God*, XIV; also, *Genesis, Literally Interpreted*, IX, 3.
  22. It might seem possible to distinguish concupiscence from desire by saying that while the latter, in its first involuntary movements, issues from nature itself, concupiscence belongs to the moral order. This would make it clear that human desires are not evil. But it would also lead to the totally unacceptable position that the disorder of concupiscence is actually evil: this, as we have seen, was the mistake of Luther, thus introducing into man as the result of original sin a definitely evil strain. But concupiscence does not belong to the moral order. It stands at the threshold of the moral order: a turmoil of desires, good in themselves in their first involuntary movements because issuing from a good nature, they need to be disciplined and regulated by the will. Only under this regulation do they obtain moral significance, leading to evil if they are not regulated in accord with the demands of reason and grace.
  23. St. Augustine, *Confessions*, II, 1.
  24. Ibid., III, 1.
  25. Ibid., II, 2.
  26. St. Augustine, *Against Julian*, IV, 14.
  27. St. Augustine, *Marriage and Concupiscence*, II, 25.
  28. Ibid., 29.
  29. Ibid., I, 8.
  30. C. S. Lewis, *The Allegory of Love*, p. 17. G. Egner (*Contraception vs. Tradition*, pp. 136ff) also suggests that that reason which Augustine would have control sexuality is a shrewd and calculating

reason. But what the saint in fact wants is control by reflective and contemplative reason—again, as he conceived it in man's original state. Is pleasure necessarily reduced because one's intelligence participates in it? Or is it not rather heightened? Perhaps even a non-Stoic would hope that reason might prevail over passion in other interpersonal activities, e.g., in interracial and international relations.

31. G. K. Chesterton, *St. Francis of Assisi*, pp. 31–33.

32. See especially Karl Stern, *The Third Revolution*; also Albert Gorres, *The Method and Experience of Psychoanalysis*; Victor White, O.P., *God and the Unconscious*; Francis Braceland, M.D., and Michael Stock, O.P., *Modern Psychiatry*.

Of course there are those who would modify or even deny the Freudian teaching. First of all the dissident psychoanalytic schools of Adler and Jung. (According to Adler, sexuality, which is central and basic in Freudianism, is but superficial and symptomatic of deeper forces.) There is also the conventional school of psychiatry, which would at least greatly reduce the Freudian claims. Then there are lay critics, such as Betty Friedan in *The Feminine Mystique*, who accuse the great liberator of sex of holding women in an inferior place by means of his theories. One recalls Harvey Wickham's book of many years ago, *The Impuritans*. Some of his criticisms, then dismissed as reactionary, are returning refreshed. A recent book (Stella Chess, Alexander Thomas, and Herbert Birch, *Your Child Is a Person*) attacks Freud in an area—infantile sexuality—in which he has hitherto been considered (although with some scandalized dissent) to have made one of his more important contributions.

Recently, Ignace Lepp made a running critique of Freud. For example: "Its greatest weakness [i.e., of the "Freudian general theory of sexuality"] lies in the fact that instead of being founded upon experience it interprets experience in the light of the exigencies of its own doctrinal postulates. Freudianism is also in error when it tries to study human sexuality without taking into account the intrinsic relationship which unites it to love: the psychic element in eroticism" (*The Psychology of Loving*, p. 87).

Nevertheless—and this is all that concerns us here—Freud has highlighted, probably once and for all, the sexual factor in human development.

33. J. Langdon-Davies, *Sex, Sin and Sanctity*, p. 300.

34. "Freudian psychoanalysis in trying to reduce love to a simple disguise of the sexual instinct, recognized in its own way the close overlapping of the two. But because of its false reductive method it cannot understand that the superior, far from being a simple disguise of the most primitive, can have its own reality which can transform the primitive to the point of making it unrecognizable" (Ignace Lepp, *The Authentic Morality*, p. 178).

35. Cf. Denis de Rougemont's books *The Devil's Share*, *Love in the Western World*, and *Love Declared*. Of course, De Rougemont has his

206   St. Augustine on Nature, Sex, and Marriage

critics. See, for example, John Updike, "More Love in the Western World," *The New Yorker* (Aug. 24, 1963); Irving Singer, "Strangelove," *The New York Review of Books* (Jan. 28, 1965); also, more extensively, John Langdon-Davies in *Sin, Sex and Sanctity*. Updike argues that some of the features of the myth, which De Rougemont traces to Catharism, can be explained by the pragmatic demands of the storyteller's art. Singer, while allowing something to De Rougemont's thesis, claims that it is vastly overstated. Langdon-Davies sees courtly love merely as a game, like chess, invented by bored courtiers. For Updike and Langdon-Davies the myth thus has no psychological or metaphysical roots, a conclusion difficult to accept. The alternative explanations given by these writers are plausible but scarcely demonstrated.

C. S. Lewis, in an early book on the subject, paralleling De Rougemont's, had treated the love-myth as a mere literary phenomenon. Later he had this to say: "Years ago when I wrote about medieval love-poetry and described its strange half make-believe, 'religion of love,' I was blind enough to treat this as an almost purely literary phenomenon. I know better now. Eros by his nature invites it. Of all loves he is, at his height, most god-like; therefore most prone to demand our worship. Of himself, he always tends to turn 'being in love' into a sort of religion" (*The Four Loves*, p. 154).

Yet even in the earlier work, *The Allegory of Love*, Lewis had noted the connection of the myth with Catharism. Incidentally, chapter 1 of that book provides a short history of romantic love.

Jean Guitton (*Great Heresies and Church Councils*, pp. 133ff) also connects the origin of courtly and romantic love with Catharism; as did Walter Pater, *The Renaissance*, chap. 1.

J. Langdon-Davies, while disputing De Rougemont's view, goes at least as far as the latter, and much farther than Augustine, in emphasizing the importance of sexuality in human life and even in the history of civilization. He interprets St. Paul's letter to the Romans, chapter 7, as referring radically and even exclusively to the tensions caused by sexuality. We have placed a text from this Pauline passage at the head of the present chapter without implying any such interpretation. The Pauline teaching, like that of St. Augustine after him, refers to concupiscence in general, although of course including sexual concupiscence.

36. St. Thomas Aquinas, *Summa theologiae*, II-II, 118, 2.

37. Dietrich von Hildebrand, *In Defense of Purity*, p. 17.

38. Bouyer, *Seat of Wisdom*, p. 89.

39. Mircea Eliade, *Patterns in Comparative Religion*, p. 405 (emphasis added).

40. Harvey Cox (*The Secular City*, chap. 9) speaks of the cultic and "tribal" meaning in our society of the Girl as goddess (and of her opposite number, the Playboy). However, his solution seems still to reflect the confusion of our age and its loss of anchorage. Pitirim Sorokin reviews the development—or retrogression—of sexual mor-

als in America in *The American Sex Revolution* (1956). There has been, of course, even further "progress" since he wrote.

CHAPTER 6

1. The plight of the individual Christian in those pagan times is strikingly described by Newman in *Callista*:

"And yet, as Agellius ascended the long flight of marble steps which led the foot-passenger up into that fair city, while the morning sun was glancing across them, and surveyed the outline of the many sumptuous buildings which crested and encircled the hill, did he not know full well that iniquity was written on its very walls, and spoke a solemn warning to a Christian heart to go out of it, to flee it, not to take up a home in it, not to make alliance with any in it? Did he not know from experience full well that, when he got into it, his glance could no longer be unrestrained, or his air free; but that it would be necessary for him to keep a control upon his senses, and painfully guard himself against what must either be a terror to him and an abhorrence, or a temptation? Enter in imagination into a town like Sicca, and you will understand the great Apostle's anguish at seeing a noble and beautiful city given up to idolatry. Enter it, and you will understand why it was that the poor priest of whom Jucundus spoke so bitterly hung his head, and walked with timid eyes and clouded brow through the joyous streets of Carthage. Hitherto we have only been conducting heathens through it, boys or men, Jucundus, Arnobius, and Firmian; but now a Christian enters it with a Christian's heart and a Christian's hopes" (chap. 10).

The description goes on at length.

2. M. D. Chenu, O.P., "Pour Lire Saint Augustine," in *La Vie Spirituelle* (1930), p. 52.

3. Vatican Council II, *Gaudium et Spes* (Pastoral Constitution on the Church in the Modern World), no. 48, no. 1.

4. St. Augustine, *Adulterous Marriages*, I, 25.

5. The remark is Louis Dupré's. See Chapter 4, note 27, above.

6. St. Augustine, *Marriage and Concupiscence*, I, 19. See also Chapter 4, p. 73, and Chapter 5, pp. 94, 98–99.

7. St. Augustine, *The Grace of Christ and Original Sin*, II, 45.

8. *Life* magazine, vol. 58, no. 16.

9. St. Augustine, *Adulterous Marriages*, II, 12; *Marriage and Concupiscence*, I, 15–17; *The Good of Marriage*, 6.

"The wish to beget children," or "intercourse for the purpose of procreation," does not mean that there must be an explicit or actual intention (which would seldom be present). It means only using the marital act naturally, according to the *finis operis*. Such an intention is presumed present unless otherwise declared. For this reason we speak of the act as being open to procreation.

10. St. Thomas writes: "If the motive for the marriage act be a virtue, whether of justice that they may render the debt, or of religion that they may beget children for the worship of God, it is

meritorious. If the motive be lust, yet not excluding the marriage blessings, namely that he would not be willing to go to another woman, it is a venial sin" (*Summa theologiae*, suppl. 41, 4).

St. Thomas may seem to open up the Augustinian teaching a little when he says that the marriage act may be carried out from "justice that they may render the debt." Does he mean that intercourse need not be referred to procreation? That faithful love—*fides*—is sufficient to justify it? He immediately adds that if the motive is lust, there is venial sin; and the sin is venial only if the marriage blessings (including procreation) are not excluded. In this the difference between Augustine and Thomas is like that between Tweedledum and Tweedledee.

Louis Bouyer remarks truly, "For this reason St. Thomas himself, in considering man as he is, is not very much more optimistic than St. Augustine about the possibility now of a sexuality that could function independently of sinfulness" (*Seat of Wisdom*, p. 74).

11. St. Augustine, *On the Grace of Christ and Original Sin*, II, 43; *Marriage and Concupiscence*, I, 16.

12. Fernand Prat, S.J. (*The Theology of St. Paul*, p. 108, and note), has given currency to an interpretation of this text that Père Allo, O.P., the most exhaustive of modern Pauline exegetes, and one of the best, calls "the least probable of all the hypotheses thus far advanced to explain Τουτο ["this"], restricting the reference as it does to a secondary detail like resuming relations in marriage": *Premièr Epître aux Corinthians*, 2d ed. (Paris, 1956), p. 159.

Prat contends that "This"—i.e., the "concession" granted by St. Paul—refers to verse 5, "and more particularly to the last clause which seemed to contain a command" (namely: "and return together again lest Satan tempt you because you lack self-control"). It is this clause that Allo calls a "secondary detail." Why indeed is a "concession" needed to resume marital relations when St. Paul has given but a cautious permission to the married to separate by consent and for a time "that you may give yourselves to prayer"?

Other exegetes refer "This"—i.e., the "concession"—to verse 2: "Yet for fear of fornication let each man have his own wife, and let each woman have her own husband." Prat says, however, that "This" cannot refer to verse 2, for the remarkable reason that it is too far off, "nor to verses 3 and 4, which deal with a duty and a debt." His reason is wholly inadequate; it would outlaw interpreting a text from its context. And it is precisely verse 2 that fixes the context for the whole passage. Paul would have all men as himself, continent; but since this is not possible, requiring a special gift, he *concedes* that they may marry since it is better to marry than to burn with concupiscence and fall into sin. Verses 3 and 4 merely extend and explain this idea as a sort of parenthesis. The concession thus refers to Paul's permission to the incontinent to marry. "The married state is for the Apostle merely a matter of advice, to which he wishes to oblige no one" (Claude J. Peifer, O.S.B., "First

Corinthians," *New Testament Reading Guide*, Liturgical Press, 1960, p. 26).

Again, "What has been said above [in the Pauline text] *about monogamous marriage* is 'by way of concession, not by way of commandment'" (Jean Continat, C.M., *The Epistles of St. Paul*, p. 55).

That this is indeed the meaning is shown further by the fact that the Apostle, immediately after giving the concession, returns to desirability of continence: "But this I say by way of concession, not by way of commandment. *For I would that you all were as I am myself....*"

Prat says that it is "incredible that St. Paul would advise one evil to avoid a greater evil, and he gives in advance absolution for all the venial sins his advice would cause." On the contrary, it is commonly considered good pastoral practice to permit a lesser evil to avoid a greater. Indeed, St. Paul himself is here speaking on the basis of this principle. He would have all men continent, but concedes that the incontinent should marry. Not that he regards marriage as evil (although it falls short of the perfect); but incontinence is evil, and the excesses of incontinence in marriage are understandable and pardonable, whereas outside of marriage they lead to serious sin. Similarly the faults that Augustine is pardoning are like those common in everyday life, e.g., exaggeration in speech, a slight excess in eating, drinking, or sleeping, talking a little too much.

The squabble over whether St. Paul means "pardon" or "concession" seems thus pretty much a tempest in a semantic teapot. The Apostle is here conceding—compassionately—something that he considers less than perfect, namely, marriage and the legitimate use of marriage by the *incontinent*. What difference does it make if he says, "I grant, I suggest [the Jerusalem Bible], I concede, that you may do this"—or "I pardon you for doing this"?

If St. Augustine's understanding of the Pauline concession was a little too narrow, it is nevertheless closer to the mark than that of his modern critics. He certainly does not, as Noonan says (*Contraception*, p. 130), "turn St. Paul against himself." But it is hard for the modern to take seriously St. Paul's clear preference for continence.

13. St. Augustine, *Sermon* 51, 22. "Married love is too often profaned by excessive self-love, the worship of pleasure, and illicit practices against human generation" (Vatican Council II, *Gaudium et Spes*, no. 47).

14. St. Augustine, *The Good of Marriage*, 9.

15. Ibid., 1.

16. St. Augustine, *City of God*, XIV, 22.

17. In recent discussions great stress is laid on the fact that not every act of coitus is procreative, as if this proves that sexuality is not inherently and objectively procreative and can thus be detached from the procreative good by contraception. But this is scarcely a finding of modern biology. St. Augustine was presumably aware of it:

he lived with one woman for twelve years at a time when, by his own confession, he was itchy with lust; yet he had only one child. In this connection, Thomas L. Hayes proves the opposite of what he sets out to prove. Pointing out that not every act of sexual coitus is procreative, he goes on to define the reproductive act as "the relationship between man and woman lasting for about one month, during which time the female produces one ovum, which finds its way to a spot suitable for combination with the sperm. The male sperm cells are delivered to this spot many times (acts of sexual intercourse), spaced at random during the reproductive act" ("The Biology of the Reproductive Act," *Cross Currents*, vol. 15, no. 4, p. 397).

So defined, it seems clear that the reproductive act is indeed reproductive and that sexuality is essentially procreative. Thus the revisionists bear reluctant testimony to the "elementary fact" that "marriage and conjugal love are by their nature ordained toward the begetting and educating of children."

18. "But he who exceeds the limits which this rule prescribes for the fulfillment of this end of marriage acts contrary to the very contract by which he took his wife. The contract is read, read in the presence of all attesting witnesses; and an express clause is there that they marry 'for the procreation of children'; and this is called the marriage contract [*tabulae matrimoniales*]" (*Sermon* 51, 22).

19. Augustine does not mention contraception in *The Good of Marriage*. He condemns it in *Marriage and Concupiscence*, I, 15. Here, however, we are less concerned with contraception than with concupiscence, which in the saint's thought drives one to the extreme of contraception but is also active to produce venial sin even when there is no intent to *exclude* procreation.

20. *Contraception and Holiness* provides many variations of this argument. See especially Kiernan Conley, O.S.B., "Procreation and the Person." See also note 14, above.

21. Inge Hegeler and Sten Hegeler, *An ABZ of Love*, p. 250. See also entries under analcoitus, cunnilingus, fellatio, homosexual, masturbation.

Even Protestantism can no longer offer a clear witness on sexual morality. "Thou shalt not exploit another person sexually." This, in effect, is the imperative that should determine the moral legitimacy of sexual intercourse, in marriage or out, says a report on "Sex and Morality" published by a committee of the British Council of Churches (*Time* magazine, Oct. 28, 1966). "Even should the report not receive a general endorsement from [the British Council of Churches], many Protestants are faced with the fact that they no longer have a clear position on the morality of premarital and extramarital intercourse" (*America*, Oct. 29, 1966). Vatican Council II has since rejected the controversial parts of the report.

22. *Gaudium et Spes*, no. 48.
23. Ibid., nos. 49, 51.
24. St. Thomas Aquinas, *Summa theologiae*, I-II, 63, 4 ad 2.

Notes 211

25. St. Augustine, *Enchiridion of Faith, Hope, and Charity*, 64.
26. St. Thomas Aquinas, *Summa theologiae*, II-II, 24, 10.
27. R. Garrigou-Lagrange, *Christian Perfection and Contemplation*, p. 430.
28. James C. Osbourne, *The Morality of Imperfections*, p. 208.
29. Our concern here is rather with the force that causes disorder—concupiscence—rather than with the nature of the disorder itself. Augustine's thoughts on the nature of the disorder may be summarized as follows: to perform an action for pleasure merely, rather than for the purpose which nature intended it to serve, is always unreasonable and therefore always wrong. Of course nature intends pleasure also, but not as an end. What therefore makes such an action wrong is the subordination of the substantive to the accessory, the inversion of nature's intention, the willing of an act while failing to will its natural effect. Fornication and adultery are radical perversions of the sexual act outside of marriage; contraception is a radical perversion within marriage. But for spouses who merely fail to will the natural purpose, without preventing it, the deflection from reason is not radical, is therefore less unreasonable (and wrong) than contraception, and does not thereby in fact exceed venial sin. Moreover, while we commonly say that the disorder of such actions arises from excess of passion, it actually results from a defect of the reasonable and right intention.

St. Augustine argues from the law of nature, but still within the order of revelation and grace. Revelation tells us the reason for that concupiscence which hinders obedience even to nature's laws, while grace enables us to overcome this obstacle in order that nature may be restored and renewed in Christ. While Augustine invariably looks at man in the context of the divine economy, which is fulfilled in the supernatural order of grace, he does not thereby attempt to exempt man from the exigencies of nature. The only way we can get free of the natural law, he says, is to step out of our nature. "Plainly they [the Hebrews] were men: they could have been without the law of nature if they could have been outside nature: *sine lege autem naturali essent, si praeter naturam humani generis esse potuissent*" (*On the Psalms*, 118, 4).

30. Dietrich von Hildebrand, *In Defense of Purity*, p. 70. Other writers known for emphasizing the value of conjugal love say substantially the same thing. For example: Ignace Lepp, *The Authentic Morality*, chaps. 23–24; *The Psychology of Loving*, chap. 8. Marc Oraison, *Man and Wife*, chap. 2. Herbert Doms, *The Meaning of Marriage*, chaps. 6–7.

Robert Adolfs, who allows that contraception may be "moral" if inspired by love, states: "[The sexual act] can be immoral when it results not from genuine love but rather from self-gratification" (*The Church Is Different*, p. 95). Although this seems to be a liberalizing of the Church's received position, it is scarcely less strict: it would certainly outlaw mere sensuality and the pandering to concupiscence.

212   St. Augustine on Nature, Sex, and Marriage

Only, since man's powers of self-delusion are almost infinite, sensuality might easily be mistaken for love. Indeed, Augustine himself agrees that love is the norm, but he would not admit that there is genuine love when a couple limit it to themselves, refusing to share it creatively with children. It is this willingness to share love, which of itself is diffusive, that provides an objective guarantee of the genuineness of love. Contraception, abortion, and infanticide, he believes, cannot issue from love.
   31. St. Augustine, *Against Julian*, V, 9.
   32. Vatican Council II, *Gaudium et Spes*, no. 49.
   33. Ibid., no. 13.
   34. See *Contraception and Holiness*, pp. 50, 75, 68, 341, 345, and passim. The charge of biologism against the Church's teaching is often made obliquely, i.e., we are told that the new and needed concept of marriage should not be merely biological, implying that the Church's position has been one of biologism: "If a marriage is truly lived according to the principle of responsible parenthood, therefore, must it be *forever* sublimated to the simple physiology of procreative function?" The contributors to this symposium rarely deem it necessary to provide evidence or documentation, it appears.
   On the other hand, one of the contributors criticizes the Church for being too "spiritual" in its outlook by overemphasizing the part of the will at the expense of sexuality in marriage (p. 280).
   Speaking of the Council's decree on marriage, Father Gregory Baum writes, "There is an attempt to avoid all that smacks of biologism" (*Commonweal*, vol. 83, no. 12, p. 369). This is true; what is untrue is the implication that the Church's stand has in the past smacked of biologism. Moreover, on Father Baum's own premise, i.e., that emphasis on procreation is "biologism," what he says here of the Council is not true; for, as we have seen, the Council places great emphasis on procreation as the fruit of conjugal love.
   35. St. Thomas Aquinas, *Summa theologiae*, suppl. 49, 4 ad 3.
   36. Anne C. Biezanek's book *All Things New*, otherwise the sad record of a mind in disintegration, at least offers some interesting testimony on this point. Suffering apparently from misandry, she sees contraception as the only possible defense of women against the unreasonable sexual demands of their husbands. "There is no natural and automatic resulting limitation upon her husband's sexual drive. With this she is well and truly walled up. There is no corresponding social pressure put upon her husband to put this drive under control" (p. 102). How this uncontrolled male sexual drive may work is also indicated: "His conscious waking mind might tell him that tonight, anyway, there should be no sex. But in the early hours of the morning the effects of sleep and feminine proximity are felt. Erection is what begins to happen. Intercourse with withdrawal at the moment of emission seems to be the obvious solution, and like as not, is what in fact occurs" (p. 104).
   For Mrs. Biezanek, the answer, a woman's only defense, is contra-

ception. But the Church wants the act initiating intercourse to be a human act, that is, rationally controlled. Can a moral teacher ask less? And can the Church of Christ fail to ask further that this human act be informed by grace? Failure to do so would indeed be "biologism." Mrs. Biezanek's complaint may throw some light on why so many replies given by the Holy See on marriage problems have been on behalf of women. Many wives have apparently found difficulty in preserving their moral and spiritual integrity against the unreasoning demands of husbands who in pursuit of a "satisfactory sex life" are unwilling to accept either the exigencies of love, the rhythms of nature, or the limitations of creaturehood.

37. St. Augustine, *Genesis, Literally Interpreted*, IX, 7 (quoted by Pius XI in *Casti Connubii*).

38. See notes 17 and 34, above; also "The Lessons of Biology" in *Contraception and Holiness*.

39. St. Augustine, *The Good of Marriage*, 9. It is hard to reconcile this teaching with Derrick Sherwin Bailey's contention that Jeremy Taylor's statement, in the 17th century, that coitus may be engaged in "to endear each other" was "probably the first express recognition in the theological literature of what may be termed the relational purpose of coitus" (*Sexual Relations in Christian Thought*, p. 208).

John T. Noonan also omits mention of this text, while denying that Augustine ever related marital intercourse to love. He then undertakes a tortuous theological investigation to discover as a modern "development" what was already in St. Augustine (*Contraception*, pp. 126ff).

G. Egner likewise omits mention of this passage and denies that there is any such teaching in Augustine, thus neutralizing his analysis also (*Contraception vs. Tradition*, pp. 145ff).

40. St. Augustine, *The Good of Marriage*, 3, 7. "Therefore, marriage persists as a whole manner and communion of life, and maintains its value and indissolubility even when despite the often intense desire of the couple, offspring are lacking" (*Gaudium et Spes*, no. 50).

41. For a discussion of how Augustine thought of the marriage-sacrament, see E. Schillebeeckx, O.P., *Marriage: Human Reality and Saving Mystery*, p. 283. A summary of the various meanings of *sacrament* Augustine applied to marriage is given in the Introduction to *The Good of Marriage*, Fathers of the Church series.

42. St. Augustine, *Marriage and Concupiscence*, I, 17.

43. *Gaudium et Spes*, no. 51.

44. All these citations are from *Gaudium et Spes*, nos. 47–51.

45. St. Augustine, *Genesis, Literally Interpreted*, IX, 7. "This good is threefold [*tripartitum*]: faith, offspring, sacrament."

46. *Gaudium et Spes*, no. 48.

47. Ibid.

48. Ibid.

49. St. Thomas Aquinas, *Summa theologiae*, suppl. 49 ad 1.

50. St. Thomas Aquinas, *Summa theologiae*, II-II, 25, 25, 3, c.

214   St. Augustine on Nature, Sex, and Marriage

51. St. Thomas Aquinas, *Summa theologiae*, suppl. 49, 3. The saint completes this statement by observing that, if we consider the goods of children and mutual faith, not in their realization, but in principle—that is, in the intention of those who marry—these goods are the more essential. Without the intention to seek such goods there would be no marriage to be indissoluble.

52. St. Augustine, *The Good of Marriage*, 19; *Holy Virginity*, 12; *The Excellence of Widowhood*, 14.

53. H. J. Denzinger, *Echiridion Symbolorum*, ed. A. Schönmetzer, 32d ed. (1953), 3707.

54. "The traditional teaching, whether expressed in the doctrine of the *bona matrimonii* or the later formula of the primary and secondary ends of marriage, has always been that no one of the essential values or ends of marriage may be deliberately excluded from the physical expression of conjugal union. The *bona matrimonii* doctrine explicitly avers that both openness to procreation and oneness in fidelity of love for one another in Christ, are equally required for virtuous and holy sexual union" (Cahal B. Daly, *Natural Law Morality Today*, p. 22).

G. Egner also acknowledges that the distinction of ends is "wholly alien to Augustine's thought" (*Contraception vs. Tradition*, p. 149).

55. *Gaudium et Spes*, no. 50. Scholars point out that the texts of Genesis 1 and 2 originate in different traditions, and that the second is older than the first (already bringing up the question of priority.) But both teachings have been united in the canonical Scripture and complete each other in one tradition. "Yet despite the difference in approach, emphasis, and hence also in authorship, the fact remains that the subject matter is ultimately the same in both versions" (The Anchor Bible, p. 19).

CHAPTER 7

1. Vatican Council II, *Gaudium et Spes* (Pastoral Constitution on the Church in the Modern World), no. 8.
2. St. Augustine, *The Good of Marriage*, III, 7. See also above, p. 129.
3. *Gaudium et Spes*, no. 49. Also: "This love is uniquely expressed and perfected through the appropriate enterprise of matrimony. The actions within marriage by which the couple are united intimately and chastely are noble ones. Expressed in a manner which is truly human, these actions promote that mutual self-giving by which spouses enrich each other with a joyful and ready will."
4. Ibid.
5. Ibid., no. 12.
6. St. Augustine, *The Good of Marriage*, I.
7. St. Augustine, *True Religion*, XVI, 30.
8. St. Augustine, *Marriage and Concupiscence*, I, 12.
9. Eugène Portalié, *A Guide to the Thought of St. Augustine*, pp. 174–176.

10. John Burnaby, *Amor Dei*, p. 113, note 3. Of Julian it has well been said that he lived fourteen hundred years before his time. Rationalist, humanist, and, although a bishop, refusing to accept the consequences of original sin, he would no doubt have found himself at home in the Enlightenment. Augustine, also a lover of the humanities, had to assume the difficult and unenviable task of demonstrating against this suave humanist the evil effects of original sin. As Julian goes on endlessly to affirm the goodness of nature, Augustine follows him step by step, affirming it also, not by way of forced concession, but by conviction; yet constantly reminding Julian that this is not the issue between them. Augustine wrote two books against Julian, the second being still incomplete at his death. In the end Julian lost his aplomb and resorted to personal attack both on Augustine and Monica.

11. *Sermon* 159, 2. The passage is as follows: "Justice ought to be loved, and in this lovable justice there are degrees of progress. The first degree is that nothing that delights should be preferred to the love of justice. This is the first step. What is it that I have said? That among all things that delight, justice itself should delight you most. For certain things naturally please our weakness, as food and drink please those who are hungry and thirsty, as the light that pours from the sky pleases us at sunrise and the light which beams from moon and stars or shines on earth from lamps enlightening the darkness of our eyes. A melodious voice and sweet song or good odor delight us. Even our touch and whatever pertains to some pleasure of the flesh are lawful. For as I said those great spectacles of nature please our eyes, but so also do the spectacles of the theatres. The former are lawful, the latter are unlawful. A sacred psalm when sweetly sung pleases our hearing, but the songs of actors also please us when we listen to them. The former is heard lawfully, the latter are heard unlawfully. Flowers and aromatics delight our sense of smell, and they are creatures of God; incense on the altars of demons delights us, too. It is lawful to smell the former, unlawful to smell the latter. Food that is not forbidden pleases our sense of taste, as also the feasts of unholy sacrifices. The one is eaten lawfully, the other, unlawfully. The conjugal embrace as well as the embrace of prostitutes gives pleasure. The first is a lawful pleasure, the second, unlawful. You see, therefore, beloved, there are licit and illicit pleasures in these bodily senses of ours. Let justice so delight you that it may surpass even lawful pleasures, and prefer justice to the pleasure you lawfully enjoy."

12. See Chapter 6, pp. 128–129.
13. St. Augustine, *The Gift of Perseverance*, 33.
14. St. Augustine, *On the Forgiveness of Sin and Baptism*, II, 26.
15. St. Augustine, *Sermon* 156, II.
16. St. Augustine, *On the Letters of St. John*, VII, 9.
17. See St. Augustine, *True Religion*, 17–18; *On Christian Doctrine*, 26–29; also the ten homilies *On the Letters of St. John*, which deal almost exclusively with this theme.

St. Thomas, distinguishing the virtues from the Gifts, shows that the former accommodate themselves to our human mode of acting, while the latter provide a "superhuman" mode of responding to the Holy Spirit (*Summa theologiae*, I-II, 68, 1, c).
18. St. Augustine, *On the Letters of St. John*, VII, 8.
19. St. Augustine, *The Lord's Sermon on the Mount*, II, 2, 3, 13.
20. This emphasis on the intention formed by love has always marked the spiritual masters of the Church. It was lost from the technical theology of the manuals through preoccupation with minimal morality and the minimal requirements for supernaturally meritorious action. "These things ought to have been done, those ought not to have been left undone."

Louis Bouyer offers an explanation of how in theology subsequent to Augustine, a minimal practice of Christianity came to be separated from the Christian vocation to holiness: "Pourrat, in the first of his four volumes on Christian Spirituality, distinguishes 'spirituality' or 'spiritual theology' not only from 'dogmatic theology which teaches what must be believed,' but also from moral theology which, according to him, teaches only 'what must be done or avoided so as not to sin mortally or venially.' 'Spirituality,' on the contrary, includes 'ascetic theology' which has 'as its object the exercises to which every Christian who aspires to perfection must devote himself,' together with 'mystical theology' which is concerned with 'extraordinary states . . . such as the mystical union and its secondary manifestations. . . .'

"These distinctions, it must be admitted, are not very satisfactory. Is it possible to define Christian morality by a merely negative idea: to 'avoid sin'? Is aiming at perfection a matter of choice for the Christian? Furthermore, is the mystical life to be reduced to the 'extraordinary'? Once we are aware of these objections, what remains of classifications that ignore them?' (*The Spirituality of the New Testament and the Fathers*, Preface, p. vii).
21. St. Augustine, *On the Letters of St. John*, VII, 6; X, 7.
22. St. Augustine, *City of God*, XV, 22.
23. St. Augustine, *On the Letters of St. John*, VIII, I.
24. St. Augustine, *Homily on the Gospel of St. John*, 82, 3.
25. St. Augustine, *On the Letters of St. John*, VI, 3.
26. St. Augustine, *City of God*, X, 3.
27. Ibid.
28. *Gaudium et Spes*, no. 51.
29. St. Augustine, *On the Letters of St. John*, VIII, I.
30. St. Augustine, *Marriage and Concupiscence*, II, 9.
31. St. Augustine, *The Good of Marriage*, 6.
32. *Gaudium et Spes*, no. 40.
33. Ibid., no. 13.
34. Ibid., no. 49.
35. *Lumen Gentium* (Dogmatic Constitution on the Church), no. 11.

36. Ibid., no. 41.
37. St. Augustine, *On the Letters of St. John*, VIII, 13.
38. St. Augustine, *Nature and Grace*, 84.
39. *Gaudium et Spes*, no. 49.
40. See Chapter 4, section 3.
41. Among the ancient pagans, C. S. Lewis maintains, erotic love was known only to be ridiculed as a weakness (*The Allegory of Love*, pp. 6ff). Of St. Thomas, this author says: "About passion in this [erotic] sense Thomas Aquinas has naturally nothing to say—as he has nothing to say about the steam engine. He had not heard of it. It was only coming into existence in his time, and finding its first expression in the poetry of courtly love" (ibid., p. 17).
The same would be true, *a fortiori*, of St. Augustine. Nevertheless, both St. Augustine and St. Thomas knew of love as friendship between two equal human persons. This is the point of view of primary interest to Catholic theology. "Firmly established in the Lord, the unity of marriage will radiate from the equal personal dignity of wife and husband, a dignity acknowledged by mutual and total love" (*Gaudium et Spes*, no. 49).
42. St. Augustine, *Confessions*, IX, 9.
43. Ibid.
44. F. Van der Meer, *Augustine the Bishop*, p. 193.
45. St. Augustine, *Sermon* 232, 2.
46. St. Augustine, *The Trinity*, XII, 7.
47. Ibid., 6. Herbert Doms, following Scheeben, seeks also to trace the analogy of the Trinity in the married couple apart from the child (*The Meaning of Marriage*, p. 16, and note 55).
48. Simone de Beauvoir, *The Second Sex*; Betty Friedan, *The Feminine Mystique*.
49. St. Augustine, *City of God*, XXII, 17.
50. St. Augustine, *Divine Providence and the Problem of Evil*, I, ii.
51. St. Augustine, *The Happy Life*, 2, 10.
52. St. Augustine, *Confessions*, IX, 10.

CHAPTER 8
1. For a study of the unity that resolves the tension between marriage and celibacy, see E. Schillebeeckx, O.P., *Marriage: Human Reality and Saving Mystery*, pp. 119ff. "Here Paul's significant contribution to dogma is to show that it was no longer possible, within the Christian order of salvation, to define marriage perfectly without at the same time calling upon total abstinence for the sake of the Kingdom of God as a correlative possibility. . . . Christian celibacy does not decline in value and ultimately disappear as marriage becomes more and more appreciated at its true worth. The very opposite is in fact true: the greater the decline in Christian celibacy, the less Christian marriage is valued" (ibid., pp. 131, 140).
For the similar views of a married layman on the relationship of

marriage and virginity, see J. Gosling, *Marriage and the Love of God*, pp. 135ff.

2. E. Schillebeeckx, *Marriage: Human Reality and Saving Mystery*, pp. 122–123: "It is thus a question of being intimately and personally tied to the Lord in apostolic service to the church, for which everything is left behind."

3. Vatican Council II, *Gaudium et Spes* (Pastoral Constitution on the Church in the Modern World), nos. 43, 44.

4. Vatican Council II, *Perfectae Caritatis* (Decree on the Appropriate Renewal of the Religious Life), no. 12.

5. *Gaudium et Spes*, no. 44. "It can aptly be said: 'The best thing that one can do with the best of things is to sacrifice it,' on condition, however, that we safeguard the hierarchy of the gifts of God and of the virtues, and that we do not sacrifice something superior to what is inferior" (R. Garrigou-Lagrange, O.P., *Christian Perfection and Contemplation*, p. 132, note 11).

And St. John of the Cross: "And, since it is true that God is exalted by the fixing of the soul's rejoicing upon detachment from all things, He is much more highly exalted when the soul withdraws itself from the most wondrous of these things in order to fix its rejoicing on Him alone.... For, the more and the greater things a man despises for the sake of another, the more does he esteem and exalt the other" (*The Ascent of Mt. Carmel*, III, 32, 2). Although this is said in a particular context, it obviously is intended as a principle of general application.

6. "It is clear that, unlike the Synoptists, Paul generalized from the idea of total abstinence, and even saw it as a positive possibility for married Christians.... Anyone who denies that Paul, deeply concerned as he was for the Kingdom of God, did not regard a life of complete abstinence as the ideal state is bound to do violence to these texts" (Schillebeeckx, *Marriage: Human Reality and Saving Mystery*, pp. 128, 130).

7. St. Augustine, *Marriage and Concupiscence*, I, 3.

8. St. Augustine, *Adulterous Marriages*, I, 2, 3, 4.

9. Albert Camus, *Notebooks: 1942–1951*, p. 36.

10. Vatican Council II, *Gaudium et Spes*, no. 41.

11. Ibid., no. 39.

12. *Lumen Gentium* (Dogmatic Constitution on the Church), no. 46.

13. Ibid., no. 44.

14. *Gaudium et Spes*, no. 13.

15. Ibid., no. 21.

16. "Therefore continence would not have been praiseworthy in the state of innocence, whereas it is praiseworthy in our present state, not because it removes fecundity, but because it excludes inordinate desire. In that state fecundity would have been without lust" (St. Thomas, *Summa theologiae*, I, 98, 2, ad 3).

17. See Cahal B. Daly, *Natural Law Morality Today*, p. 25, for

criticism of this alleged predominance of celibate theologians in Catholic marriage theology. See also ibid., note 1.

18. See Ernest Cassirer, *Rousseau, Kant, and Goethe,* pp. 13ff, for a dissenting voice from what he nevertheless calls the "traditional view" of Rousseau's teaching.

19. Louis Bouyer, *Seat of Wisdom,* p. 72—an observation that perhaps points up a certain inconsistency in Bouyer's criticism of Augustine (see Chapter 5). Father Bouyer's own admirable spirituality has, in fact, a pungent Augustinian flavor.

20. S. C. Callahan, *The Illusion of Eve,* p. 104. To be sure, such a remark is not to be compared with the utterly irresponsible statement of Canon F. H. Drinkwater: "But 'concupiscence' remains a grand bogey-word for orotund missioners to roll around their tongues and terrify adolescents with" (*The Catholic Worker,* vol. 32, no. 6, February 1966, p. 8).

21. *Gaudium et Spes,* no. 40.
22. St. Augustine, *Nature and Grace,* 21.
23. Étienne Gilson, *The Christian Philosophy of St. Augustine,* p. 143.
24. John Henry Newman, "Abraham and Lot," *Parochial and Plain Sermons,* vol. 3, sermon 1.
25. *Gaudium et Spes,* no. 37.
26. Ignace Lepp, *The Psychology of Loving,* p. 156.
27. *Gaudium et Spes,* no. 49.
28. Inge Hegeler and Sten Hegeler, *An ABZ of Love,* p. 194.
29. F. J. Sheed, "Marriage and the Family," in *Society and Sanity,* pp. 8, 18.
30. *Gaudium et Spes,* no. 48.
31. Romano Guardini, *The Conversion of St. Augustine,* p. 175.
32. St. Augustine, *Homily on the Gospel of St. John,* 65, I.
33. *The Nation* 134 (Jan. 27, 1932), 102.
34. St. John of the Cross, *Ascent of Mt. Carmel,* book 3, chap. 32, no. 2.
35. His renunciation included what might not seem great in a saintly pastor but is almost unimaginable in anyone else: "Augustine was a servant of servants, if ever man was. Even as an author he was ready to descend to the level of the uneducated. For them he did something that surely no other man of his literary stature has ever done; he completely denied his own style" (Van der Meer, *Augustine the Bishop,* p. 258).
36. Louis Bouyer, *Seat of Wisdom,* p. 55.
37. Vernon J. Bourke, *Augustine's Quest for Wisdom,* p. 68.
38. F. Van der Meer, *Augustine the Bishop,* 216.
39. St. Augustine, *Soliloquies,* 17.
40. C. S. Lewis, *Miracles: A Preliminary Study,* p. 165.
41. St. Augustine, *Confessions,* VI, 15.
42. Ibid., 46.
43. Ibid., 12.

220   St. Augustine on Nature, Sex, and Marriage

44. Ibid., 13.
45. St. Augustine, *Holy Virginity*, 35.
46. Ibid., 21.
47. Ibid., 45, 47.
48. St. Augustine, *Confessions*, X, 6.
49. St. Augustine, *Holy Virginity*, 27.
50. St. Augustine, *Confessions*, X, 17.
51. Guardini, *Conversion of St. Augustine*, p. 302.
52. St. Augustine, *Confessions*, I, 1. We have noticed that the Fathers of Vatican II made these words of Augustine their own. Moreover, despite the demand by "progressives" today to "dehellenize" Christian teaching, it is interesting to note that the first part of that very progressive work, the *Dutch Catechism*, is but a commentary on the Platonic eros as Christianized by Augustine, reaching its climax (of course) in these words of Augustine.
53. *Gaudium et Spes*, no. 19.
54. Ibid., nos. 10, 13.
55. John L. Thomas, S.J., "What Did the Council Say on Contraception?" *America* (Feb. 26, 1966), p. 296.

Life and Works of St. Augustine

In this schematized treatment, only those works referred to in the study have been mentioned. Excellent bibliographies and "suggested dates" can be found in Hugh Pope's *St. Augustine of Hippo* and in Étienne Gilson's *Introduction to the Study of St. Augustine*.

LIFE

	354	Born in Tagaste
	370	Studied in Carthage
	372–382	Manichaean period
	380	Went to Rome; taught rhetoric
Platonic period	386	Retreat at Cassiciacum; Conversion
	387	Baptized in Milan; Returned to Rome; Monica dies at Ostia
Manichaean polemic		
	388	Returned to Tagaste
Donatist polemic	391	Ordained at Hippo
	395	Consecrated Bishop of Hippo
	400	
Pelagian polemic	405	
	412	
	430	Death of Augustine

WORKS

386	*Against the Academics*
386	*The Happy Life*
386	*Divine Providence and the Problem of Evil*
387	*Soliloquies*
388–389	*Morals of the Manichees*
388–389	*Morals of the Catholic Church*
388–395	*The Problem of Free Choice*
389	*On Genesis, Against the Manichees*

389	The Teacher
389–391	True Religion
391–392	Two Souls, Against the Manichees
391–430	Psalms
393	Genesis Literally Interpreted (incomplete)
393	The Lord's Sermon on the Mount
394–395	Continence
394–430	Sermons (1–363)
397	Christian Doctrine
397	The Christian Combat
397–401	Confessions
400	Against Faustus the Manichee
400–401	The Good of Marriage
401	Holy Virginity
401–415	Genesis Literally Interpreted (12 books)
405	The Nature of Good
412	The Spirit and the Letter
413–426	City of God
414	The Good of Widowhood
415	Nature and Grace
415	The Perfection of Righteousness
416	On the Gospel of St. John
416	On the Letters of St. John
417	The Deeds of Pelagius
418	The Grace of Christ and Original Sin
418–419	The Trinity
419	Marriage and Concupiscence
419	Adulterous Marriages
420	Against Two Letters of the Pelagians
421	Against Julian
421	Enchiridion of Faith, Hope, and Charity
426	Retractations
426–427	Grace and Free Will

Bibliography

Adolfs, Robert, O.S.A. *The Church Is Different.* New York: Harper & Row, 1964.
Bailey, Derrick Sherwin. *Sexual Relations in Christian Thought.* New York: Harper & Brothers, 1964.
Bainton, Roland H. *Here I Stand: A Life of Martin Luther.* New York: New American Library, 1964.
Biezanek, Anne C. *All Things New.* New York: Harper & Row, 1965.
Bloy, Leon. *The Woman Who Was Poor.* New York: Sheed & Ward, 1947.
Boehmer, Heinrich. *Martin Luther: Road to Reformation.* Trans. John Dobertstein and Theodore Tappert. Cleveland: World Publishing Co., 1960.
Bourke, Vernon J. *Augustine's Quest for Wisdom.* Milwaukee: Bruce, 1945.
Bouyer, Louis. *Dictionary of Theology.* New York: Desclée, 1963.
———. *Seat of Wisdom.* New York: Pantheon, 1962.
———. *The Spirit and Forms of Protestantism.* Cleveland: World Publishing Co., 1964.
———. *The Spirituality of the New Testament and the Fathers.* Vol. I of *A History of Christian Spirituality.* New York: Desclée, 1963.
Braceland, Francis, M.D., and Michael Stock, O.P. *Modern Psychiatry: A Handbook for Believers.* New York: Doubleday, 1963.
Burnaby, John. *Amor Dei: A Study of the Religion of St. Augustine.* London: Hodder, Stoughton, 1938.
Callahan, Sidney Cornelia. *The Illusion of Eve.* New York: Sheed & Ward, 1965.
Camus, Albert. *Notebooks, 1942–1951.* New York: Alfred A. Knopf, 1965.
Cassirer, Ernst. *Rousseau, Kant, and Goethe.* New York: Harper Torchbooks, 1963.

Cayre, F., A.A. *Manual of Patrology*. Vol.1. New York: Desclée, 1935.
Chesterton, G. K. *St. Francis of Assisi*. London: Hodder, Stoughton, 1923.
Continat, Jean, C.M. *The Epistles of St. Paul Explained*. New York: Alba House, 1966.
Contraception and Holiness. Introd. by Archbishop Thomas B. Roberts. New York: Herder & Herder, 1964.
Cox, Harvey. *The Secular City*. New York: Macmillan, 1965.
Daly, Cahal B. *Natural Law Morality Today*. Dublin: Clonmore & Reynolds, 1965.
de Beauvoir, Simone. *The Second Sex*. Trans. H. M. Parshley. New York: Alfred A. Knopf, 1961.
de Lestapis, Stanislas, S.J. *Birth Regulation: The Catholic Position*. London: Burns, Oates, 1963.
de Rougemont, Denis. *The Devil's Share*. New York: Pantheon, 1944.
———. *Love Declared*. Boston: Beacon Press, 1963.
———. *Love in the Western World*. New York: Pantheon, 1956.
Doms, Herbert. *The Meaning of Marriage*. New York: Sheed & Ward, 1939.
Dupré, Louis. *Contraception and Catholics*. Baltimore: Helicon, 1964.
Dyer, George J. *Limbo: Unsettled Question*. New York: Sheed & Ward, 1964.
Egner, G. *Contraception vs. Tradition*. New York: Herder & Herder, 1966.
Eliade, Mircea. *Patterns in Contemporary Religion*. Cleveland: World Publishing Co. 1963.
Eyes on the Modern World. Ed. John Deedy. New York: P. J. Kenedy & Sons, 1965.
Fargot, J. "Jansenius." *Catholic Encyclopedia*. New York: Appleton, 1909.
Friedan, Betty. *The Feminine Mystique*. New York: Dell Books, 1964.
Fromm, Erich. *The Art of Loving*. New York: Harper & Row, 1962.
Garrigou-Lagrange, Reginald. *Christian Perfection and Contemplation*. St. Louis: B. Herder Book Co., 1939.

Gilson, Étienne. *The Christian Philosophy of St. Augustine.* New York: Random House, 1960.
———. *The Spirit of Thomism.* New York: P. J. Kenedy & Sons, 1964.
Gorres, Albert. *The Methods and Experience of Psychoanalysis.* New York: Sheed & Ward, 1962.
Gosling, J. *Marriage and the Love of God.* London: Geoffrey Chapman, 1965.
Grisez, Germain. *Contraception and the Natural Law.* New York: Bruce, 1964.
Guardini, Romano. *The Conversion of St. Augustine.* Westminster, Md.: Newman Press, 1960.
Guitton, Jean. *Great Heresies and Church Councils.* New York: Harper & Row, 1965.
Häring, Bernard, C.SS.R. *Christian Renewal in a Changing World.* New York: Desclée, 1964.
———. *Marriage in the Modern World.* Westminster, Md.: Newman Press. 1965.
Hegeler, Inge, and Sten Hegeler. *An ABZ of Love.* New York: Medical Press of New York, 1963.
Henry, Paul, S.J. *St. Augustine on Personality.* New York: Macmillan, 1960.
"The Human Reality of Sacred Scripture." Vol. X of *Concilium.* New York: Paulist Press, 1965.
Klein, Abbé Felix. *Americanism: A Phantom Heresy.* Cranford, N.J.: Aquin Bookshop, 1951.
Kung, Hans. *Justification: The Doctrine of Karl Barth with the Catholic Reflection.* New York: Thomas Nelson, 1964.
Langdon-Davies, John. *Sin, Sex, and Sanctity.* London: Gollancz, 1954.
Lepp, Ignace. *The Authentic Morality.* New York: Macmillan, 1965.
———. *The Psychology of Loving.* Baltimore: Helicon, 1963.
Lewis, C. S. *The Allegory of Love.* New York: Oxford University Press, 1958.
———. *The Four Loves.* New York: Harcourt, Brace, and World, 1960.
———. *Miracles: A Preliminary Study.* New York: Macmillan, 1947.

Maritain, Jacques. *Three Reformers*. New York: Scribners, 1920.
Marshall, John, M.D. *Catholics, Marriage, and Contraception*. Baltimore: Helicon, 1966.
Mink, Louis. Introd. to *Of True Religion* (St. Augustine). Trans. J. H. S. Burleigh. Chicago: Regnery, 1959.
Newman, John Henry. *An Essay on the Development of Christian Doctrine*. London: Longmans, 1885.
Noonan, John T. *Contraception*. Cambridge, Mass.: Harvard Univ. Press, 1965.
Novak, Michael. "The Break with Platonic Religion," *Eyes on the Modern World*. Ed. John Deedy. New York: P. J. Kenedy & Sons, 1965.
Oakes, Whitney. ed. *Basic Writings of St. Augustine*. New York: Random House, 1958.
Oraison, Marc. *Man and Wife*. New York: Macmillan, 1965.
Osbourne, James C. *The Morality of Imperfections*. Baltimore: Carroll Press, 1950.
Pfurtner, Stephen, O.P. *Luther and Aquinas on Salvation*. New York: Sheed & Ward, 1965.
Pius XI, Pope. "On Chaste Wedlock." *The Church and the Reconstruction of the Modern World*. Ed. Terence McLaughlin, O.S.B. New York: Doubleday, 1957.
Pohle-Preuss. *God the Author of Nature and the Supernatural*. St. Louis: Herder, 1965.
———. *Grace: Actual and Habitual*. St. Louis: Herder, 1941.
Pope, Hugh, O.P. *St. Augustine of Hippo*. New York: Doubleday, 1961.
Portalié, Eugène, S.J. *A Guide to the Thought of St. Augustine*. Chicago: Regnery, 1960.
———. "Augustine." *Catholic Encyclopedia*. New York: Appleton, 1909.
Pourrat, Pierre. *Christian Spirituality*. 3 vols. London: Burns, Oates, & Washbourne, 1922.
Prat, Fernand, S.J. *The Theology of St. Paul*. 2 vols. Westminster, Md.: Newman Press, 1926.
Rahner, Karl. *Theological Investigations*. Vol. I. Baltimore: Helicon, 1963.
Rahner, Karl, and Herbert Vorgrimler. *Theological Dictionary*. Trans. Richard Strachan. New York: Herder & Herder, 1965.

Reuter, Amandus, O.M.I. *Sancti Aurelii Augustini doctrina de bonis matromonii*. Rome: Gregorian University Press, 1942.
St. Augustine: His Age, Life, and Thought. Cleveland: World Publishing Co., 1961. Formerly *A Monument to St. Augustine*. London: Sheed & Ward, 1930; New York: Sheed & Ward, 1945.
St. Francis de Sales. *Treatise on the Love of God*. 7th ed. London: Burns, Oates & Washbourne, n.d.
St. John of the Cross. *Complete Works*. Trans. and ed. by E. Allison Peers. Westminster, Md.: Newman Press, 1953.
Scheeben, Mathias. *The Mysteries of Christianity*. St. Louis: Herder, 1946.
———. *Nature and Grace*. St. Louis: Herder, 1954.
Schillebeeckx, E., O.P. *Marriage: Human Reality and the Saving Mystery*. Vols. I, II. Trans. N. D. Smith. New York: Sheed & Ward, 1965.
Selected Sermons of St. Augustine. Trans. and ed. Quincy Howe, Jr. New York: Holt, Rinehart and Winston, 1966.
Sheed, F. J., *Society and Sanity*. New York: Sheed & Ward, 1953.
Sixteen Documents of Vatican II. Trans. NCWC. Boston: Society of St. Paul Press, 1966.
Sorokin, Pitirim. *The American Sex Revolution*. Boston: Porter Sargent, 1956.
Stern, Karl. *The Third Revolution*. New York: Harcourt, Brace, 1954.
Stone, Irving. *The Nature of Love: Plato to Luther*. New York: Random House, 1966.
Teilhard de Chardin, Pierre, S.J. *The Phenomenon of Man*. New York: Harper & Brothers, 1959.
Thomas, John L., S.J. *The Council, the Family, and the Community of Man*. Colloquium of Vatican Council II. Washington, D.C.: Georgetown Univ. Press, 1966.
———. "What Did the Council Say on Contraception?" *America*, Feb. 26, 1966. p. 296.
Tixeront, J. *History of Dogma*. Vol. II. St. Louis, Herder, 1923.
Todd, John M. *Martin Luther*. Westminster, Md.: Newman Press, 1964.

Van der Marck, William., O.P. *Towards a Christian Ethic.* Westminster, Md.: Newman Press, 1967.
Van der Meer, F. *Augustine the Bishop.* New York: Sheed & Ward, 1961.
Von Hildebrand, Dietrich, *In Defense of Purity.* Baltimore: Helicon, 1962.
White, Victor. *God and the Unconscious.* Cleveland: World Publishing Co., 1952.
Widengren, George. *Mani and Manichaeism.* New York: Holt, Rinehart and Winston, 1965.
Williams, Charles. *The Descent of the Dove.* London: Longmans, 1939.
———. *He Came Down from Heaven.* London: Heinemann, 1938.

Index of Topics

aggiornamento
 and Pope John XXIII, 18, 42
anthropology, Christian
 Augustine as founder of, 24
 how formulated, 40, 41, 58
Augustinism
 "phantom heresy," defined, 60
 Jansenistic mentality and, 60
 consequences of, 61, 196n15
biologism, 31
 defined, 132-133, 160
 charge of, 212n34
canon law, 132
 ends of marriage in, 139-141, 143
 Canon 1013, 132, 172
Catharism
 and love-myth, 109
 de Rougement's thesis, 109
 critics of, 205n35
celibacy
 and marriage, 168-170, 217n1
 and chastity, 171-174
 vows and mystical death, 174-175
 renunciation of a good, 178
 Augustine's celibate love, 178
 service to Church in, 217n2
 See also continence.
charity
 poured forth by Holy Spirit, 79
 a work of love of neighbor for God, 85
 order of, in marriage, 134
 conjugal love and, 146-151
 licit and illicit, 199n4
 See also friendship; love.
chastity
 "surpassing gift of grace," 168
 in marriage, 169
 evangelical counsels, 170
 "dying we live," 174
 See also celibacy; continence.

Church
 assimilates truth from every age, 18
 dogmatic definitions from Augustine, 24
 doctrine of the Fall (Thomas Aquinas), 58
 contains Augustine *eminenter*, 60, 61, 66, 68, 77
 teaching on concupiscence, full notion of, from Augustine, 66-67
 marriage, development of, in Augustine framework (Pius XI, Vatican Council II), 119-121, 160, indispensable, 187
 celibacy, value reaffirmed by, 171
 unity and integrity of the person, 132, 176-177
 emphasized pastoral office, 178
 See also Trent, Council of; Vatican Council II; theology.
concupiscence
 background teaching, 54-57
 the sources of sin (Trent), 54, 62, 72, 77
 four wounds of (Thomas Aquinas), 54, 58-61, and passim
 full Augustine notion of, 61, 65-66
 Augustine "exaggeration," 66, 105-106
 a crucial, dynamic principle, 74
 not original sin, 75-78
 Luther's error, 75, 77-78, 204n22
 sexual, 94-97
 Fr. Bouyer's charge, 97-99, 203n1
 disorder of, 210n29
 See also desire; Fall.

229

continence
    Manichaean notion of, 38, 118
    Augustine definition, 95
    restrains all passions, 100
    St. Paul's teaching on, 169
    "better part," 178
    final fulfillment in, 184
    and Thomas Aquinas, 218n16
    See also celibacy; chastity.
contraception, 21
    critics of Augustine, 126
    "evil appliance," 136
    deluded love, 153, 211n30
    Augustine's view of, 210n19–20
    disorder of, 210n29
created good
    Augustine's praise of, 49
    of the body, 18–21, 79–82, and passim; 190n9
    love of, 79–89
    use and enjoyment, 79–85, 99–100
    conjugal union, a supreme, 94–95, 107–108
    and concupiscence, 96–97
    See also nature; pleasure.
Cross, 54–55
    and remedial grace, 61, 73–74, 174
    "dying with Jesus," notion of concupiscence indispensable to, 73–74
    St. Paul's teaching on, 74–75
    sharing in, 173–175
desire
    purification of, 74–76
    concupiscence and, 76–77, 98–99, 101, 111, 204n22
    Augustine teaching, critical decision, 80
    sexual, 94–97
    and sin, 97–105
    lust, 102–104
    See also concupiscence.
dualism
    Platonic, 40–42
    Augustinian and evangelic (St. Paul, Vatican Council II), 41–43
    Manichaean, 52
eroticism
    Confessions (Augustine), 101–102, 107

erotic love, myth of, 108
Vatican Council II, 128
"love excels," 147
integrated with marriage, 175–176
ethic of love
    Augustine's, 86, 156, 186
    as situation ethic, 150–154
evil
    Augustine's concept of (privatio boni), 44–50, 69–78, 98, 193n9
existentialism
    of Augustine, 35, 37–40, and passim; 192n27
faith
    mutual and loving, as marriage blessing, 132
    rooted in love, 133
    not mere legalism, 133–134
Fall
    and Adam, 53–59
    consequences of, 48–63, and passim
    Jansenism and, 58–61, 67, 95, 173
    misreading in catechisms, 60
    See also concupiscence; sin.
feminism
    and Augustine, 161–164
    dignity of sexes, 163–164
    Monica, 164–166
    See also paganism; personalism.
Freudianism
    and sexuality, Augustine's anticipation of, 106–108
    theological concepts and, 107
    sex and maturity in, 170, 171–173, 205n32 and n34
friendship
    promoted in marriage, 125, 126
    procreation includes, 133
    communion of works (Thomas Aquinas), 141
    Augustine's teaching developed by Vatican Council II, 147
    in Augustine's day, 158–159
    See also love; personalism.
goods of marriage
    St. Augustine's teaching on, 119, 120, 136

one good, three-faceted, 132,
    138–145
  Thomas Aquinas, 141–143, and
    passim
  "concomitant and coordinate,"
    143–144
  and *Casti Connubii* (Pius XI),
    143–144
  ends of marriage, 214n54
  See also marriage.
grace
  before Fall, elevating, 53, 58
  Augustine's emphasis on
    remedial, 55
  neglect of, 61
  need of, 65, 71, 73–75
  Aquinas's assimilation of
    Augustine teaching, 59
  and Vatican Council II, 155
  Pelagians and Jansenists on,
    62–64, 196n15, 197n16
holiness
  purification of desire as first
    step, 73
  marriage and, 126–129, 149
  in the home, call to perfect love
    (Pius XI, Vatican II), 155
  Augustine on divine love, 156,
    177, 183
  fulfills deepest aspirations, 183–
    185, 216n20, 218n5 and n6
Jansenism
  falsifies Augustine's teaching,
    25, 66, 197n17
  modern misunderstandings, 58,
    60, 61–63
  fundamental error, 59
  Jansenist mentality, 60
  Pelagianism and, 62–64
  Lutheran interpretation, 75
  17th-century attitudes, 198n19
  See also concupiscence; grace;
    sin.
love
  of God, 80–81, 84–85
  of neighbor, 84–85
  final happiness in, 86
  concupiscence and, 101–105
  erotic, 107–110
  mystical, 110
  conjugal, 132–135, 157, 160,
    178
  in Augustine's thought, 213n39

Manichaeism
  flesh and spirit, 38
  Augustine's deliverance from,
    44
  refuted in Augustine, 46–47, 50,
    52, 63, 118, 119
  view of sex and marriage in, 51–
    52, 118–119
  implicit in Jansenism, 61
  See also evil; Pelagianism.
Mariology, 148
  virginal integrity, 167
  Mary and Joseph, 168
marriage
  and sexuality, 93
  concupiscence and, 104–106
  theology of, 118–119
  Casti Connubii (Pius XI), 120
  and holiness, 126
  "love in the service of life," 137
  "community of love" (Vatican
    Council II), 137
  marriage act (Thomas
    Aquinas), 207n10
  Pauline concession, 208n 12
matrimony
  in Roman Catechism, 144
metaphysics
  Christian heritage from Plato,
    41
  valuable tools of, 42–43
  substantial evil as metaphysical
    impossibility, 50
  in modern theologians, 193n34
  See also evil; Platonism.
nature
  goodness of, 33, 45–46, 49, 50–
    52
  Platonic, Pelagian notions of, 38
  wounded (Thomas Aquinas),
    54–61, and passim
  See also created good.
paganism
  Augustine's efforts to protect
    marriage against social evils
    in, 120, 156–157
  plight of Christians, 158–159,
    207n1
  See also feminism.
Paradise
  loss of gifts, 55
  concupiscence in, not
    disordered, 73, 79, 94

Paradise (cont.)
  marriage in, 94, 103–105
  marital intercourse in (Thomas Aquinas), 100–101, 121
  before the Fall, 199n21
Pelagianism
  errors of, combated by Augustine, 46–49, 58, 66, 190n22
  notion of original sin, transmission of, 46–48
  Jansenism and, opposing forms of naturalism, 61–63
  modern forms of, disregard of concupiscence, 63, 71
  idyllic view of marriage, 126
  old and new, 174
  See also concupiscence; sin.
personalism
  Augustine theology of, 35–36, 85
  free and equal persons, 146–150
  and conjugal love, 147
  Trinity and, 161–164
  personal fulfillment, 170
  personalist teaching on man, 186
Platonism
  influence on Augustine, 32–43, 190n8
  unity of human person, 35–37
  flesh and spirit, 190n22
  See also dualism; personalism.
pleasure
  moral assessment of, 86
  rule for regulating, 86–88
  within marriage, 99, 101
  delight of saints in, 100
  and holiness, 104, 149
  rational control of, 204n30
  licit and illicit, 215n11
  See also concupiscence; Paradise.
procreation, 109, 124–126
  Thomas Aquinas on, 122–124
  sanctifies intercourse, 124
  responsible human act, 132
  Augustine and Vatican Council II, 138–139
  "creative love shared," 211n30
sacrament
  Augustine's understanding of, 134–135, 213n41

development of (Thomas Aquinas), 142
  in St. Paul, 157
  See also goods of marriage.
Scholasticism
  refinements of, 23
  tended to be static, 40
  view of abstract nature, 60
  influence on Luther, 77, 201n33
  later, and Augustine, 66
  and unfallen sexuality, 104
Scripture
  and Augustine, 23, 34
  orthodoxy safeguarded by, 38–39
  demythologizing of, 42
  St. Paul on concupiscence, 74; union of Christ and Church, marriage a type of, 145; continence, value of, 169; Pauline concession, 208n12
  Genesis, three goods of marriage, 145
  feminism in, 161
sexuality
  a created good, 94
  sexual desire, 94–97
  sexual concupiscence not sin, 97
  sexuality today, 113–117
  development of, 206n40
  not intrinsically evil, 123
  function and end of, 125
  and perfection, 170
  procreation and, 209n17
  morality of, Protestant position, 210n21
sin
  origin in will, 47
  original, 47–48, 54
  two consequences of, 56
  defined by Augustine and Thomas, 67, 200n26
  material and formal elements in (Thomas Aquinas), 77
  sexual desire and, 97
  sexual intercourse and, 122–124
  venial, 127
  mortal, 129
  diminishes man, (Vatican II), 170–171
  and concupiscence, 200n27
  See also concupiscence; will.

theology
  Catholic, definition of, 19, 42
  development of Augustine
    synthesis, 22–26, 56
  misunderstanding Augustine,
    57, 59–61, 66, and passim
  contributions, 58, 61, 73, 116
  and notion of conjugal love, 146
  and marriage, 160, 186
  See also Scripture; Trent,
    Council of; Vatican
    Council II.
Trent, Council of
  incorporated Augustine's
    teaching, 24
  the *fomes* of sin, 54–55, 62, 72
  consequences of Fall, 55, 61
  principle of evil, 69
  and concupiscence, 72
  authorized Roman Catechism,
    144
Trinity
  Augustine doctrine of
    personality and, 35, 74
  peak of Augustine synthesis,
    39
  supreme enjoyment in, 80, 84,
    85, 161–163
  analogues of, 161–163, 217n47
unity
  psychophysical, new sense of,
    31
  in Augustine, 34–36

of flesh and spirit, Augustine's
  teaching on, 37–40
and concupiscence, 74
in Freud, 107
See also personalism;
  Platonism.
Vatican Council II
  and Augustine, 22, 186
  citing Augustine on marriage,
    120–121
  marriage ordained to
    procreation, 138
  no priority of ends, 139–140
  conjugal love, personalism,
    146–149, and passim
  divine life of grace, 155
  and Pius XI, 155
virginity, 45
  need for humility, 175
  consecration, 184
  See also celibacy; continence.
will
  origin of sin and evil in, 47–48,
    190n22, 194n10
  free will and desire, 54, 69, 78,
    79
  freedom, established by grace,
    57–59, and passim
  good and evil love in, 85
  and sexuality, 95, 99
  Augustine emphasis on, 101
  rationale, 193n6
  See also desire; sin.

Index of Authors

Omitted from this index are references to St. Augustine.

Adolfs, Robert, O.S.A., 211n30
Bailey, Derrick S., 192n33, 213n39
Bainton, Roland H., 201n33, 203n11
Baum, Gregory, 212n34
Biezanek, Anne C., 212n36
Bloy, Leon, 111
Boehmer, Heinrich, 201n32
Bourke, Vernon J., 27, 56, 178, 192n29, 219n37
Bouyer, Louis, 97–98, 99, 111, 123, 127, 178, 201n33, 216n20, 219n19
Braceland, Francis, 205n32
Burnaby, John, 193n9, 215n10

Callahan, Sidney C., 219n20
Camus, Albert, 170, 218n9
Cassirer, Ernst, 219n18
Chenu, M. D., O.P., 207n2
Chesterton, G. K., 26, 40, 105–106, 116, 134
Conley, Kiernan, O.S.B., 210n20
Continat, Jean, C.M., 208n12
Cox, Harvey, 193n34, 206n40

Daly, Cahal B., 214n54, 218n17
de Beauvoir, Simone, 217n48
de Lestapis, Stanislas, S.J., 203n13
de Rougement, Denis, 108–110, 205n35
Doms, Herbert, 211n30, 217n47
Dupré, Louis, 200n27, 207n5

Egner, G., 204n30, 213n39, 214n54
Eliade, Mircea, 112–113

Fargot, J., 197n16
Francis De Sales (St.), 51, 72, 82, 156
Freud, Sigmund, 106–108, 170, 172, 205n32 and n34
Friedan, Betty, 205n32, 217n48

Garrigou-Lagrange, Reginald, O.P., 211n27, 218n5
Gilson, Étienne, 26–27, 32, 35, 38, 46, 59, 61, 76, 189n2, 190n7, n9, n14, and n15, 192n25 and n30, 195n7, 198n18 and n21, 199n3, 202n44, 219n23
Gorres, Albert, 205n32
Gosling, J., 217n1
Grou, Jean, S.J., 198n23
Guardini, Romano, 56, 192n27, 220n51
Guitton, Jean, 206n35

Häring, Bernard, C.SS.R., 61
Henry, Paul, S.J., 190n18 and n19
Hughes, Philip, 189n7

John of the Cross (St.), 72, 75, 110, 131, 218n5

Klein, Abbé Felix, 60
Kung, Hans, 202n33

Langdon-Davies, John, 205n33 and n35
Lepp, Ignace, 205n32, 211n30, 219n26
Lewis, C. S., 19, 104, 180, 206n35, 217n41

Maritain, Jacques, 58, 106, 190n3, 196n15
Marshall, John, M.D., 195n6
Mink, Louis O., 194n19

Newman, John Henry, 7, 26, 115, 189n2, 200n26, 207n1
Noonan, John T., 22, 189n4, 192n31, 198n19, 213n39
Novak, Michael, 192n31

235

Oakes, Whitney, 189n13
Oraison, Marc, 211n30
Osbourne, James C., 211n28

Peifer, Claude, O.S.B., 208n12
Pfurtner, Stephen, O.P., 202n33
Pius XI (Pope), 21, 22, 120, 133, 140, 143–144, 146, 160, 177
Pope, Hugh, O.P., 194n22
Portalié, Eugène, S.J., 27, 32, 75, 76, 189n1, 190n4 and n8, 197n15, 201n28, 214n9
Pourrat, Pierre, 195n1, 216n20
Prat, Fernand, S.J., 191n24, 208n12

Rahner, Karl, S.J., 18, 191n24, 196n9, 197n16, 200n27
Reeves, John B., 189n9

Sanger, Margaret, 11, 177
Schillebeeckx, E., O.P., 213n41, 217n1, 218n2 and n6
Sheed, F. J., 176
Singer, Irving, 205n35
Sorokin, Pitirim, 206n40
Stern, Karl, 205n32
Stock, Michael, O.P., 205n32
Stone, Irving, 202n47

Teilhard de Chardin, Pierre, S.J., 18, 193n33
Thomas Aquinas (St.), 54–55, 57, 59, 60, 66, 67, 68–69, 76–77, 82, 100, 123, 128, 141–142, 207n10
Tixeront, J., 189n11, 196n14, 199n12
Todd, John, 201n33

Updike, John, 205n35

Van der Marck, William, O.P., 203n1
Van der Meer, F., 27, 178, 190n5, 195n25, 203n55, 217n44, 219n38
Von Hildebrand, Dietrich, 111, 206n37, 211n30

White, Victor, 205n32

Acknowledgments and Credits

I wish to express my sincere thanks to J. Edward Coffey, S.J., Professor of Family Ethics at the Gregorianum University, Rome, for his critical reading of the manuscript of this hook and for many helpful suggestions; also to Father Marion Casey of New Ulm, Minnesota, for his perceptive comments; to Sister M. Angelica, S.C., of the De Paul Institute, Pittsburgh, for invaluable assistance in preparing the manuscript; to Sister Rose de Lima, Seton Hill College, Greensburg, Pennsylvania, for assistance in translation; and to Mrs. Lloyd Fisher of Pittsburgh for typing the manuscript.

I also wish to thank the publishers who graciously gave me permission to quote from their publications as follows:

William B. Eerdmans Publishing Company: *Select Library of the Nicene and Post-Nicene Fathers,* 1956

Paulist-Newman Press: *The Ancient Christian Writers* and the *Fathers of the Church* volumes; also, Pierre Pourrat, *Christian Spirituality,* 1922

Confraternity of Christian Doctrine, Washington, D.C.: *The New Testament,* 1941

Doubleday & Company: Jerusalem Bible, 1966; also, G. K. Chesterton, *St. Francis of Assisi,* 1923

Fortress Press: Heinrich Boehmer, *Martin Luther: Road to Reformation,* 1960

Herder & Herder: Karl Rahner and Herbert Vorgrimler, eds., *Theological Dictionary,* 1965

Hodder & Stoughton Ltd., London (and Miss Dorothy Collins, owner of the Chesterton copyrights): G. K. Chesterton, *St. Francis of Assisi;* also, John Burnaby, *Amor Dei: A Study of the Religion of St. Augustine,* 1938

Pantheon Books: Louis Bouyer, *Seat of Wisdom,* 1962

Random House: Étienne Gilson, *The Christian Philosophy of St. Augustine,* 1960

Henry Regnery Company: Eugène Portalié, S.J., *A Guide to the Thought of St. Augustine,* 1960

Sheed & Ward: F. Van der Meer, *Augustine the Bishop,* 1961

U.S. Catholic Conference News Service (formerly National Catholic Welfare Conference): *Sixteen Documents of Vatican II,* 1966